Literature and the World

Literature and the World presents a broad and multifaceted introduction to world literature and globalization. The book provides a brief background and history of the field followed by a wide spectrum of exemplary readings and case studies from around the world. Amongst other aspects of World Literature, the authors look at:

- New approaches to digital humanities and world literature
- Ecologies of world literature
- Rethinking geography in a globalized world
- Translation
- Race and political economy

Offering state of the art debates on world literature, this volume is a superb introduction to the field. Its critically thoughtful approach makes this the ideal guide for anyone approaching World Literature.

Stefan Helgesson is Professor of English Literary Studies at Stockholm University, Sweden.

Mads Rosendahl Thomsen is Professor of Comparative Literature at Aarhus University, Denmark.

Literature and Contemporary Thought

Literature and Contemporary Thought is an interdisciplinary series providing new perspectives and cutting edge thought on the study of Literature and topics such as Animal Studies, Disability Studies and Digital Humanities. Each title includes chapters on:

- why the topic is relevant, interesting and important at this moment and how it relates to contemporary debates
- the background of and a brief introduction to the particular area of study the book is intended to cover
- when this area of study became relevant to literature, how the relationship between the two areas was initially perceived and how it evolved

A glossary of key terms and annotated further reading will feature in every title.

Edited by Ursula Heise and Guillermina De Ferrari this series will be invaluable to students and academics alike as they approach the interdisciplinary study of Literature.

Available in this series:

Literature and Disability
Alice Hall

Literature and Emotion
Patrick Colm Hogan

Literature and Food Studies
Amy L. Tigner and Allison Carruth

Literature and Law
Mark Fortier

Literature and the World
Stefan Helgesson and Mads Rosendahl Thomsen

Literature and the World

Stefan Helgesson and
Mads Rosendahl Thomsen

First published 2020
by Routledge
2 Park Square, Milton Park, Abingdon, Oxon OX14 4RN

and by Routledge
52 Vanderbilt Avenue, New York, NY 10017

Routledge is an imprint of the Taylor & Francis Group, an informa business

© 2020 Stefan Helgesson and Mads Rosendahl Thomsen

The right of Stefan Helgesson and Mads Rosendahl Thomsen to be identified as authors of this work has been asserted by them in accordance with sections 77 and 78 of the Copyright, Designs and Patents Act 1988.

All rights reserved. No part of this book may be reprinted or reproduced or utilised in any form or by any electronic, mechanical, or other means, now known or hereafter invented, including photocopying and recording, or in any information storage or retrieval system, without permission in writing from the publishers.

Trademark notice: Product or corporate names may be trademarks or registered trademarks, and are used only for identification and explanation without intent to infringe.

British Library Cataloguing in Publication Data
A catalogue record for this book is available from the British Library

Library of Congress Cataloging-in-Publication Data
Names: Helgesson, Stefan, 1966- author. | Thomsen, Mads Rosendahl, 1972- author.
Title: Literature and the world / Stefan Helgesson and Mads Rosendahl Thomsen.
Description: New York : Routledge, 2019. | Includes bibliographical references and index.
Identifiers: LCCN 2019020545 (print) | LCCN 2019981526 (ebook) | ISBN 9780815384656 (paperback) | ISBN 9780815384649 (hardback) | ISBN 9781351203678 (ebook)
Subjects: LCSH: Literature–History and criticism. | Literature and globalization.
Classification: LCC PN56.G55 H45 2019 (print) | LCC PN56.G55 (ebook) | DDC 809–dc23

ISBN: 978-0-8153-8464-9 (hbk)
ISBN: 978-0-8153-8465-6 (pbk)
ISBN: 978-1-351-20367-8 (ebk)

Typeset in Sabon
by Taylor & Francis Books

Contents

List of figures		vi
Introduction: Why world literature?		1
STEFAN HELGESSON & MADS ROSENDAHL THOMSEN		
1	Paradigms: World literature and its others	24
	MADS ROSENDAHL THOMSEN	
2	Ecologies of literature: The cosmopolitan-vernacular nexus	45
	STEFAN HELGESSON	
3	Genre: Strangeness and familiarity	62
	MADS ROSENDAHL THOMSEN	
4	Geographies: Reading the oceans	81
	STEFAN HELGESSON	
5	Media and method: The digitized library of Babel	109
	MADS ROSENDAHL THOMSEN	
6	Translation: Duration and cosmopolitan reading	131
	STEFAN HELGESSON	
7	Unfinished business: A dialogue	152
	STEFAN HELGESSON & MADS ROSENDAHL THOMSEN	
Index		168

Figures

5.1 Ted Underwood, *Why Literary Periods Mattered* 121
5.2 Nouns that most typically occur with the concept "epiphany" on Google Books Ngram Viewer 128

Introduction
Why world literature?

Stefan Helgesson and Mads Rosendahl Thomsen

The question in the heading should really be phrased like this: why *world* literature? If we speak of *literature*, a ragtag collection of objects, both tangible and intangible, will probably come to mind. Books, obviously: shelves filled with editions of Homer, Jo Nesbø, Virginia Woolf, the *Arabian Nights* and Honoré de Balzac. Genres, just as evidently: drama, lyric, the novel, short stories, crime fiction, chick lit. Formal properties such as poetic metre and rhyme could be included, as should discourses *about* literature: criticism, theory, literary history. Literature, it seems, is a thing consisting of many things – a composite entity, or, to use a term derived from the philosopher Ludwig Wittgenstein, a cluster concept. Just as Wittgenstein observed that the word "game" could refer to activities as diverse as playing cards and playing tennis, so one could argue that "literature" refers to a variety of phenomena that bear some family resemblances, but cannot be reduced conclusively to any single shared property (Wittgenstein 2009, 36).

Literature, then, as a general concept, is already capacious. Indeed, its flexibility is such that it apparently has the capacity to include all forms, varieties and periods of verbal art in its domain. So why complicate matters with the qualifier "world"? Isn't "world literature" already covered by the concept of "literature"? Or, to phrase this with greater precision: what kind of explanatory value might "world literature" have in relation to literature? In this book, we will answer that question by presenting an extended argument in favour of world literature as an essential paradigm for literary studies today. We won't do so uncritically, however, but are guided by the ambition both to present some of the main tendencies in world literature studies today, and to identify blind spots and problems in its current phase of development.

There are in fact a number of historical, theoretical and disciplinary motivations for using the concept of "world literature." Historical, because the term itself has a history – first as *Weltliteratur* in Germany around 1800 – but also because our current historical moment, shaped by migration, digital media and forms of uneven economic globalization, has accelerated the cross-border traffic of (some) literature, genres, writers, and so on. The dramatic revival of "world literature" as a critical term around the turn of the millennium is indeed directly linked to these contemporary developments. Then there are theoretical motivations, since "world literature" can allow precisely for an interrogation of literature as a culturally and linguistically distinct but also changeable concept. Our chapters on translation, geographies and digital humanities will all push the boundaries of the concept by pursuing exploratory practices of reading. Finally, and more pragmatically, in this age of rapid cultural change, world literature is in the process of enabling new disciplinary formations, both of literary scholars with different geographical and linguistic specializations, and across the domains of literary studies, media studies, anthropology, translation studies, and so on. These historical, theoretical and disciplinary aspects, which frame the larger argument in this book as a whole, are what we aim to touch upon in the present chapter. Before getting there, however, let us begin in true literary fashion: with a story.

The making of a modern classic

In 1956, a young employee of the Nigerian Broadcasting Company in Lagos spent his evenings composing a novel in longhand. These were the waning days of colonialism in Nigeria, a time full of promise for that young, urban generation to which our hero belonged. He had previously published a few short stories in a campus magazine, but that was all. He was not recognized as an author, nor did he really think of himself as a writer. Still, he had this inner compulsion to complete his novel, and once his handwritten manuscript was finished, he felt it should be typed up professionally to be presentable. An advertisement placed by a UK firm convinced him to send off the manuscript to London for "polishing" – a service that cost the hefty sum of £32. But the weeks and months went by without notice from London. This was, moreover, the one and only copy of the manuscript. It seemed more than likely that it had gone astray. Only thanks to an English friend, who visited the typing agency in London and demanded to know what had happened, was the manuscript recovered, typed out, and duly delivered. All that remained now was to get it accepted, but it was rejected off-hand by numerous publishers. Eventually, it reached an editor at Heinemann, who endorsed the manuscript enthusiastically.[1]

The rest, as the phrase goes, is history. The young Nigerian's name was Chinua Achebe, and his manuscript became the novel we know as *Things Fall Apart*, one of the most widely read and highly canonized novels of the twentieth century. When the 50th anniversary of its publication was being celebrated in 2008, it had been translated into 50 languages and had sold more than 11 million copies. It has spawned an entire library's worth of scholarship, and the novel can be found on reading lists at schools and universities around the world, often as the exemplary first (or only) book from Africa that students read. Intriguingly, even Harold Bloom, in his influential but idiosyncratic *The Western Canon* (1994), included *Things Fall Apart* in a much-debated list of canonical works. It is unusually easy to agree, in other words, with the assessment of *Things Fall Apart* as an example of "world literature." At the same time, both the story of its production and subsequent reception, as well as its thematic and stylistic aspects, raise a number of challenging questions concerning the possible meanings of world literature.

To refer back to our introductory remarks, *Things Fall Apart* is easily pinned down as an instance of literature, pure and simple. It is published as a book, written in prose, identifiable as a novel with characters and plot development. It relates also to other literature, as in the title's citation of a line from W. B. Yeats's poem "The Second Coming," or in the Igbo tales that are recounted by female characters in the novel. But here we begin to discern an important anomaly: the novel's intertextuality is not restricted to any single tradition, language, or form. The modernist lyric of Yeats is juxtaposed here with an English-language rendering of an oral storytelling practice in the Igbo language. Here, not only the general polysemy of the term "literature" becomes evident, but also its diverse cultural, geographical and media-technological aspects. Literacy and orality, African and Irish literature, the languages of English and Igbo all combine to form the novel that we read. If we then add the circumstances of how the manuscript was sent off to England and eventually became read across the world in numerous translations, this should begin to clarify the analytical relevance of discussing *Things Fall Apart* not just as literature, but as an instance of world literature. It is the kind of work that quite spectacularly resists identification with any *single* unit such as a nation, language, genre or tradition, but emerges instead in the interstices between multiple poles of belonging.

However, Achebe's novel also invites two different possibilities for discussing world literature, and this distinction will be of importance to our line of reasoning in the rest of this book. The first possibility is what could be called the *affirmative*, or even idealistic, account of world literature. This entails a focus on the success of *Things Fall Apart* – its canonization. The story of its precarious beginnings and subsequent valorization as the great classic of modern African literature would in that respect be seen as an example of how world literature works to the benefit of a cosmopolitan broadening of cultural horizons. This affirmative account would resonate with Johann Wolfgang von Goethe's optimistic notion of world literature (which we discuss below), and places a premium on literature as a sanctioned realm of intercultural dialogue. Such a view also conceives of translation as a fundamentally benign practice that participates in the gradual cosmopolitan construction of world literature as a shared planetary domain.

The other possibility, which is more in line with most recent scholarship, is to develop a *critical* account of world literature. Remaining with our example, this would adopt a sceptical view of *Things Fall Apart*'s rags-to-riches story, focusing on gaps, occlusions, inequalities, conflicts, and contradictions. The most obvious conflict here concerns British colonialism. The novel is read as a paradigmatic story of the African experience of colonization, beginning as it does in the self-contained lifeworld of Umuofia village, and ending with the brutal reduction of its inhabitants to colonial subjects under British rule at the tail end of the nineteenth century. But to this should be added also the colonial circumstances of its production: Achebe's choice to write in English and try his luck with publishers in London – despite his own location in Lagos – are not neutral facts, but historically salient ones that testify to a particular conjunction of political power and cultural hegemony within which Achebe was bound to operate. The interesting detail of the manuscript first having been handwritten by Achebe, then intermediated in London through the technology of the typewriter, and eventually published in 2,000 hard copies by Heinemann also tells the story of uneven resources within the bounds of what was then the British empire – resources that could be technological and economic in nature, but also symbolic. There were obviously typewriters in Nigeria. Still, Achebe let himself be convinced that the typescript would be prepared more "properly" by the London firm. But besides this, it was – and still is – the case that the publishing infrastructure, in terms of the number of publishers, their variety and their resources, was far more established and robust in London than in Lagos. One could in this way, as far as institutions of publication and literary recognition are concerned, speak of an undeniable centre-periphery relationship between London and Lagos at this moment in history.

If we then look at the subsequent circulation and canonization of *Things Fall Apart*, a related set of critical questions can be asked. The fact that it becomes the *exemplary* novel of Africa, for example, can raise suspicion. At least until the recent global success of Chimamanda Ngozi Adichie and others, African literature has not enjoyed a high profile among readerships in Europe or the Americas. This can lead to the conclusion that *Things Fall Apart* has been accorded a representative status, thereby functioning as an alibi for not engaging more thoroughly – from the outside – with African literature. The production of "the postcolonial exotic" has, in Graham Huggan's account (2001), been a recurring feature of how writers from the formerly colonized world have been positioned in the literary markets of Europe and North America. Their entry to these markets has been conditional, subject to "technologies of recognition" (Shih 2004) that produce visibility or invisibility in the dominant literary fields of the contemporary world.

When translation is added to the discussion, a critical analysis can also be developed both in relation to Achebe's own text, which could be claimed to perform a cultural translation of an Igbo world into English, and in relation to subsequent translations, which then could be described as translations of translations. The cliché has it that something always gets lost in translation; a more refined understanding claims instead that translation is by definition a transformation – and the analytical question would then be what characterizes the multiple transformations of *Things Fall Apart*.

As we can see, already the single example of *Things Fall Apart* invites an astonishing range of questions that all attach to "world literature" understood as a combination of methodological frameworks. As precisely just one example, it also allows us to intimate the exceptional complexity of world literature as a field of inquiry. It should therefore be obvious that we cannot hope to cover every facet of the field in this book. What we will do in our chapters, however, besides accounting for some of the more important previous contributions to world literary thinking, is to provide updated points of orientation in what has emerged as one of the most consequential recent developments in the humanities. Although the critical dimension of world literature sketched out above is more in tune with the professional identity of scholars and intellectuals, the affirmative understanding is not irrelevant to our endeavour. One could argue that if critique has run out of steam, as one scholar famously argued (Latour 2004; see also Anker and Felski 2017), then this might be true when critique has lost sight of what it in the long run wants to affirm. In other words, if the critical study of world literature is justified in insistently drawing our attention to the silences and gaps in an uneven world of reading and writing, this justification may or may not derive from a desire to establish *better* modes of cross-cultural literary appreciation and translational exchanges. In our case it does, even though such a blunt formulation may be accused of courting naivety. But this same problem could also be phrased as a question with an aesthetic slant: should the global success of *Things Fall Apart* be understood as a result of its intrinsic qualities as a novel (an affirmative view), or is it merely an external construction, attributable to a particular conjunction of uneven power relations between continents, languages, literary fields and systems of knowledge production (a critical view)? The only defensible answer, it seems to us, is that both dimensions are combined in the world literary making of Achebe's classic. It is also such a stereoscopic view of world literature that informs our argument in this book.

The history of a concept

"World literature" as a term has a distinctly, if not exclusively, European provenance. This is an historical fact and an inescapable problem. It was first a German word, *Weltliteratur*, that formed in the philosophical cauldron of late eighteenth-century Enlightenment and pre-Romantic thinking. Theo D'haen (2012, 5) has dated the earliest recorded use of *Weltliteratur* to 1773, in a book by the historian August Ludwig von Schlözer (1735–1809). Much more famous, however, are the scattered remarks by the ageing Johann Wolfgang von Goethe (1746–1832) in Johann Peter Eckermann's *Gespräche mit Goethe* (*Conversations with Goethe*; published between 1836 and 1848, but the conversations took place mainly in the 1820s). This is where Goethe speaks of the eclipse of national literature by the advent of *Weltliteratur*. In the conversation with Eckermann dated 31 January 1827 (we should imagine it as a bitingly cold winter's day), he expresses his conviction that "poetry is the common property of all mankind and that it is manifest everywhere and in all ages in hundreds of hundreds of people" (D'haen, Domínguez and Thomsen 2012, 11). Hence, "[n]ational literature means little now, the age of Weltliteratur has begun; and everyone should further its course" (2012, 11). These statements are so familiar that they have become almost formulaic. They create thereby the somewhat problematic impression that Goethe *inaugurated* world literature, whereas contemporary scholarship has increasingly shown how his musings are better understood as emerging out of wider intellectual and historical developments at the time. To begin with, the immediate historical moment is significant: Goethe had lived through the Napoleonic wars, a new order of nation-states was emerging in Europe, and it is as though he wished to counter the destructive potential of nationalism by envisioning an elevated, convivial concert of voices among the distinct literatures of the world. Pointing to European conditions alone is, however, insufficient, since Goethe's invocation of "all mankind" and "all ages" is explicitly universalizing and global: he first speaks to Eckermann on the topic after having read a "Chinese novel," finding in its characters a distant mirror of his own. His cycle of poems *West-Östlicher Divan* (1819), inspired by the Persian poet Hafez, was written in that same spirit of "Orientalist" discovery. Even more important than the post-Napoleonic reconstruction in Europe, therefore, is the exceptional transformation and expansion of the epistemological horizons of European thought in the eighteenth and nineteenth centuries. This expansion was cultural as well as temporal and geographical: humanity was not just far more diverse than earlier antique and Christian canons of knowledge had acknowledged, nor was it only the case that the entire planet now constituted the spatial horizon of inquiry, but the planet and humanity were also far *older* than earlier Christian dogma had allowed for. Comte de Buffon and Immanuel Kant were among the many eighteenth-century thinkers who explicitly contested earlier Bible-based calculations of the age of the Earth – a knowledge revolution which would accelerate with Darwin's evolutionary theory, presented in 1859. It is within this reconfiguration of the very conditions of knowledge that one can discern the deeper motivations behind the world literary thinking of this epoch.

The knowledge revolution, however, was not a neutral phenomenon, but tied in complicated ways to the expansion of European power. With Columbus's voyage to the Americas in 1492 and the Portuguese seafarers' establishment of the Cape route to India, European colonialism became a global affair, culminating in the era of high imperialism around 1900 and extending into the twentieth century with the hegemony of the United States. This world-historical process defies neat summary, but one of its more obvious consequences was the accelerated occurrence of asymmetrical transcultural encounters between Europeans and their "others." Within the often mundane, sometimes sharply conflictual, practice of colonial rule – such as the managing of the East India Company's business in Calcutta in the late eighteenth century – there emerged also a need for and interest in new forms of scholarly inquiry. The Calcutta example is particularly instructive, since this is where the polyglot William Jones (1746–94) founded the Asiatic Society of Bengal and established the philological study of Asian languages, particularly Sanskrit. This Orientalist knowledge-formation would have extremely far-ranging consequences for the study of language, culture and literature in the nineteenth century and beyond – leading in its most destructive iterations to the consolidation of a racial "Aryan" myth of origin (Arvidsson 2006). We will discuss this scholarly development and its imbrication with power at greater length in our account below of current critiques of world literature. Suffice it at the moment to say that Goethe's appreciation of Asian literary cultures was connected to this development – and thereby to the world-historical dimension of European national concerns at that time – as was his predecessor Johann Gottfried von Herder's (1744–1803) insistent accommodation of human cultural diversity under one philosophical umbrella (Noyes 2015). In Herder's case, interestingly, European colonialism was not only an unstated condition of possibility for an acute awareness of diversity – he also attacked colonialism relentlessly as one of the great threats to this diversity. Herder was prescient in this regard, intuiting what we might call a structuring irony of world literature: if it is the planetary consciousness and asymmetrical cultural encounters of the modern era that make world literature thinkable as a concept, it is this same condition of possibility that threatens the integrity of distinct linguistic and cultural traditions.

For Karl Marx and Friedrich Engels, in *The Communist Manifesto* (1848), this irony is treated in dialectical fashion as a consequence of market forces and globalized capital: "The intellectual creations of individual nations become common property. National one-sidedness and narrow-mindedness become more and more impossible, and from the numerous national and local literatures, there arises a world literature" (Marx and Engels 2012, 39). A century later, another German scholar, Erich Auerbach, burdened by the historical experience of two world wars and the onset of the Cold War, would present the problem in a more mournful key:

> The presupposition of *Weltliteratur* is a *felix culpa*: mankind's division into many cultures. Today, however, human life is becoming standardized. The process of imposed uniformity, which originally derived from Europe, continues its work, and hence serves to undermine all individual traditions. [...] Should mankind succeed in withstanding the shock of so mighty and rapid a process of concentration – for which the spiritual preparation has been poor – the man will have to accustom himself to existence in a standardized world, to a single literary culture, only a few literary languages, and perhaps even a single literary language. And herewith the notion of *Weltliteratur* would be at once realized and destroyed.
>
> (1969 [1952], 2–3)

Plus ça change, plus c'est la même chose. These formulations from earlier eras demonstrate two things. One is how many of the contemporary concerns in the world literature field are in fact old and familiar, and could be understood simply as a sharpening and acceleration of a dynamic between cosmopolitan and vernacular values in the literary domain that has a much longer history (see Chapter 2). Another point is paradoxically opposed to this: world literature is never old, but belongs in the future. For Goethe, Marx and Auerbach, world literature has never quite yet arrived. It is always in the process of happening, be it as a promise or a threat, but still without being fully realized. These dual temporal trajectories are enabling insofar as they prohibit us from reifying world literature as an object and make us recognize that the problematic as such is embedded in the longer yet always unfinished history of modernity. In other words, it is as though world literature will inevitably return again and again as a question in a world shaped by entangled histories, accelerated communication and technological transformation.

Two contributions by writers located culturally in South Asia and West Africa, respectively, however, do provide a counterpoint to the European narrative, while nonetheless supporting our reading of world literature as a particularly modern, and global, problematic. In 1907, Rabindranath Tagore (1861–1941) gave a lecture in India on the topic of "vishva sahitya," a Bengali term that translates – albeit imperfectly – as "world literature," and is invoked today as a guiding principle of the Comparative Literature Association of India. The first English translation of Tagore's lecture appeared as late as 2001, and apparently it still lacks a translation that does it justice. The gist of his argument, nonetheless, is universalizing and affirmative. Presented well before the two world wars, which would push him towards a more sombre view of humanity, Tagore's idea of world literature derives from an explicitly anti-utilitarian conception of creativity and expression. He identifies three modes of connection with the world: intellect, need, and joy or delight (*ananda* – a particularly difficult term to translate). The intellect "places truth in a witness box of its own making and interrogates it to extract its secrets," whereas need is driven by self-interest (Tagore 2015, 277). *Ananda*, which is the domain of literature and aesthetic expression, is characterized instead by "incautious spending," a giving without calculation that enables communion between the inner and outer world, and between self and other: "What is this connection of joy? It is to know another as our very own, and to know ourselves as if we were another's" (282, 278). It is from this standpoint that literature, for Tagore, manifests a literally unending process of externalization and internalization of man's being in the world: "Thus one must view literature as a temple that the universal man (*vishva-manav*) has built; writers have come from all times and all nations to work as labourers in that project. The plan of the building is not available to us, but whatever is wrong is immediately demolished" (286). "World literature" becomes in this way not an add-on or an epiphenomenon, but rather an aesthetic outlook that regards the boundaries between people, languages and cultures as epiphenomena. Tagore's stated ambition is to understand what man accomplishes "through his work," and in order to achieve this, it is insufficient to focus on isolated cases such as the reign of Akbar or Queen Elizabeth (286). More pointedly, at least in Bhavya Tiwari's reading (2011, 44), it was the religiously motivated divisions imposed on Bengal by the British administration that drove Tagore to denounce what he saw as the threat of parochialism:

> just as the world is not merely the sum of your plough field, plus my plough field, plus his plough field – because to know it that way is only to know with a yokel-like parochialism – similarly world literature is not merely the sum of your writing, plus my writing, plus his writings. We generally see literature in this limited, provincial manner. To free oneself of that regional narrowness and resolve to see the universal being in world literature, to apprehend such totality in every writer's work, and to see its interconnectedness with every man's attempt at self-expression – that is the objective we need to pledge ourselves to.
>
> (Tagore 2015, 288)

Reading this through Western eyes, Tagore can come across as an idealist in the Hegelian sense, a position which easily attracts condemnation from the "critical" camp. We should be wary of such hasty conclusions, however. Of more importance to our current argument is instead to recognize that these formulations – once again – emerge out of an historical moment of increasing entanglements between histories and cultures. Tagore himself had lived several years in Britain; through the combined processes of European colonialism and the Orientalist upsurge in European scholarship from the late eighteenth century onwards, intellectual traffic between Bengal and Europe had intensified. Both the European romanticist interest in India – manifested by Schlegel, Goethe, Schopenhauer and others – and the Bengal renaissance (with Tagore at its tail end) need therefore to be read as outcomes of a yoking together of the world in the modern era. Tagore's lecture is one attempt, from within a profoundly local, linguistically specific position, at articulating the literary consequences of world-historical transformations. Globalization is an old story, as is world literature. Importantly, however, Tagore once again presents world literature in the aspirational, future-oriented mode – "the objective we need to pledge ourselves to" – but adds to this a more thoroughly articulated self-other dialectic than we find in Goethe. His faith in the capacity of the self continually to develop through this dialectic, and through literature, by enabling such creative exuberance or joy, can never be closed off but becomes instead a site for the continuous overflow, or excess, of man's becoming.

Four decades after Tagore's speech, in 1949, the Senegalese poet and statesman Léopold Sédar Senghor (1906–2001) would give a lecture at UNESCO (the United Nations Educational, Scientific and Cultural Organization) in Paris that resonated in uncanny ways with Tagore. Senghor never discussed the actual term "world literature," but his lifelong practice of reading across numerous languages, continents and cultural traditions was thoroughly world literary. The "civilization of the universal" – which he contrasted against imperialist forms of "universal civilization" – became his central concern in the 1960s and 1970s, and retraces all the familiar challenges of human diversity and the self-other dialectic that we recognize by now from the conceptual history of world literature. His 1949 lecture is of particular interest here, given not only the symbolically important venue – a manifestation of post-Second World War globalism under Western hegemony (McDonald 2017, 153–72) – but all the more because of its pointed thematization of reading under conditions of conflict. He recounted here his experience, in 1941, of being imprisoned in a Nazi camp in Poitiers – a camp designated for prisoners from the French colonies. The conditions seem to have been bearable. He taught himself German during this time, and was allowed to keep a "minuscule library" that contained Virgil's *Aeneid*, Pascal's *Pensées* and Plato's dialogues. To these volumes he would add Goethe's *Faust* and *Iphigenia*, as his reading fluency in German gradually improved.

He describes his encounter with Goethe as a conversion, a strong word for someone with such close ties to religion as Senghor. But a conversion from what? "Two years previously," he writes, "I had still been immersed in a mad passion for the Kingdom of Childhood, for the rediscovery of negritude, consumed by the burning lava of my inner volcano. [...] Two years previously, my quest, our quest, had been only for ourselves. [...] We stalked only the grounds of those who were like us" (Senghor 1964, 83; Helgesson's translation).[2] With the German anthropologist Leo Frobenius – much admired by Senghor – as a mediating link, Senghor approached Goethe as an other who yet seemed familiar. The otherness here should be understood not least as an intra-European otherness. For the French-trained Senghor, Goethe represented something alien in relation to France – for Senghor the Senegalese negritudinist, Frobenius had made him inclined to imagine a cultural affinity between Germans and Africans. In that respect, Senghor was already favourably inclined towards Goethe. He even speaks of the prior engagement with Frobenius in terms of a *Sturm und Drang*. The world literary dynamics operating here are surprisingly complicated. At first glance, Senghor's library of European classics seems to be little more than a predictable outcome of the canonical force of the French and German literary fields, hence reproducing an established Eurocentric hierarchy of world literature. But add to this the immediate context: Senghor is a Senegalese held captive by the Nazis. His political response to that situation could have been to reject German culture altogether, yet he does the opposite.

Senghor's cultivation of this paradoxical openness provides us, we want to suggest, with a clue to how we might read his reading. To begin with, his predicament in the war camp could be seen as an allegory of his colonial situation: held captive by French culture and French state power, his strategy all along had been to absorb more and more of French literature. His reading of Goethe in the war camp repeats in this way a pattern one can trace throughout his early career. It is a reading, moreover, aiming at transformation both of the self and of the self's political context. Confronted by the Nazi "hatred of reason and bloodcult," the lesson that Goethe taught him in that moment was "the danger of cultural isolation, of self-preoccupation, of the risks of building only on one's own race, one's own nation, one's native virtues." The story that Senghor tells his audience at a UNESCO conference in 1949 is thereby one of openness, transcultural receptivity and, indeed, the virtue of deep reading – even under the most conflictual of circumstances. Without, most likely, being aware of Tagore's lecture, Senghor's approach echoed the Indian writer's emphasis on continual becoming.

The subtle approaches of Tagore, Auerbach, and Senghor notwithstanding, in the decades prior to the late 1990s, world literature was typically used as little more than shorthand for either the best and most universal literature, or simply as all literature that does not belong to your own nation. More significant than the *theory* of world literature in the Cold War era, however, was the institutional broadening of the field of literature with a cosmopolitan ambition. The fact that Senghor held his speech at UNESCO testifies to this, and UNESCO collaborated also with the scholar René Étiemble in the creation of a series of translations of Asian and Middle Eastern literature. Other key interventions by Ahmadou Hampâté Bâ, Ahmed Sekou Touré and Gabriel García Márquez also took place under the auspices of UNESCO (McDonald 2017, 159–65). The organization has since continued to promote an agenda of internationalism in literature, for example through its City of Literature

Introduction: why world literature? 13

programme. Also in the Cold War era, PEN International consolidated its role as a cosmopolitan network of writers supporting writers against state intervention (Svedjedal 2013). Another less familiar yet intensive engagement with world literature occurred in the Soviet Union. Both prior to the Second World War and after, the Soviet Union was observant of the importance of literature and invested early, with Maxim Gorky as a driving force, in translations of literature that would support a programme of universal values but with respect for the local histories and evolved forms (Khotimsky 2013, 142). The influence on Chinese literature in the post-war period, marked by a literature committed to a socially engaged realism, was also significant. At the other side of the Iron Curtain, the Central Intelligence Agency (CIA) took an interest in literature and sought to influence major writers and magazines (Whitney 2016). Still, the world of the Cold War and the whole rhetoric of the Earth being divided into different worlds constituted a major obstacle to thinking of the relevance of a world literature.

Revival

The revival of world literature seems in hindsight to be an almost logical consequence of how the world opened after 1989 and globalization gathered pace. Cultures and literatures that had previously worked on very different premises, either as part of closed political systems or restrained by limited resources, were now opening up and becoming affluent and free enough to take a greater interest in literature. The introduction of the Internet further added to a sense that the world was becoming smaller or more interrelated.

Scarcely used until the late 1990s, the concept of world literature rapidly became a focal point for discussions among literary disciplines, not least comparative literature. One of the first books to become a centre of attention of the newfound interest in world literature was Pascale Casanova's *La République mondiale des lettres* from 1999. It was not as such involved with the idea of world literature, but essentially showed how literature circulated and how an international literary field had emerged that was detached to some degree from the national scenes (Casanova 1999, 119). Casanova's work focused on how dominant centres in the international literary circuit, such as Paris, London and New York, functioned as hubs for the further dissemination of works. Casanova lamented that some of the values of literature had been replaced by a focus on the demands of the market in the shift from the domination of Paris to the anglophone metropolises. The focus in her book, translated in 2004 as *The World Republic of Letters*, were those writers who despite writing from the semi-periphery of the larger nations, made a lasting impact on literature in the centres. Two of Casanova's monographs concern Samuel Beckett and Franz Kafka, who are both emblematic of having been able to change literatures to which they were outsiders. Finally, she also showed how useful the sociological thinking of Pierre Bourdieu was to the field of literary studies and how it could bring awareness and a methodology to the study of the complex structures generated by high and low genres, of artistic and economic forces, of the perpetual renewal of the field, and not least the role of critics (Casanova 1999, 127).

Franco Moretti's article "Conjectures on World Literature" from 2000 framed the methodological challenge of world literature to comparative literature, which had often been less global in its orientation than it had nominally claimed. Moretti's diagnosis was that world literature could not be studied by merely reading more, because of the sheer magnitude of printed matter. Hence, he saw it as a provocation to the discipline to find new ways to study literature at a remove ("distant reading") by compiling results from studies that had already been carried out and by working collectively on a shared set of interests. In "Conjectures on World Literature," Moretti suggested focusing on the spread of genres, in particular that of the novel, as one approach that would reveal patterns of influences, which could rely on collective work, or "distant reading" of the works of others in order to test hypotheses of how literary genres became influential. This perspective was quite different from other approaches to world literature that traditionally had been interested in reading outstanding works from various parts of the world. Moretti never advocated that distant reading should be the only way to study literature, but saw it as part of a necessary condition for being able to generate new knowledge about world literature (Moretti 2013, 48).

In 2003, David Damrosch published *What Is World Literature?* which presented three definitions of world literature that became recurrent focal points in debates (Damrosch 2003, 281). The three definitions emphasized that world literature is "a refraction of national literatures," whereby the connections to local roots were stressed but also the distance that makes another perspective necessary. Damrosch suggested the ellipsis as a graphic model for reading world literature in which the figure is constructed from two focal points: the reader's own perspective, and her or his projection of different, foreign viewpoints. Damrosch's second definition underlined the importance of translation to world literature studies, which in many ways was the most decisive challenge to the discipline of comparative literature. Finally, the third definition of world literature as a mode of reading rather than a canon was perhaps the most influential

Introduction: why world literature? 15

idea, suggesting that world literature studies should create a space for reading where highly canonized and overlooked works could be compared across time and space. Damrosch also worked to put theory into practice as the lead editor of the six-volume *Longman Anthology of World Literature*, which replaced the usual division of world literature into regions with a thematic organization that mixed different literatures. Since the establishment of the Institute for World Literature in 2011, Damrosch has also worked to train teachers and build an international community of world literature studies.

Half a decade into the new millennium, world literature studies had been established as an emerging paradigm for studying literature. Two very different examples could be invoked here: on the one hand, the four-volume Swedish publication *Literary History: Towards a Global Perspective* (Pettersson et al. 2006); and on the other, the American Comparative Literature Association's decennial report edited by Haun Saussy, *Comparative Literature in an Age of Globalization* (2006). World literature also became a target of criticism for its methodological and political implications alike, which we will address in the following sections. It has nonetheless continued to be influential with a steady number of works being published within the field, e.g. Alexander Beecroft's *An Ecology of World Literature* (2015), B. Venkat Mani's *Recoding World Literature* (2017), Sandra Richter's world history of German literature, *Eine Weltgeschichte der deutschsprachigen Literatur* (2017), and Helena Buescu's massive seven-volume undertaking *Literatura-mundo comparada: perspectivas em português* (the first four appeared in 2018), which analogously to Richter inflects world literature through the Portuguese language – understood as a global language.

World literature and its discontents: theoretical challenges

Given the double optic of this book – affirmative yet critically self-reflexive – critiques of world literature will be addressed throughout, in individual chapters. What needs to be outlined here are some key trajectories of this criticism, particularly in its more recent iterations. Ever since the post-millennial revival of world literature, debates have been lively. Criticism has sometimes been very specific, as when Christopher Prendergast (2004) took Franco Moretti and Pascale Casanova to task for what he saw as flawed theoretical assumptions. There have also often been terse exchanges between specialists in various fields and proponents of world literature (Orsini 2015). As we discuss in Chapter 1 and the concluding dialogue, one of the main fault lines has been between postcolonial studies and world literature. The criticism of world literature has been quite explicit from scholars working with both postcolonial literature and translation studies. In recent years, three main tendencies in the debate on world literature have emerged. The first is the critique of translatability, a line of argument particularly associated with Emily Apter. The second is the interrogation of the under-theorized notion of "world" by critics such as Gayatri Spivak (2012) and Peter Hitchcock (2010), as well as Eric Hayot (2012), Debjani Ganguly (2016), and Pheng Cheah (2016). Third, a group of scholars have focused on the genealogy of "literature" and its complicity with colonialism. We will discuss these three critical debates in turn, although they tend to be interrelated in various ways.

Gayatri Chakravorty Spivak warned in *The Death of a Discipline* from 2003 of a world literature dominated by American academia and commercial interests, and she expressed her concern about the uneven conditions that the Global South faces with a multitude of languages compared to the relatively few dominant Indo-European languages (Spivak 2003, 12). Instead, she hoped for a comparative literature that would broaden its scope and become a discipline concerned with the performativity of cultures through narratives (Spivak 2003, 13). A decade later, Emily Apter published *Against World Literature*, in which she shared the hope for a wider and less Western canon as the foundation of comparative studies, but also raised concerns about the institutional conditions under which the new world literature was promoted in academia. Apter's arguments revolve around the question of the untranslatable and the resistance of literature to being adapted to a different language and different cultural context (Apter 2013, 3). While both Spivak and Apter have been criticized for being too idealistic in their demands on the discipline, their critique remains an important reminder of the blind spots that even a well-intended attempt to broaden the field of comparative literature carries with it.

Not unlike critics of translatability, scholars who have focused on the world concept have cautioned against the assumed "smoothness" of common-sensical assumptions about the world as a unified space. Against speed and interchangeability, and against the homogenizing grid of a mapped globe, these critics insist instead on conflict, density and difference. Peter Hitchcock lamented the "studiously neutral" conception of the world in world literature (2010), and Gayatri Spivak has for a long time problematized the impulse of conflating the world with the globe of capitalism, or of confusing what one assumes about the world with the world as such (2003 and 2012; see also Chapter 2). This line of reasoning has informed much of our argument in this book – world literature, we insist, is always a matter of perspective – and will also be discussed at greater length particularly in Chapter 2. It is important, moreover, to note how more recent interventions have spent considerable amounts of theoretical labour on refining and elaborating various notions of the world. Pheng Cheah's *What Is a World?* (2016) engages at length with the canon of Western philosophy to arrive at a temporal, rather than spatial, understanding of "world" as something that is humanly made and sustained, not least through narrative. He argues forcefully against the "conflation of the world with market processes of global extensiveness" (37), and views "world" instead as a normative horizon with the potential, through literature, to resist the world-destroying forces of globalized capitalism. Similarly, in *This Thing Called the World* (2016), Debjani Ganguly strives to distinguish the globe of contemporary capitalism from the forms of world-making achieved by literary texts. Her point is also to relieve the reading of world literature from a purely mimetic relationship with globalization, insisting on the non-reductive nature of literature – she differs from Cheah, however, by paying more concrete attention to form and narrative. In her discussion, Ganguly identifies (at least) four possible meanings of the word "world":

> [T]he world as spatial amplification and systemic interconnection across the globe through the circuits of informational capitalism; the world as an aesthetic remainder of the globe that resists the space-time compression of global commodity circuits; the world as an ethical site of human relationality and humanitarian connectivity; and the world a self-contained totality analogous to a Leibnizian monad whose many parts are compossible with each other and that is not reducible to the materiality of the actual world we inhabit.
>
> (2016, 69)

The last of these – the Leibnizian understanding – emerges out of the separate field of "possible worlds" theory, which has become increasingly relevant for revised methods of world literary reading that otherwise focus on the second meaning, "world" as an aesthetic remainder of the globe. These methods clearly have future potential, and this book could have been devoted to unpacking and exploring Ganguly's and Cheah's world definitions. Our purpose, however, is less philosophical and focused instead on the range of current methods and perspectives within world literature *as a practice*. The specific meanings of "world" in this book therefore tend to result from the delimitation and purpose of the research questions, rather than the other way round. In the chapter on digital media and methods, for example, "world" relates to the geographical distribution and accumulation of texts in diverse languages; in Chapter 4, "Reading the oceans," world has rather to do with the "significant geographies" (Laachir, Marzagora and Orsini 2018) shaped through histories of conquest, trade and cultural contact. A basic conceptual tension worth keeping in mind, however, is that between "world" as a self-enclosed set of systemic relations and "world" as the unfathomable ground of being (Hayot 2012, 30–7). It is the former meaning that has been foregrounded in much post-millennial world literature theory. Both Moretti's literary world-system and Casanova's world republic of letters refer in the main to literary worlds (or fields) themselves, not the world at large. They are in that sense inward-looking and self-referential. This is the understanding that has been further developed by the Warwick Research Collective, whose *Combined and Uneven Development* (2015) posits world-literature (with a hyphen) as the literature of the capitalist world-system, thereby implicitly excluding all other literatures, contemporary and above all ancient, that are not evidently formed within that world-system. "World-literature" in this sense will not encompass Dante or the Persian poet Rumi, in other words, but does include Doris Lessing and Vladimir Mayakovsky. To take a different example, translation studies could also be described as a field primarily concerned with relations between literatures and languages. "World" in that context will primarily refer to those systemic relations, whereas other approaches discussed in this book, such as literary ecologies and oceanic studies, relate to "world" in a wider, not strictly systemic sense.

The genealogical critique of world literature, finally, has been pursued primarily by Aamir Mufti (2016), Siraj Ahmed (2018), and Bhaidik Bhattacharya (2016). Differences in emphases notwithstanding, all three return to the same source: the emergence of Orientalist philology in late eighteenth-century Bengal. With William Jones's establishment of linguistic connections between Sanskrit and European languages, a tremendously influential line of philological inquiry was inaugurated. It is through this "knowledge revolution," in Mufti's words, that "non-Western textual traditions made their first wholescale entry *as literature*, sacred and secular, into the international literary space that had emerged in early modern times in Europe as a structure of rivalries between the emerging vernacular traditions" (2016, 58). Aligning himself closely with Edward Said, this is what Mufti identifies as the Orientalist logic of world literature, which established literature as a flattening "plane of equivalence," allowing for conceptual mastery of human diversity. Ahmed is more critical of Said's attachment to philology, but makes a related argument when he claims that this period saw the development

Introduction: why world literature? 19

of a form of "philological power" that "disembedded native literatures from their tradition in order to dissever native subjects from their forms of life" (2018, 39). In Bhattacharya's formulation, what began with William Jones as the discovery of the Indo-European language family, developed "into an epistemic habit of the colonial state in the subsequent decades and saturated the daily business of running the empire" (2016, 679). All three scholars make a Foucauldian argument about how comparative literature and/or philology instituted an episteme – a knowledge/power paradigm – that then explains the "logic" of contemporary world literature. Their analyses of the eighteenth- and nineteenth-century materials are compelling and contribute significantly to the understanding not only of the early globalization of the humanities, but also of their complicity with colonialism. They are, however, less convincing as *general* critiques of contemporary practices of world literature, for two reasons. The first is that their own mode of enquiry is dependent on philological methods of linguistic historicization, archival retrieval and comparative analysis to make their case – which implies that there are better and worse ways of doing philology and comparatism, not that it is by definition doomed to replicate colonial methods of governance. The second (as this book tries to demonstrate) is that no single "master approach" to world literature is being practised today, only overlapping and sometimes even contradictory methods. Related to this, if one investigates the archives of literary criticism in, say, Latin America, Africa and South Asia over the last century, "literature" emerges as a work in progress and a site of contestation, not as an unchangeable paradigm (Chaudhuri 2014; Helgesson 2017, 2018; McDonald 2009, 2017). This requires a more dynamic, dialectical and actor-oriented mode of critique than the identification of a Foucauldian episteme tends to allow.

The way forward

As should be evident, world literature today is the site of a complex renegotiation of the object of literary studies. Its current configuration is unthinkable without the postcolonial turn in the 1980s and 1990s, but it is for all that not just postcolonialism under another name – its cultural, geographical and temporal scope goes beyond the formative paradigms of postcolonial studies. Nor is it simply an extension of comparative literature, whose diverse disciplinary traditions tended to be firmly entrenched in a Western, canonical frame of reference. At a high level of abstraction, world literature can be described as the ongoing redefinition of literary studies in the era of globalization. But if "globalization" counts here as the turbulent historical predicament that prompts disciplinary reappraisal, one should not commit the mistake of viewing literature as a stable term that simply needs to accommodate globalization and then continue with business as usual. On the contrary, the value of literature and literature as a value are equally at stake, not least in the domain of higher education, when confronted with the effects of migration, digital media, ecological deterioration, weakening nation-states and resurgent nationalisms. It is at this nexus of literature and social flux that much of the energy in contemporary scholarship is focused, and it is such an understanding of world literature today that informs our endeavour in this book.

The chapters that follow describe a distinct trajectory from meta-disciplinary to more hands-on concerns. The following two chapters position world literature studies in relation to the history of literary studies and its spatial orientations. In Chapter 1, "Paradigms: world literature and its others," we discuss four other approaches to literary studies in relation to world literature. The seasoned national and comparative schools of thought as well as the relatively newer focus on postcolonialism and translation are juxtaposed with the world literature paradigm in a search for the blind spots of each mode of inquiry. Chapter 2, "Ecologies of literature: the cosmopolitan-vernacular nexus," builds on Alexander Beecroft's typology of the related spheres of the world of literature, which both connect and separate environments at various scales. Literary ecologies, which are formed by factors such as language, politics, economy and religion, are arguably what determines the meaning of "literature" in given historical moments. They enable in that way a meta-perspective on world literature itself. Chapters 3 and 4 are devoted to modes of interpretation. "Genre: strangeness and familiarity" focuses on the value of strangeness and how genres play a role in mitigating the unfamiliar, sometimes at the risk of promoting stereotypes. "Geographies: reading the oceans" shows how the routes of literature cross with the patterns laid out by historical power relations and influences, which are particularly visible along the Atlantic and Indian Ocean trading routes. The next chapters take on two central methodological challenges to world literature studies: the role of digitization and of translation. Chapter 5, "Media and method: the digitized Library of Babel," addresses the impact of digitization on world literature studies in terms of accessibility, translation, and scholarship, an aspect that has not drawn much attention although the digital revolution and the re-emergence of world literature that occurred at the same time. Chapter 6, "Translation: duration and cosmopolitan reading," shows how the complexity of language and the choices of the translator are a central issue for world literature studies. Using cases from Brazilian literature, the cosmopolitan desire is brought forward as a pivotal aspect of translation practices. Finally, the volume ends with a dialogue between the authors, "Unfinished business," that brings a number of the key issues of the book together and lays bare the considerations, choices and challenges that cannot simply be solved but should be part of an ongoing exchange about how literature and the world make sense and make a difference.

Acknowledgement

Stefan Helgesson gratefully acknowledges funding from the Swedish Foundation for Humanities and Social Sciences (Riksbankens Jubileumsfond) that has supported the writing of this book.

Notes

1 This account paraphrases Chinua Achebe's own (Achebe 2012, 33–9).
2 "Deux ans auparavant, j'étais encore plongé dans l'ivresse du Royaume d'Enfance, de la Négritude retrouvée, en proie aux laves brûlantes du volcan intérieur. [...] Deux ans auparavant, ma quête, notre quête n'était que de nous-mêmes [...] Nous ne hantions que nos congénères."

References

Achebe, Chinua. 2012. *There Was a Country: A Personal History of Biafra*. New York: Penguin.
Ahmed, Siraj. 2018. *Archaeology of Babel: The Colonial Foundation of the Humanities*. Stanford, CA: Stanford University Press.
Anker, Elizabeth S. and Rita Felski, eds. 2017. *Critique and Postcritique*. Durham: Duke University Press.
Apter, Emily. 2013. *Against World Literature: On the Politics of Untranslatability*. London: Verso.
Arvidsson, Stefan. 2006. *Aryan Idols: Indo-European Mythology as Ideology and Science*. Translated by Sonia Wichmann. Chicago, IL: Chicago University Press.
Auerbach, Erich. 1969. "Philology and Weltliteratur." Translated by Maire and Edward Said. *The Centennial Review* 13, no. 1: 1–17.
Beecroft, Alexander. 2015. *An Ecology of World Literature*. London: Verso.
Bhattacharya, Bhaidik. 2016. "On Comparatism in the Colony: Archives, Methods, and the Project of Weltliteratur." *Critical Inquiry* 42: 677–711.
Bloom, Harold. 1994. *The Western Canon: The Books and School of Ages*. New York: Harcourt Brace.
Buescu, Helena, et al., eds. 2018. *Literatura-mundo comparada: perspectivas em português*, vols. 1–4. Lisbon: Tinta da China.

Casanova, Pascale. 1999. *La République mondiale des lettres*. Paris: Seuil.
Casanova, Pascale. 2004. *The World Republic of Letters*. Cambridge, MA: Harvard University Press.
Chaudhuri, Rosinka. 2014. *The Literary Thing: History, Poetry and the Making of a Modern Cultural Sphere*. Oxford: Peter Lang.
Cheah, Pheng. 2016. *What Is a World? On Postcolonial Literature as World Literature*. Durham: Duke University Press.
Damrosch, David. 2003. *What Is World Literature?* Princeton, NJ: Princeton University Press.
D'haen, Theo. 2012. *The Routledge Concise History of World Literature*. London: Routledge.
D'haen, Theo, César Domínguez and Mads Rosendahl Thomsen, eds. 2012. *World Literature: A Reader*. New York: Routledge.
Eckermann, Johan Peter. 1929. *Gespräche mit Goethe in den letzten Jahren seines Lebens 1823–1832*, vols. 1 and 2. Leipzig: Tempel.
Ganguly, Debjani. 2016. *This Thing Called the World: The Contemporary Novel as Global Form*. Durham: Duke University Press.
Hayot, Eric. 2012. *On Literary Worlds*. Oxford: Oxford University Press.
Helgesson, Stefan. 2017. "Ngugi wa Thiong'o and the Conceptual Worlding of Literature." *Anglia* 135, no. 1: 105–121.
Helgesson, Stefan. 2018. "'Literature,' Theory from the South and the Case of the São Paulo School." *Cambridge Journal of Postcolonial Literary Inquiry* 5, no. 2: 141–157.
Hitchcock, Peter. 2010. *The Long Space: Transnationalism and Postcolonial Form*. Stanford, CA: Stanford University Press.
Huggan, Graham. 2001. *The Postcolonial Exotic: Marketing the Margins*. London: Routledge.
Khotimsky, Maria. 2013. "World Literature, Soviet Style: A Forgotten Episode in the History of the Idea." *Ab Imperio* 3: 119–154.
Laachir, Karima, Sara Marzagora and Francesca Orsini. 2018. "Significant Geographies: In Lieu of World Literature." *Journal of World Literature* 3: 290–310.
Latour, Bruno. 2004. "Why Has Critique Run out of Steam? From Matters of Fact to Matters of Concern." *Critical Inquiry* 30: 225–248.
Mani, B. Venkat. 2017. *Recoding World Literature: Libraries, Print Culture, and Germany's Pact with Books*. New York: Fordham University Press.
Marx, Karl and Friedrich Engels. 2012 [1848]. *The Communist Manifesto: A Modern Edition*. London: Verso.
McDonald, Peter D. 2009. *The Literature Police: Apartheid Censorship and Its Cultural Consequences*. Oxford: Oxford University Press.
McDonald, Peter D. 2017. *Artefacts of Writing: Ideas of the State and Communities of Letters from Matthew Arnold to Xu Bing*. Oxford: Oxford University Press.
Moretti, Franco. 2013. *Distant Reading*. London: Verso.
Mufti, Aamir. 2016. *Forget English! Orientalisms and World Literatures*. Cambridge, MA: Harvard University Press.

Noyes, John K. 2015. *Herder: Aesthetics against Imperialism*. Toronto: Toronto University Press.
Orsini, Francesca. 2015. "The Multilingual Local in World Literature." *Comparative Literature* 67, no. 4: 354–374.
Pettersson, Anders et al., eds. 2006. *Literary History: Towards a Global Perspective*, vols. 1–6. Berlin: De Gruyter.
Prendergast, Christopher, ed. 2004. *Debating World Literature*. London: Verso.
Richter, Sandra. 2017. *Eine Weltgeschichte der deutschsprachigen Literatur*. München: C. Bertelsmann.
Saussy, Haun. 2006. "Exquisite Cadaver Stitches from Fresh Nightmares: Of Memes, Hives, and Selfish Genes." In *Comparative Literature in an Age of Globalization*. Baltimore, MD: Johns Hopkins.
Senghor, Léopold Sédar. 1964. *Liberté 1: Négritude et humanisme*. Paris: Seuil.
Shih, Shuh-mei. 2004. "Global Literature and the Technologies of Recognition." *PMLA* 119, no. 1: 16–30.
Spivak, Gayatri Chakravorty. 2003. *Death of a Discipline*. New York: Columbia University Press.
Spivak, Gayatri. 2012. "The Stakes of a World Literature." In *An Aesthetic Education in the Era of Globalization*, 455–466. Cambridge: Harvard University Press.
Svedjedal, Johan. 2013. *Bland litteraturens förenade nationer: kring svenska PEN-klubbens historia*. Stockholm: Wahlström & Widstrand.
Tagore, Rabindranath. 2015. "Vishva Sahitya." Translated by Rijula Das and Makarand R. Paranjape. In *Rabindranath Tagore in the 21st Century*, edited by Debashish Benerji, 277–288. New Delhi: Springer.
Tiwari, Bhavya. 2011. "Rabindranath Tagore's Comparative World Literature." In *The Routledge Companion to World Literature*, edited by Theo D'haen, David Damrosch and Djelal Kadir, 41–48. New York: Routledge.
Warwick Research Collective (WReC). 2015. *Combined and Uneven Development: Towards a New Theory of World-Literature*. Liverpool: Liverpool University Press.
Whitney, Joel. 2016. *Finks: How the C.I.A. Tricked the World's Best Writers*. New York: OR Books.
Wittgenstein, Ludwig. 2009. *Philosophical Investigations*, 4th ed. Translated by G. E. M. Ascombe, P. M. S. Hacker and Joachim Schulte. Oxford: Wiley-Blackwell.

1 Paradigms
World literature and its others

Mads Rosendahl Thomsen

Cultural globalization is an ongoing and differentiated process that has obviously not arisen out of nowhere. In literary studies the re-emergence of world literature can be seen as a reaction to and a critique of other ways of addressing the international dimensions of literature. In this chapter, world literature is framed in terms of its relations to four central paradigms or modes of study: national literature, comparative literature, postcolonial studies, and translation studies. These approaches to literature overlap in many ways, but also contain significant differences in terms of how literature should be understood in an international context: differences in terms of ideological stance, sense of purpose and perspective, and the inclusion and exclusion of canons, for instance. Such differences can be fruitful when they highlight choices that have significant consequences for scholarship and education; but some differences appear to create divisions where there should be dialogue.

National literature

Johann Wolfgang von Goethe's emphatic prediction in the late 1820s that national literature would come to an end and be replaced by world literature is an unavoidable moment in the history of world literature studies (Goethe 2012, 11). Goethe's bold assertion may be guilty of doing some damage, leading people to perceive world literature as a threat with almost imperial ambitions. The implicit suggestion that national literature and world literature cannot coexist has caused a lot of often unnecessary debate about which of the two should prevail. Both perspectives, one local and one universal, have merits and continue to challenge each other, no matter what they are called. As Kwame Anthony Appiah has explained, ruthless cosmopolitanism is very rare in practice, and this is certainly true in the study of a specific field such as literature (Appiah 2005, 220).

Goethe was not just wrong, but extremely wrong in thinking that national literature would soon cease to be of importance. Instead of a cosmopolitan utopia, there followed a period of national orientation in Europe, and literary history as a genre played a significant role in building national identities in nineteenth-century Europe. Instead of chronicling conflict and power struggles, as history traditionally has done and still does, literary history presents a more positive narrative of artistic mastery of language and stories of individuals and their emotions grounded in a larger culture. The golden age of literary history in the second half of the nineteenth century (if it is possible to talk of a golden age) took place during a period when literature was a dominant medium. There was no television, radio, Internet, recorded music or cinema to compete with the written word. And yet despite the existence of such media today, there are probably more readers now than ever before, thanks to the prevalence of better education and more leisure time for more people.

The prominence of national literature in Western academic circles began to wear off at the beginning of the twentieth century; and while it has been ideologically tainted – as a perspective on literature that is narrow-minded, xenophobic, provincial and just wrong in its portrait of how influences flow among writers – it has in practice been (and still is) influential. Educational systems, book markets, funding for authors and (not least) the existence of publishing houses with an interest in publishing in the vernacular have all supported a structure that gave so much prevalence to local authors that even neighbouring countries with shared languages were marginalized, a situation that still prevails to some extent today. The enthusiasm for a globalized world of the 1990s has waned, and the strong impact of nationally funded institutions has proven more powerful than expected. It now seems likely that the national frame will continue to be very important, depending, among other things, on how educational systems fortify national narratives or open up their curricula towards the world. The rise of a new nationalism is a tendency in the 2010s that takes many different shapes: from the newfound self-confidence of China and Russia and the xenophobic populism of politics in both East and West Europe, to the disillusioned nations around the world that feel marginalized and instead turn inwards.

In Shuyu Kong's study of the changed and more liberal Chinese book market, *Consuming Literature*, the most interesting observations may be not that the *Harry Potter* series does well or that Shakespeare is being translated in often competing versions, but rather that there is a large market for a new urban literature that draws on American and European genres but is written by and for a young Chinese audience (Kong 2004, 31). There is nothing wrong with authors turning their backs on a wide international audience, focusing instead on being of interest to people who can relate directly to what it is like to live at a certain moment in history in China, Chile or Canada, with references to local phenomena, intricate details of history and everyday customs being picked up easily by their compatriots but not necessarily by other readers – even readers from neighbouring countries. This complicates matters from a world literature perspective, since the traditional interpretation of world literature as the most universal and most accomplished form of literature is at odds with the idea of a literature that is highly regarded locally but of little interest to the rest of the world. Should not all literature aspire to speak universally? Can there be more than one scale for measuring value in literature? This is particularly complicated because works that are considered to be world literature by this definition almost always rise out of local environments. An old maxim – "all good art is national, all national art is bad" – suggests that one should not aspire to write literature that is unconnected to real times and places. However, this does not mean that there cannot be valuable, original works that for a number of reasons do not have a broad appeal but are primarily part of a national canon. This may change as writers have a late breakthrough internationally, but it may also remain as it is. Changing the attitude towards the hierarchy implicitly suggested by "world literature" would be beneficial not only with regard to promoting the values of a rethought version of national literature, but also in terms of the idea that world literature is not bound to one standard of literary value.

In "Die Weltliteratur," the Czech-French author Milan Kundera speaks of two kinds of provincialism: that of small nations, and that of large ones. The provincialism of the small nation makes it turn inwards because it does not think that it has anything to offer to the world and instead concentrates on its own life, whereas the provincialism of the large nation finds that it has everything it needs and ignores the world. Both stances are problematic to Kundera: "A nation's possessiveness toward its artists works as a *small-context terrorism*, reducing the whole meaning of a work to the role it plays in its homeland" (Kundera 2012, 293). Kundera not only adopts a general orientation towards world literature, but also highlights particular contexts that go beyond the nation. He has argued, for example, that Central European literature provides a more meaningful framework than national literatures, which in many cases are marked by the unstable and changing maps of their region of origin. But the question is whether a compromise is possible:

Between the *large context* of the world and the *small context* of the nation, a middle step might be imagined: say, a *median context*. Between Sweden and the world, that step is Scandinavia. For Colombia, it is Latin America. And for Hungary, for Poland? In my emigration, I tried to work out a response to that question, and the title of a piece I wrote at the time sums it up: *A Kidnapped West, or The Tragedy of Central Europe.*

(Kundera 2012, 295)

Kundera's suggestions align, most likely unintentionally, with the field of area studies that has emerged as an important alternative to nationally based studies of history and literature. The International Comparative Literature Association has made the regional perspective the focus in a series of comprehensive volumes of literary history. Rather than writing on the literature of single countries, these volumes are organized by regions and seek other ways to explore the characteristics of literature across national borders. The Iberian Peninsula, Latin America, Central Europe, Africa (south of the Sahara), and the Nordic countries are examples of the regional ordering of literary history. This framing has often worked well as a productive compromise that breaks with nationalism but remains manageable in ways that a global perspective does not. Rather than presenting itself as a new natural frame of reference, the regional perspective is concerned with the contingency and historically unstable nature of its object. It is of course also a weakness, at least rhetorically, that the borders of these literary histories can be criticized for their excessive breadth and their failure to build on the hard currency of nationhood, or for being too narrow compared to a world literature perspective. (We will address this issue in Chapter 4.) Unlike the world and the nation, or a language for that matter, it is difficult to see the region as a close-knit unit, although that could be contested. Some national borders have varied a great deal over time, but the regional unity of, say, the Iberian Peninsula or Scandinavia could be a better fit for writing on the *longue durée* of the history of literature. As a pragmatic frame seeking to do more than just reproduce things that have already been explored, without attempting to take on a huge project on a global scale, the regional perspective can use its lack of any metaphysical claim to be the true frame to venture into productive critique and deconstruction of national monoliths and infinite worldliness.

While world literature as a paradigm has never been at odds with place-specific, locally based literature, it has been more in conflict with nationalism. But is it even possible to argue in favour of national literature nowadays? It may be. One argument would be that younger nations should develop their own identity and that the literary world – institutions, academics, etc. – should bear that in mind. The call for world literature and cosmopolitanism is much easier to make when one already has a literary tradition extending back centuries or even millennia to stand on, and the uneven playing field of literature is very apparent here. While the age of some literatures is measured in hundreds or thousands of years, the print-based literary history of a good number of the world's national literatures is essentially still measured in decades. There is obviously no natural development and no fixed number of steps that have to be taken along the path to becoming a "mature" literature; but even so, young literatures still have to face a situation in which a new global agenda is being promoted while their local foundation is still being built.

The dilemma of the importance of local context has deep roots. Goethe's hope for world literature may even have been born out of frustration with the immature development of German literature in his day and age compared with the role model of Greek, Latin, and Chinese literature, as well as other modern European literatures with a far more established tradition – in particular Renaissance classics. In this perspective, world literature could be seen as a different and more glorious framing of Goethe's work. Eventually, Goethe succeeded in both ways: as a figure of world literature and as the central author of German literature. The question is whether Goethe would have become part of world literature without the development of German literature into a strong tradition of its own.

The importance of literature to the reinforcement of national identities in the nineteenth century is unlikely to be repeated in the twenty-first century, owing to the reduced influence of literature in a much more diverse media landscape. Freedom from the burden of creating identity may be a way forward, but also implies a significant new role for literature, not least in educational systems. It may be the only way to go, as the historian of nationalism Joep Leerssen has suggested in *National Thought in Europe*:

> The most coherent states may in the future well be those that are most flexible about their inner diversity, and most efficient in giving citizens a civic, rather than a cultural, focus for their shared loyalty and solidarity.
>
> (Leerssen 2006, 241)

Instead, the implicit hope is that literature could flourish by becoming more transnational and less dependent on providing identity, or (more positively) by providing a different, more fluid kind of identity that is in sync with the way people navigate their lives in the twenty-first century.

Comparative literature

In practice, comparative literature has become a generic description of a field in literary studies that goes beyond national philologies rather than being defined by distinct methods. The idea of comparing literatures does not reflect what is actually going on in the field, at least not in the sense of juxtaposing different national traditions and finding evidence of the influence of different literatures on each other. One could argue that all literary scholarship involves comparing of some sort, although such comparison has also been neglected and remained a tacit element of the discipline that has needed more reflection. It has recently received detailed study in Rita Felski and Susan Stanford Friedman's edited volume *Comparison*, which re-energized the field of comparative literature by taking up questions of comparison on a multitude of subjects, from linguistic structures to political inequalities (Felski and Friedman 2013, 2).

The openness of the discipline to new impulses has made it a home for many cross-disciplinary scholars and a centre for important theoretical work that has had an influence across the humanities (Saussy 2006, 34). However, this theoretical curiosity has not always been matched by an openness towards the world's literatures. Ideally, comparative literature should entail an approach to literary studies that would make world literature unnecessary as a revitalised paradigm; but it may be the lack of curiosity and de facto reliance on a Western canon that led to a reorientation towards world literature.

One of the merits of comparative literature is its demand that literature should be read in its original language; but this has also shaped the field in ways that have hindered a global outlook. The question of translation provides a real dilemma: working directly with literature sets the bar high (appropriately so for academic work), but it also makes it difficult to conduct fruitful discussions among scholars and students, since their linguistic competences will have as many gaps as overlaps. There is therefore a need for a more flexible attitude towards translation in order to include more literatures in the conversation. In "The (Really Big) Shape of Comparative Literature Now, Or, a Discipline's Totalizing Conceit," Jerry Varsava has called for a necessary expansion of the way in which comparative literature should be organized:

> Comparative literature can no longer define itself simply as comparative research involving literary works drawn from two or more

linguistic traditions. Such an enterprise has great merit, as the history of the discipline shows, and we need to promote and conserve it. Still, it is not the only way to conduct research in comparative literature. When the world was a smaller (Eurocentric) place, it was much easier to achieve competence in a small handful of notionally exemplary, "high-canonical" languages, mostly western European for, as no less of an authority than Goethe opined pithily, "European, in other words, World Literature." The world is bigger today than it has ever been. An understanding of two or three languages can help one to achieve great insights but, given what John Tomlinson has called "complex connectivity," there are many major issues and challenges that are culturally, and dare one say linguistically, overdetermined. No adequate understanding of contemporary global economic affairs, of contemporary ideological differences and tensions, of the contemporary political novel, can be achieved by a "reading knowledge," or even mastery, of a small clutch of languages.

(Varsava 2017, 498–9)

Varsava's arguments for change in the field could also be read as a conflict between comparative literature and world literature studies in defining the fundamental units in their object of study. Although it is hardly the practice any more, the original foundation for comparative studies was national literatures considered as whole entities that could be compared. This is of course easier said than done, and in practice the discipline has produced focused studies with the overarching ambition of representing national literary identity. One way of characterizing world literature studies would then be that it has come up with several ideas for creating a new space for comparison. David Damrosch has suggested the inclusion of works from several different literatures and comparing these works not by neglecting their specific origins and contexts, but without seeing them as representatives of a larger literature (Damrosch 2003, 299–300). By setting up constellations of works for comparison, this approach carves out a space for comparison that relies not on representing national literatures, but rather on tendencies in world literature that will become apparent thanks to the common traits shared by the works in question. Franco Moretti has placed much emphasis on the spread of genres, techniques and devices, rather than on individual works (Moretti 2013, 111). For example, the novel, which Moretti's research has focused on, has been adopted by literatures that did not have a strong tradition in this particular mode of prose narration. Although the modern form of the novel has many forerunners, the spread of the genre and the complex history of influences makes it a form that is truly global as well as dominant in some literary cultures, relegating poetry, drama and short fiction to niche genres. In a call for a more global engagement with modernist literature that is applicable to literature in general, Andreas Huyssen has suggested that the idea of high and low literature and genres needs to be abolished without giving up on demands for aesthetic quality (Huyssen 2007, 202–3). This is obviously quite a challenge, but it also appears to be a worthwhile direction for literary studies – and in particular for the broader field of cultural studies. Whereas the former has held on too strongly to a limited canon and particular preferences for certain genres and modes, the latter has been more thematically driven and has not focused sufficiently on why and how certain aesthetic forms have greater impact and longevity.

The 2017 decennial report *Futures of Comparative Literature* from the American Comparative Literature Association did not try to summarize the most pressing challenge facing the field, but presented itself as simply a discussion of the futures of comparative literature, acknowledging the range and lack of coherence of the discipline by using the plural form (Heise 2017). By contrast, the two previous reports singled out a new cultural situation. "Multiculturalism" was the keyword in the 1995 report (Bernheimer 1995), while "globalization" framed the debates on world literature in 2006 (Saussy 2006). The generic "futures" acknowledges the number of minor changes that are shaping the field and the way in which the different scales of investigation – world, area, nation, locality – shape the practices of investigation. Two other trends are also significant: the increased importance of other media for literature (in terms of both the media landscape in which literature is studied and the remediation of literature), and the way in which digitization changes access to works and the study of literature (including its circulation). In many respects, it is a healthy sign for a discipline that it is not concerned with defining one decisive direction, but focuses instead on a wider fabric of shaping issues. A number of topics are still of great importance, even though they entered the field of discussion decades ago. The canons are still gender biased, the world's resources are still distributed very unevenly, and xenophobia has become a pressing issue in new ways as migration and more diverse societies have become more influential. The question of languages has assumed new configurations as the dominance of English has become more pronounced, and even traditional world languages are being marginalized outside their base.

It is difficult to find a new consistent framework for a more multifaceted comparative approach. The German scholar Ottmar Ette has provided original suggestions for seeing places as culturally encoded sites where vectors from other places criss-cross and exert their influence on specific cultural configurations. Ette thereby opts for a model that does not do away with site specificity, but describes places as complex and subject to numerous influences: cultures, languages, media, temporal consciousness, and the organization of space and activity of travelling (Ette 2005, 21–2). Ette's central point is that the most realistic semantics in the analysis of place and literature have moved from a focus on relations between separate entities (often using the prefix "inter"), via the co-habitation of unlike cultural phenomena (often determined by being "multi"), to a situation in which influences from other entities have mixed (usually designated by "trans"). Ette's distinctions reflect significant movements in comparative studies convincingly, but they also provide a much more complex landscape of distinctions that are difficult to develop into a stable set of principles. However, the general direction in Ette's diagnosis of the semantics of identity construction is telling, as is his call to take in multiple perspectives in the analysis of literature's cultural location. The flexibility of the idea of comparative literature is certainly one of its strengths, but also raises the question of what is at its core: what makes this activity valuable beyond reacting to how the world changes?

Postcolonial studies

It is an open question whether there would have been a renewed interest in world literature if it had not been for postcolonial studies. Postcolonial studies – which cannot be reduced to one movement but is widely used as a category – raised the most sustained and impactful critique of the Western-centric canon in the late 1970s. This led to an institutional reorganization of the degree programmes conducted by many English departments in the 1980s, with programmes in colonial and postcolonial literature supplementing the traditional emphasis on British and American literature and thus effectively arguing that studies in English literature should cover the whole world. Postcolonialism emerged as a movement with many strong figures who have given it a complex identity in terms of artistic accomplishment (V.S. Naipaul, Derek Walcott and Chinua Achebe, for instance), and academic achievement (Frantz Fanon, Édouard Glissant, Edward W. Said, Gayatri Spivak and Homi Bhabha, for instance). Some of these individuals were explicitly involved with world literature. Said translated Erich Auerbach's essay on world literature into English, while in his preface to *The Location of Culture*, Bhabha draws on Goethe to redefine the potential for a new world literature:

[W]orld literature could be an emergent, prefigurative category that is concerned with a form of cultural dissensus and alterity, where nonconsensual terms of affiliation may be established on the grounds of historical trauma. The study of world literature might be the study of the way in which cultures recognize themselves through their projections of "otherness." Where, once, the transmission of national traditions was the major theme of a world literature, perhaps now we can suggest that transnational histories of migrants, the colonized, or political refugees – these border and frontier conditions – may be the terrains of world literature.

(Bhabha 1994, 12)

Like many scholars of world literature, Bhabha asks whether or how the unhomely, understood as a radical experience of not feeling at home in the world that is often related to the political situation of an individual, can become an international theme without claiming universality; but by contrast with other world literature scholars, he also stresses the importance of politics in its institutionalization.

This institutionalization was followed by a number of dilemmas that may explain why world literature became another focal point in studies of literature that wanted to break free from the assumptions of comparative literature. First of all, the integration of the object of postcolonial studies with other literatures remains complicated. If we take postcolonialism to be the academic response to anticolonialism and decolonization, then we need to recognize that literature is just one of its various focal points. In that sense, it is almost a category mistake to compare the disciplinary agendas of postcolonialism and world literature – their purposes are constitutively different. When they do overlap, however, there are potential contradictions. What the two fields share, one might say, are complex hopes for diversity and a common ground. But juxtaposing the literatures of the old colonial powers with those of the former colonies risks reiterating power relations and the unequal terms on which literatures and works accumulate canonical authority. The question of language is also problematic: while Indian literature in English has been very influential internationally, the same cannot be said of the hundreds of languages used on the Indian subcontinent. The same dilemmas surround African literatures, only more so, given the continuing need for African writers to publish in Europe or North America if they wish to reach a wider audience. For this reason, the use of formerly colonial languages has been singled out as problematic in itself – as argued particularly by Ngugi wa Thiong'o (1986) – although English, French and Portuguese are increasingly regarded as African languages in their own right. Literatures in, say, Wolof, Yoruba, Hausa or Amharic remain mostly invisible outside their linguistic communities, which also contributes to making Europhone literatures less inclusive of other languages.

This leads to the fundamental question of what kind of postcolonial writing should be valued. One dividing distinction goes between migrant writers and non-migrants. For better or worse, a significant number of the internationally circulated writers from formerly colonized nations are migrants who no longer live in the countries that they draw upon for their literature; and their experience as migrants having to adapt to a new culture is often central to their writing, rather than the experience of taking part in the life of a developing nation. But many migrant writers have also established themselves as powerful voices whose works circulate very broadly, in part because they have published from within the Western markets and write about issues that have multiple contexts and highlight how to navigate these. This tension between the cosmopolitan and the local or national remains.

Increasingly, "world literature in English" has become a subject in many university programmes, thereby (in principle) breaking down the tri-partite division into British, American and postcolonial literature and creating a single space for the study of literature. However, one might fear that it will be easy to take away the foothold that postcolonial literature has gained in such educational programmes unless it is given its own designated position. The optimistic view would be that a postcolonial literary canon has developed that is strong enough to be integrated into British and American literature, while the pessimist would claim that this is still an uneven playing field: Western literature is backed by a much longer tradition, and the ethnocentrism of markets and readers tends to shift the balance back in favour of Western writers with Western experiences. As such, there are irreconcilable disagreements between postcolonial and world literature studies.

The strong political commitment of postcolonial studies may make it more relevant in the years to come. Whereas world literature studies has focused to some extent on the virtues of literature and its manifold expressions, the darker sides of globalization have not been addressed extensively. Postcolonial studies, on the other hand, has proposed a powerful narrative of how accumulated capital exploits the most vulnerable in societies, formerly through colonization, theft and slavery, and in the twenty-first century through the outsourcing of jobs, tax evasion and automation: an ongoing history of injustice which today also needs to account for China's neo-imperial clout. The sustained interest in the writing of Frantz Fanon, whose *The Wretched of the Earth* is a modern classic conveying the experience of being subaltern, is just one indication of how the political perspective is a dimension of literary studies that engages scholars. Nonetheless, the question is whether literature is still the most relevant medium for political critique. While the number of imprisoned writers throughout history speaks volumes about the close connection between literature and political struggle, the public field today seems more dispersed and seems to have many other actors and media.

As we have been arguing, then, world literature studies and postcolonial studies have much in common, but also distinct interests and perspectives. In her 2018 book *Postcolonial Poetics*, Elleke Boehmer sums up what she sees as the main differences between postcolonial and world literature critique:

> World literature embraced "the diversity of literary cultures," yet without abandoning the authority of the western reader and the centrality of Europe, a space that for postcolonial studies would necessarily always be contested. Whereas postcolonial critique ultimately always returned and returns critics to political and geohistorical questions of power and agency – who has voice?, whose land is this? – world literary studies with its commitment to concepts of an interconnected globe, a unified if uneven literary field, or a single world-system, and to methods of generic overview and modular reading, effectively bypassed or conflated such often historically specific, culturally calibrated, and ethically difficult concerns. In place of postcolonial studies' often dark and driven preoccupations, its exploited peripheries, disruptive interfaces, partitions, and schisms, world literature upheld stable literary entities like canons and classics, bulwarked by tried-and-tested procedures of formal and comparatist literary analysis. Its universal cultural values comfortably overrode, or overwrote, the difficult, fraught, and fussy specificities of the postcolonial.
>
> (Boehmer 2018, 163)

The pronounced dichotomies are outlined more emphatically than elsewhere in Boehmer's book. While it is debatable whether she provides an accurate account of current world literature studies, her description does identify some crucial points of contention. The question of Western authority and centrality in world literature studies is an inherent risk in a field where so much of the research is being carried out in Western countries. But the accusation of Western-centrism has sometimes been aimed at the postcolonial field itself, and not without good reason (Lazarus 2011;

Gikandi 2011). On the one hand, the often reduced political emphasis in world literature studies is a fair description of a difference in the practices of world literature. On the other hand, the field deals to a wide extent with issues of global inequality, including the unequal access to become world literature.

Boehmer's last sentence is interesting for its implicit scale of value. Stability is viewed as problematic, whereas disruption and "fussy specificities" are seen as positive; the universal must give way to the specific, and so on. An alternative view would claim that canonicity is always a stake in the game, and that multiple canons (among multiple interpretive communities) are in operation at any given moment. One would be hard pressed to imagine a postcolonial scholar claiming, in the name of anti-canonical critique, that we should *refrain* from reading Mulk Raj Anand's *Untouchable*, Chinua Achebe's *Things Fall Apart*, or Tsitsi Dangarembga's *Nervous Conditions*. Or to take a different example: literature on the Holocaust has developed a clearly identifiable canon, although a rigorously ethical position would hold that every witness should be seen as equal. But in practice this is not the case, as Imre Kertész has pointed out (Kertész 2001, 268), and the same goes for postcolonial literature. The hopes for expanding the canon and finding new connections are what has driven world literature as well as postcolonial studies, and it seems odd to want to give the latter credit for this ambition alone, even if one may have productive disagreements on how the structure of the literary field is perceived (disagreements that also depend on the purpose of a particular investigation.) And even then, the ways in which canonicity has been perceived in world literature studies vary a great deal. David Damrosch's insistence on matching distant works, often canonical and non-canonical, is quite different from Pascale Casanova's penchant for authors from minor countries that have made a mark on the larger literatures, which again is very different from Franco Moretti's explicitly non-canonical interest in the spread of genres. Neil Lazarus's critique of the strictures of the *postcolonial* canon (2011) resulted not only in a critical expansion of his corpus, but also in a decisive turn towards "world-literature" (with the hyphen indicating its connection to world-system theory – see WReC 2015). So it would seem that unity in these respective fields is often only observable at a distance.

The most relevant question, and one that applies very broadly, is how one can be open to the unknown in a way that creates meaningful connections. There will always be some context in which one locates the new, but if works from the Western canon serve de facto as the norm by which other works are measured, then that is obviously not genuine openness. Promotion of universals does not seem like a way forward either, and it will in reality become a question of what one finds to be a better balance between untenable positions. To make sense of literature in an international perspective, it is not enough to insist on the extremely local or to suggest that comparative practices are not viable. And it is also important to acknowledge that readers come from all kinds of backgrounds, even within national borders. So it is more a question of how to cultivate the openness of literary communities in a way that enables them to respond to something new without abandoning their own values – even while they question whether they are doing things well enough.

Finally, if there is no interest in the quality of writing and the aesthetics of literature, why bother with literature and poetics? Naturally, Boehmer does bother with them, praising the quality of Achebe's work (Boehmer 2018, 138) and singling out various productive strategies – hybrid and resistance writing, for instance – that deliver a certain energy to the texts. The positive valuation of hybrid writing and resistance writing, presented elsewhere by Boehmer (2018, 80), could also just as well be ascribed to works of world literature as to postcolonial writing. Nor is it entirely clear why she promotes a strong preference for complication. What makes for interesting, enlightening and joyful reading? Clarity or complexity? Mysticism or simplicity? The diversity of literature is something that usually comes across as a value in any paradigm.

The nub of Boehmer's claim, then, is that world literature studies has not been sufficiently open to the postcolonial field. The reverse criticism could also be made, but that is a matter of opinion and perspective. In fact, we ultimately agree with Boehmer's suggestion that both fields can learn from each other, and that there is no obstacle to combining world literature's capacity to "track shared textual features across wide geographies" with "radical postcolonial energies" in the service of a "more horizontal conception of the world" (Boehmer 2018, 165). At the end of the day, the relative lack of political interest in prevailing inequalities may be the point at which the critique of world literature studies stings the most, even if some of the past expressions of imperial dominance no longer exist except as historical memories. Echoing the concerns of many postcolonialists, Indian writer and scholar Tabish Khair has suggested that xenophobia has been reinvented in our day:

> Old xenophobia constructed the stranger in terms of a physicality or a materiality that was different and had to be feared, and obviously this construction applied to strangers who were already, as implied by my concept of border/contact, not "unknown." With new xenophobia, the greater abstraction of capital has shifted the zone of border/contact: we

are no longer talking of physical or material differences in such circles, but of a difference between the abstract operation of capital as power – an operation that increasingly marginalizes producing and laboring bodies as well as money today – and the materiality and physicality of human existence. The difference then being constructed is based on the fear of the physical and the material when not mediated through abstract capital.

(Khair 2016, 179)

Khair is not optimistic with respect to eradicating the new xenophobia, not least because he sees it as a result of capitalism. But this simply strengthens the urgency of the political dimension in postcolonial studies and beyond.

Translation studies

Robert Frost famously dismissed translation in his definition of poetry as "that which is lost out of both prose and verse in translation" (Frost 1995, 856). Today, translation has become a central issue in literary studies, and as the Bosnian-American writer Aleksandar Hemon has drily remarked, Frost did not speak languages other than English. He has softened his view on Frost, though, explaining that:

> The strange, brilliant thing with language is that it is at the same time very personal, but also it belongs to all the people who speak it. So that even within the same language the personal value of certain words cannot be transmitted to anyone outside the experiential domain inside which that word operates. So that we all know what "beach" means, but for each of us it conjures up a different set of images and smells. But that also means that it is precisely this failure to transmit the exact personal meaning that allows for the negotiations between the writer and the reader that amount to poetry. So yes, there are Bosnian words or phrases that don't have the same emotional value for me when translated into English. But then there are those who don't have it in Bosnian but attain it in English. For instance, "black wine" is the idiomatic way in Bosnian of describing what is "red wine" in English. In Bosnian, "black wine" therefore does not sound strange at all, but in English it does. Robert Frost said: "Poetry is what is lost in translation." But then Joseph Brodsky said: "Poetry is what is gained in translation." Both of them are right.
>
> (Hemon 2015)

The field of translation studies has undergone a significant transformation in the past decades, developing from a peripheral part of literary studies to one of its key components (and we will address the topic at length in its own chapter). First of all, the field has grown along with world literature studies because there cannot be a meaningful idea of world literature without translation. No person can master all languages, or even more than just a fraction of them; so translations are necessary to prevent works of literature from being written off in advance as part of world literature, not least in the non-academic literary culture, where many people prefer to read in their own vernacular. Even in populations that read English quite well, there is a strong demand for translations from English. What has also changed is that translation is now regarded as a much more creative process than it was in the past: translation is a valuable rewriting of works that adds to the understanding of the original. In various ways, Susan Bassnett, Lawrence Venuti and Svend Erik Larsen have drawn attention to the importance of translation studies in a world literature perspective, just as it has been a red thread throughout David Damrosch's work:

> Particularly when we read a work in translation, the book already comes to us shaped by the translator's choices and the publisher's framing of the text for its new market. An assimilative edition can adapt the foreign work strongly toward host-country norms, while a "foreignizing" translation can emphasize the work's difference, its violation of local expectations. Writers and readers alike often turn to world literature to provide resources and aesthetic experiences beyond what is available at home. Even as readers reach out in this way, they may not realize how strongly their prior expectations affect the way they read, and people who have a good knowledge of the foreign work's language and culture are often distressed to find how the original work has become distorted in the process, whether by mistranslation or by culturally obtuse misreading, whether assimilative or exoticizing in character.
>
> (Damrosch 2018, 110)

Let us now proceed from the way authors themselves are influenced by the stories of others to the actual task of producing new works. When works are translated (translated well, of course), the result is a larger corpus of texts that has new meanings and new expressions even though it refers back to the same point of origin. Dante is not just Dante in the original, but a corpus of works in many languages, including translations into contemporary Italian. Sandra Bermann has called this the polyvalence of the text, and she argues that "transnational dialogues tend to subvert the singleness and 'purity' associated with 'foundational' texts. No longer a fixed and stable 'root,' it reveals instead a multi-directional reach to other languages, texts and cultures" (Bermann 2011, 97).

Furthermore, translation is increasingly connected with adaptation and remediation, which has a significant impact on the reception of works. Drama benefits in particular from not only being translated but also staged locally. Whereas poetry and prose will always be received in translation as both distant in time and language, the staged play will carry with it both a sense of the original and the newness and here and now of the performance. The global restaging of Henrik Ibsen or William Shakespeare gives new life to their texts in ways that are unheard of in other genres. Edwin Gentzler has stressed how post-translation studies must be considered, adding to the complexity of the field as:

> post-translation studies is not bound by fixed objects – source and target texts – but is more fluid and includes looking at the pre-textual components, the multilingual aspects and multicultural ideas that comprise an original. ... Importantly, post-translation studies looks at the after-effects of the translation in the target culture.
>
> (Gentzler 2017, 230)

Translation has also become more important in the theory of literature. While the craft of translation is generally recognized, the theory of translation is a more complicated battleground. Emily Apter's *The Translation Zone* even has contradictory theses at the beginning of the book, claiming, with some humour, that everything can be translated and nothing can be translated (Apter 2004, xi–xii). In her later work, Apter has focused increasingly on what cannot be translated, most notably in *Against World Literature*, where she stresses a certain humility towards the idea of being able to comprehend everything, not least in light of how complex the context of a concept or a text can be (Apter 2013, 63ff).

One of the most important distinctions in translation is between domestication and foreignization, which Lawrence Venuti has written about at length (Venuti 2004, 483; see Chapter 6). Translators have to make a key choice in choosing their strategy: either to produce a new text that has been assimilated to the traditions and norms of the receiving culture, or to produce a text in which the difference and strangeness are allowed to figure. This is not a trivial choice, and while Venuti advocates for tipping the balance towards the foreignization that will make it clear to the readers that there is a cultural distance at play, it can also be argued that what is obvious and trivial in one culture should not be translated in a way that makes it seem mysterious and exotic in another. A telling example of this dilemma can be found in the works of the Turkish Nobel Prize laureate Orhan Pamuk. He has stressed to his translators that they should not use Turkish words in their translations in order to make them seem more authentic or produce an effect of estrangement by implying that certain words cannot be translated into other languages. However, in *Istanbul* he did make an exception and insisted that *hüzün*, a word that signifies melancholia, should remain as it was, indicating a particular Turkish sense of the word (Ece 2010, 299).

Translation studies is often a battleground where dubious claims of authenticity and well-intentioned suggestions for a deeper engagement with other languages and literatures collide. Without translation, large parts of the world's literature would be inaccessible to most people. But if we relied solely on translations, world literature would be flatter, culturally more determined by fewer languages (or only one). In *Forget English!*, Aamir Mufti is highly critical of the effects of translation:

> The modes of circulation of Anglophone world literature today, including as (supposedly "neutral") medium of translation, thus serve to *naturalize* this specific version of the international or global, which is predicated on, and helps to reproduce, reading publics oblivious of the possibility of historical alternatives in the past or the present, even and especially in the Global South. My argument here rests on a view of English as a language of translation that does not fully correspond to either side of the quarrel between protagonists of the efficacy of translation and those who emphasize the stubbornly ineffable and untranslatable in language.
> (Mufti 2016, 92)

As a contrast to Mufti's view, in his 2003 article "More Conjectures," Franco Moretti pointed out that literary criticism is produced primarily by scholars and authors writing in English, but added that their cultural background is highly diverse and that the topics they address also make sense in English. If the alternative is silence and invisibility, translation with all its flaws is preferable. Interestingly, following Ottmar Ette's focus on the translinguistic turn, there could be a middle ground in thinking of languages as impure and themselves involved with processes of translation and loans, as Haun Saussy has stressed:

> Loan words are an opposite to translation in the following sense: with translation, interpretation always precedes the restatement; but

with loan words, incorporation occurs without interpretation. Translation works out what the meaning of the foreign text is, then elaborates a corresponding set of meanings that will suitably address the speakers of the target language. With transliteration, foreigners are putting words in your mouth: pure mimicry, as when English speakers imitated the sounds of *amok, ketchup, kayak,* or *samurai*. (Not to mention *gavagai*.) The fact that incorporation can be separated from interpretation installs a strangeness in language, a zone of vocabulary where the mouth acts independently of the mind and where the native speaker and native competency are no longer in command.

(Saussy 2017, 19)

Unlike the other paradigms commented on in this chapter, including world literature studies, translation studies comes across as a modest, focused area of study concerned with a particular activity that is necessary for an international perspective on literature, and which is closely related to the use of language itself with no way to hide behind a thematic agenda. Translation studies stands outside the battle for the dominant position between comparative, postcolonial and world literature, and it cannot exist without considering the writing itself. And these may be two of the main reasons why it has become a pivotal issue.

References

Appiah, Kwame Anthony. 2005. *The Ethics of Identity*. Princeton, NJ: Princeton University Press.
Apter, Emily. 2004. *The Translation Zone: A New Comparative Literature*. Princeton, NJ: Princeton University Press.
Apter, Emily. 2013. *Against World Literature: On the Politics of Untranslatability*. London: Verso.
Bassnett, Susan. 2013. *Translation Studies*, 4th edition. London: Routledge.
Bermann, Sandra. 2011. "In the Light of Translation: on Dante and World Literature." In *Foundational Texts of World Literature*, edited by Dominique Jullien. New York: Peter Lang.
Bernheimer, Charles. 1995. *Comparative Literature in the Age of Multiculturalism*. Baltimore, MD: Johns Hopkins Univ. Press.
Bhabha, Homi. 1994. *The Locations of Culture*. London: Routledge.
Boehmer, Elleke. 2018. *Postcolonial Poetics: 21st-century Critical Readings*. Basingstoke: Palgrave.
Damrosch, David. 2003. *What Is the World Literature?* Princeton, NJ: Princeton University Press.

Damrosch, David. 2018. "Frames for World Literature." In *Tensions in World Literature: Between the Local and the Universal*, edited by W. Fang. Basingstoke: Palgrave Macmillan.

Ece, Ayse Fitnat. 2010 "Orhan Pamuk's hüzün in English and French." *Perspectives: Studies in Translatology* 18, no. 4: 297–306.

Ette, Ottmar. 2005. *Zwischenweltenschreiben: Literaturen Ohne Festen Wohnsitz.* Berlin: Kulturverlag Kadmos.

Fanon, Frantz. 2001. *The Wretched of the Earth.* London: Penguin.

Felski, Rita and Susan S. Friedman, ed. 2013. *Comparison: Theories, Approaches, Uses.* Baltimore, MD: Johns Hopkins University Press.

Frost, Robert. 1995. *Robert Frost: Collected Poems, Prose, and Plays*, edited by Richard Poirier and Mark Richardson. New York: Library of America.

Gentzler, Edwin. 2017. *Translation and Rewriting in the Age of Post-Translation Studies.* London: Routledge.

Gikandi, Simon, 2011. "Theory after Postcolonial Theory: Rethinking the Work of Mimesis." In *Theory after "Theory,"* edited by Jane Elliott and Derek Attridge, 163–178. London: Routledge.

Goethe, Johann Wolfgang von. 2012. "On World Literature." In *World Literature: A Reader*, edited by Theo D'haen, César Domínguez, and Mads Rosendahl Thomsen. London: Routledge.

Heise, Ursula K. et al., ed. 2017. *Futures of Comparative Literature.* London: Routledge.

Hemon, Aleksandar. 2015. "Interview." *Deltona Howl*, 28 August.

Huyssen, Andreas. 2007. "Geographies of Modernism in a Globalizing World." *New German Critique* 100 (Winter): 189–207.

Kertész, Imre. 2001. "Who Owns Auschwitz?" *The Yale Journal of Criticism* 14, no. 1: 267–272.

Khair, Tabish. 2016. *The New Xenophobia.* New Delhi: Oxford University Press.

Kong, Shuyu. 2004. *Consuming Literature: Best Sellers and the Commercialization of Literary Production in Contemporary China.* Stanford, CA: Stanford University Press.

Kundera, Milan. 2012. "Die Weltliteratur." In *World Literature: A Reader*, edited by Theo D'Haen, César Domínguez, and Mads Rosendahl Thomsen. London: Routledge.

Larsen, Svend Erik. 2017. *Literature and the Experience of Globalization: Texts Without Borders.* London: Bloomsbury.

Lazarus, Neil. 2011. *The Postcolonial Unconscious.* Cambridge: Cambridge University Press.

Leerssen, Joep. 2006. *National Thought in Europe: A Cultural History.* Amsterdam: Amsterdam University Press.

Moretti, Franco. 2013. *Distant Reading.* London: Verso.

Mufti, Aamir. 2016. *Forget English! Orientalisms and World Literatures.* Cambridge, MA: Harvard University Press.

Ngugi wa Thiong'o. 1986. *Decolonising the Mind: the Politics of Language in African Literature.* London: Heinemann Educational.

Pamuk, Orhan. 2004. *Istanbul: Memories and the City*. New York: Alfred A. Knopf.
Saussy, Haun. 2006. "Exquisite Cadavers Stitched from Fresh Nightmares: Of Memes, Hives and Selfish Genes." In *Comparative Literature in an Age of Globalization*, edited by Haun Saussy. Baltimore, MD: The Johns Hopkins University Press.
Saussy, Haun. 2017. *Translation As Citation: Zhuangzi Inside Out*. Oxford: Oxford University Press.
Varsava, Jerry. 2017. "The (Really Big) Shape of Comparative Literature Now, Or, a Discipline's Totalizing Conceit." *Symploke* 25, no. 1–2: 493–503.
Venuti, Lawrence. 2004. "Translation, Community, Utopia." In *The Translation Studies Reader*, 2nd edition. Edited by Lawrence Venuti. New York: Routledge.
Warwick Research Collective (WReC). 2015. *Combined and Uneven Development: Towards a New Theory of World-Literature*. Liverpool: Liverpool University Press.

2 Ecologies of literature
The cosmopolitan-vernacular nexus
Stefan Helgesson

On the tercentenary of William Shakespeare's death in 1916, Oxford University Press published a lavish volume entitled *A Book of Homage to Shakespeare*. Comprising more than 550 pages, it was edited by Israel Gollancz, then a professor of English at King's College, and was the outcome of the joint labour of the "Shakespeare Tercentenary Committee," which had formed as early as 1904. As Gollancz explains in the preface, the committee's aim was to celebrate Shakespeare "in a manner worthy of the veneration in which the memory of Shakespeare is held by the English-speaking peoples and by the world at large" (Gollancz 1916, vii).

The resulting book achieved this goal by gathering 166 tributes from virtually all parts of the world. Although English dominates the volume, it rubs shoulders with 22 other languages and seven additional scripts besides the Latin alphabet. Famous male figures in Western Europe at the time such as Henri Bergson, Georg Brandes, Thomas Hardy, Rudyard Kipling and Rabindranath Tagore share the pages with writers and scholars from Finland, Japan, Denmark, Burma, Persia, Iceland, Italy, Romania, the United States, and so on. They write most frequently in their own languages, with translations or summaries often but not always provided in English. Besides the Romance, Germanic and Slavic languages of Europe, and alongside Finnish, Persian, Japanese and Mandarin, there are, as Gollancz points out, "tributes, not only in the classic dead languages of antiquity, Greek, Latin, Hebrew, Sanskrit, but also in the living languages of Ireland, Wales, India (Bengalee, Urdu, and Burmese), Egypt (Arabic), and South Africa (the Bechuana dialect)" (Gollancz 1916, viii). Hence, the book is a tower of Babel in its own right, impossible for any single reader – however erudite and polyglot – to read in its entirety. The hierarchy of languages, judged by quantity but also by the *absence* of translation, is nonetheless evident: English comes first, untranslated French second, some additional untranslated Western European languages third – and then a long tail of translated languages and scripts less easily placed, but divided between "classical" and "vernacular" languages. This hierarchy produces, in and of itself, an image of the prevailing world-literary relations at that historical moment.

The editor is candid about one obvious effect of politics on this literary endeavour. The spirit of the committee's work was avowedly cosmopolitan, he writes. But "[t]hen came the War; and the dream of the world's brotherhood to be demonstrated by its common and united commemoration of Shakespeare, with many another fond illusion, was rudely shattered" (Gollancz 1916, vii). This made it impossible to include any German contributions, an absence barely compensated for by the Manchester professor C. H. Herford's essay "The German Contribution to Shakespeare Criticism" (1916, 231–5). The reality of conflict unceremoniously dashed the idealism of the tercentenary; what remained of its cosmopolitan aspirations relied heavily on the imperial authority of Britain.

Printed only in 1,250 expensive copies – of which 1,000 were for sale – *A Book of Homage* presents a contradiction also in material and economic terms. While it projects an image of a globe-girdling community of readers, united in their appreciation of Shakespeare, the book itself was never intended to circulate widely, except among an exceptionally reduced elite readership.

As previous scholars have noted, *A Book of Homage* is possible to examine from a potentially endless number of angles (Kahn 2001; Seddon 2004; Helgesson and Kullberg 2018). The conclusions one might draw from the diverse modes of address of the (often eminently forgettable) contributions, as well as their heterogenous collation of genres and languages, are sometimes banal, sometimes surprising. If it is thought of as a *representative* book, then we must ask *what* it represents: hardly any broad and popular literary culture, nor any particular national literature. As a manifestation of the globalization of Shakespeare, it is both dauntingly capacious and extremely narrow – a textual collage for the benefit of the few. The suggestion in this chapter is that it represents two different things, namely the impossible *dream* of world literature, and the heterogeneous, contradictory *reality* of world literature (in its historical moment). The impossibility should be evident by now: published amid the strife and conflict of the First World War, almost zero circulation, unreadable in its multilingualism. The reality, however, is its material manifestation of multiple connections between languages and literary cultures. In that respect, it can serve as a springboard for sustained reflection on the different modes – or ecologies – through which literatures circulate and connect. As a book-object, the

Ecologies of literature 47

Book of Homage also serves as an idiosyncratic exemplar of the anthology, which – together with the journal – is a particularly strategic collective form through which world literature can be approached. To explore this, the chapter begins by discussing the circulation paradigm of world literature. Recent work on "ecologies" of literature – particularly by Alexander Beecroft – helps to further the discussion by providing distinctions within the understanding of circulation. Conceptually, Beecroft's nuanced understanding of circulation encompasses both the minor and the major, both the contemporary and the historically distant, in ways that do not just confirm the success of success. Secondly, building on this, the chapter will demonstrate how *A Book of Homage* juxtaposes diverse literary ecologies in a way that complicates the hierarchy referred to above. What do we make, for example, of the book's combination of hierarchy and pluralism? What does it tell us about the construction of world literature in 1916 in comparison with our constructions a century later? An intriguing aspect of the book is how it demonstrates not just the incompatibility but also the interaction between ecologies – especially the cosmopolitan, vernacular and national varieties. In idiosyncratic fashion, then, *A Book of Homage* demonstrates what we argue is a driving force in the world histories of literature: the dynamic between cosmopolitan and vernacular scales of literary value.

Circulation in general and ecologies in particular

As we saw in the Introduction, it was primarily through the work of David Damrosch – but also Franco Moretti – that "circulation" became a dominant concern in the post-millennial revival of world literature. Damrosch's point was to focus on the "phenomenology" rather than the "ontology" of literary texts: in other words, how they appear in the world, rather than how they originate. As a variant of reception studies, albeit writ large, the circulation perspective allows for any number of investigations of critical reception, translations, libraries, book markets, and so on. It views literature from the readerly perspective, taking it for granted that literature is a social construction and that its value derives from its readers.

Damrosch suggested that world literature encompasses "all literary works that circulate beyond their culture of origin, either in translation or in their original language" (2003, 4). He further elaborated this definition by insisting that a work "only has an *effective* life as world literature whenever, and wherever, it is actively present within a literary system beyond that of its original culture" (2003, 4; emphasis in the original). As the chapters in this book show, each of the terms in these definitions prompts a set of separate questions. How do we delimit a literary system? What counts as a culture of origin? Can the notion of literature itself be disconnected from culture? If it can, to what extent is culture a relevant factor in literary appreciation? If it can't, what enables us even to recognize a "literary work" across cultural contexts?

These questions, which concern tensions between cultural (or national or linguistic) integrity, the apparent transportability of literature, and inequalities of power, inform most of the chapters in this book. What needs to be noted here is that numerous scholars have levelled sharp criticism at the circulation paradigm of world literature *as such*. Among the more prominent critics are Emily Apter and Pheng Cheah (also mentioned in the Introduction). In her 2013 book, *Against World Literature*, Apter accused world literature theory of an unexamined "translatability assumption" (3). Rather than celebrate the flows of literary works across geographical and linguistic borders, Apter was more interested in the ways circulation was disrupted or resisted, particularly at the linguistic and conceptual level. Such disruption, if one follows the logic of Apter's argument, is a product of theory as much as of inherent properties of literary texts and languages themselves. If, in her view, "World Literature … is an encapsulating model of literary comparatism that, in promoting an ethic of liberal inclusiveness of the formal structures of cultural similitude, often has the collateral effect of blunting political critique," her preferred alternative is to focus on how languages "create small worlds of idiom and creative idiolect that ford the divide, often imposed on postcolonial writers, between those deferring to the experimental modernity of the West (stream of consciousness, wordplay) and those adhering to a colonial realism informed by local custom, tradition, and the romance of political aspirations to national self-determination" (2013, 42–3). Such an approach, accordingly, might enable "a planetary approach to literary history that responds to the dynamics of geopolitics without shying away from fractious border wars" (43).

In a similar vein, Pheng Cheah sees an "analogy between world literature and the circulation of commodities in a global market," which implies that world literature simply "reflects and is conditioned by the global character of political economy" (2014, 308). This view reiterates, in effect, Marx and Engels's observation in *The Communist Manifesto* that "from the numerous national and local literatures, there arises a world literature," as a result of the boundlessness of capital (Marx and Engels 2012, 39). For Cheah, however, this form of literature is no cause for celebration, insofar as it is produced by and retraces prevailing structures of domination and wealth. As he puts it with a Heideggerian twist, conceiving of world literature "solely in terms of global circulation intensifies globalization's unworlding of the world" (Cheah 2016, 193). His interest lies instead in literature's "normative vocation of opening new worlds," which might be glossed as the capacity to introduce alternative temporal (rather than spatial) logics in the ongoing process of "making" the world and achieving human freedom (2016, 16). In a philosophical register not unrelated to Apter's, Cheah speaks therefore in favour of viewing the literary as an active, productive force in the world – indeed, in the "worlding" of the world – and not merely as an after-effect of capitalist rationality.

Both Apter's and Cheah's critical perspectives could be linked to the concerns Gayatri Spivak expressed in an earlier phase of the debate about the "globe" as a projection of the interests of capital. "Globalization," Spivak suggested, should be understood as "the imposition of the same system of exchange everywhere." Within such a context,

> [i]n the gridwork of electronic capital, we achieve that abstract ball covered in latitudes and longitudes, cut by virtual lines, once the equator and the tropics and so on, now drawn by the requirements of Geographical Information Systems. [...] The globe is on our computers. No one lives there. It allows us to think that we can aim to control it.
>
> (Spivak 2003, 72)

Against this, Spivak posited the planet, which we inhabit "on loan," and a conception of literature that resists "the rational destruction of the figure, the demand for not clarity but immediate comprehensibility by the ideological average" (2003, 71). In a later essay, she similarly moved against the grain of global thinking by pointing out (with reference to Kant) that "the concept of the *world in general* is a regulative idea of merely speculative reason" (2012, 457; emphasis added). Instead, what she calls the "intuition of literature" comes "from what I would like to believe, from what little I know of the world I assume" (2012, 458). The key to these rather difficult statements is the notion of "the world in general": while the world, by definition, is where each human subject is emplaced, any attempt at conceptualizing the world will always be incomplete and partial. This philosophical truism, Spivak is saying, must inform also the field of world literature.

Apter, Cheah and Spivak all present us with a normative understanding of literary reading that is incommensurable with what could be called objectifying, external approaches to literature and the world. Moretti's "distant reading" is, in their view, a means of bypassing and ignoring the linguistically singular, situated qualities of literature; the same applies supposedly to Damrosch's model. These debates on circulation present a rift between varieties of radical, theory-driven critique and Damrosch's more pragmatic pluralist and liberal approach. But if the question is regarded in methodological rather than political terms, the opposition seems if not false, then at least overstated. Is there really a mutually exclusive relationship between textual appreciation and a more "external" conception of circulation? Or is it rather the case that they serve different but equally legitimate purposes?

The premise for much of the critique summarized above is that world literature is shaped by and addressed to *contemporary* historical conditions: world literature is here understood to be the literature of globalization. Other scholars, such as Galin Tihanov (2017), Alexander Beecroft (2015) or indeed Damrosch himself (2003), have instead resisted the presentism of this conception and argue rather for the antiquity of world literature: it is not something that comes (only) after but rather *before* the emergence of distinct vernacular and national literatures. Literature in classical Chinese, Akkadian, Sanskrit, Greek, Latin, Arabic or Persian was – on this understanding – already "world literature" long before the self-aware identification of deliberately particularist literatures that renounced "the larger world for the smaller place," as Sheldon Pollock has phrased it (2000, 590).

This long-term, historical understanding of world literature is apparently at odds with the contemporary focus of the critics discussed here. Indeed, it would seem that their criticism doesn't even apply to Homer or the Bhagavadgita, which alerts us to the need to keep two things separate in this discussion. The first concerns the *disciplinary motivation* for world literature. The prominence of world literature today derives very obviously from a number of material, social and technological conditions prevailing in our contemporary world. The post-1989 moment of accelerated globalization, the advent of the Internet and digital media, increased mobility (both forced and voluntary) and the long-term effects of decolonization (including the resurgence of "race" as a category of exclusion and differentiation) have all been powerful motivators for the renewed attention to world literature, be it in a critical or affirmative spirit, be it from liberal, postcolonial or Marxist standpoints. But this inescapably present-day dimension of its disciplinary motivation, which may involve geopolitics (9/11, Sino–American rivalry) as well as university-centred concerns about how to teach the humanities to the smartphone generation, should be kept distinct from the second aspect, namely the *definition* of world literature as an object of study. The phenomenon of "circulation," after all, is not exclusive to the late capitalist era. Working historically through deep time comes with its own problems, but the critique of globalization or translatability does not automatically apply in that context.

In addition, it is not the case that "circulation" – as it can sometimes appear in Apter's and Cheah's discussions – is an effortlessly accessible domain. Actual studies in book history or the sociology of translation demonstrate both the methodological complexity of such undertakings and the unpredictable nature of transfers across languages and borders: an awareness of, for example, the national idiosyncrasies of book markets and uneven access to intellectual property rights will militate against the understanding of words such as "flows" and "circulation" as seamless and undifferentiated (Davis and Johnson 2015; Nauwerck 2018). As will be discussed further in Chapter 6, Gisèle Sapiro and Johan Heilbron are among the more important scholars on translation exchanges in the contemporary world. Their results can only be achieved empirically, yet they invite theoretical conclusions on how literature does and does not travel across borders. Confirming Itamar Even-Zohar's earlier theoretical claims, Heilbron observed in 1999 (a year before Moretti's famous article) that the international translation system functions according to a core-periphery model, and hence that its structure is hierarchical, with "central, peripheral and semi-peripheral languages" (Heilbron 1999, 433). But in addition, it is also "a historical system, marked by a specific genesis and minor and major transformations over time" – such as the relative decline of French and the rise of English to a hyper-central position in the system (434). There is a considerable and, as yet, underexploited potential for book history to further our understanding of world literature in this regard.

Circulation, in other words, is always a differentiated phenomenon. One productive way to conceptualize this is the ecologies approach suggested by Alexander Beecroft. In a bold attempt to describe the meta-system of circulation, Beecroft focuses on the constraining and enabling factors of literature in relation to its environment. The word "ecology" has a metaphorical, or more precisely analogical function here: Beecroft is not engaging in ecocriticism, but rather proposing that the conditions of literature can be described along similar lines as ecosystems or biomes, discernible as "particular patterns of ecological constraints operating on the circulation of literary texts in a variety of different historical contexts" (2015, 25). The point to bear in mind is the operative function of the term "constraints": as in economic theory, Beecroft's ecological view of literature is governed by a logic of scarcity and cost-benefit calculations. Expanding on his discussion, determining factors for literary ecologies can be glossed as follows:

- *Language.* The spread of a language, the scope and prestige of its literary history, its degree of standardization, its relationship to other languages in the environment, and so on, all contribute to the impact and meaning of its literary production.
- *Politics.* How do structures of governance promote certain forms of literary circulation and discourage others? Two examples are, on the one hand, the transregional prestige of Arabic achieved through the rapid spread of Islamic rule in the seventh and eighth centuries CE, and, on the other, current-day state support of literary production in small (and not-so-small) national languages in Europe.
- *Economics.* Patterns of trade, economic inequality, relations of exploitation between systemically central and peripheral regions, and so on, all contribute to shaping the constraints for literary production and reception. An obvious case would be how writers and readers in postcolonial African nations have depended on publishing infrastructures in Europe and the United States.
- *Religion.* Throughout history a number of different languages have served as vehicles for religion – Latin, Church Slavic, Sanskrit, Hebrew, Ge'ez. As such, they have tended to create linguistic communities of a different order than ethnically or regionally contained ones. Also, the languages of religion valorized and regulated the *use* of language in ways that resonate with literary values.
- *Cultural politics.* The point here, it seems, is that culture has its own mode of politics which may or may not, for example, value literature at the expense of other cultural forms; or which insists that literature should be an elite practice rather than a popular art, or vice versa. Historically, one can see the difference between the scribal cultures of, say, early China or fifteenth-century Ethiopia, where writing was an esoteric practice reserved for the select few, and the rise of mass literacy in the nineteenth and twentieth centuries, which also produced the ideal of literature for and of the people.
- *Technologies of distribution.* As Chapter 5 makes clear, media technologies play a key role in shaping literature. From the spoken word, carried only by the voice of an individual and memorized in the minds of listeners, to a variety of writing systems, to the development of print technology, and finally to the digital media of our day, distribution can range from minimal and slow to instantaneous and global. But as media theorists such as N. Katherine Hayles (2004) and Jan-Dirk Müller (1994) have established, these technologies are not just neutral conduits. Orality requires forms that aid

memory; low-cost printing methods enable the best-seller; digital media must accommodate distracted reading.

If these are the overall conditions shaping literary ecologies, Beecroft's discussion results in a list of six ideal-typical literary biomes. The first he calls epichoric literature, which is a "limit case" for literary circulation. This remains restricted to a "single, small-scale, political and/or cultural context" and is the oldest literary ecology, epitomized by oral delivery in a small community (Beecroft 2015, 37). By contrast, the maximized version of circulation is global literature, an ecology still in the process of being formed. Between these two extremes, we find the panchoric ecology, which ties together distinct polities through a common cultural repository of myths and stories; the cosmopolitan ecology, tied to a prestige language and (normally) a centre of imperial power; the vernacular ecology, which typically emerges in reaction against a cosmopolitan dominance; and the national ecology, which was the default mode of literary reception in the nineteenth and twentieth centuries.

This selection of headings is intriguing and somewhat counter-intuitive, but not entirely arbitrary. At the core of Beecroft's argument we find an engagement with Sheldon Pollock's theorization of cosmopolitan and vernacular literature along a South Asian-European comparative axis. This is a productive starting point, given Pollock's counter-Herderian claim that cosmopolitan literature has historical priority over vernacularization, but Beecroft's six ecologies demonstrate that the cosmopolitan-vernacular dynamic is not the only game in town – or, rather, that our conception of the cosmopolitan and the vernacular needs to be refined. National literature, which long remained the default mode of organizing literary studies, may draw on the vernacular but is dependent on the nation-state, which was emphatically not the case with the vernacular interventions of Dante or the Korean monk Kyunyŏ in the tenth century CE. Similarly, what Beecroft terms the panchoric – exemplified by the literatures of Ancient Greece and pre-Qin China – bears comparison with cosmopolitan literature, but whereas cosmopolitan languages such as Latin, Sanskrit or Arabic were adopted by elites in diverse linguistic environments, panchoric literature is characterized by uniting smaller polities through a common language, a canonized set of texts (such as the *Canon of Songs*), and a mythology (such as the Trojan war) that enables the construction of a shared cultural identity.

Beecroft's model is shaped by taking into account the variables of language, script, literary form, religion, economic resources, technologies of reproduction and circulation, and political organization. In any given ecology, these variables are subject to different constraints. Orality, unless technologically mediated, is constrained by the reach of the human voice, the reliability of memory and the availability of forms that aid memory. Vernacular literature is constrained by the reach of its language, but has the potential to penetrate much deeper into a particular speech community. Literature in a cosmopolitan language, by contrast, can reach widely but thinly. Written literature is by definition constrained not just by language but by the reach of literacy within that particular script. The circulation of printed books is constrained by the buying power of the readership – or the relative spread of public libraries, which in turn depends on the political system. And literary recognition, that greatest prize of all, is inevitably limited by the available amount of attention, aesthetic preferences, as well as political interests.

It is in the political dimension of literary reception, moreover, where constraints are most flexible and amenable to external pressure. Beecroft keenly observes that "[o]ne of the chief tasks for each ecology as it emerges is to reduce the quantity of information within the system; some existing texts cannot survive in the new environment, others survive in a marginal or altered role, while others still flourish in their new and unexpected surroundings" (2015, 198). In national ecologies, cosmopolitan sources are obscured and the vernacular canon is streamlined to fit the narrative of national emergence. But when in our day English literature transforms into Global Anglophone literature, the national dimension of English must, by contrast, be suppressed – even if this might also, as a defensive reflex, strengthen national literary ecologies in other languages.[1] Literatures (in the plural, as identifiable groupings of texts) are in other words produced to no small degree through politically inflected information management – an observation which boomerangs back at those of us whose bread and butter it is to teach and write about literature.

This system of ecologies is open-ended and amenable to criticism as soon as one looks at empirical cases. But before doing precisely this (by returning to *A Book of Homage*), two premises of Beecroft's argument are worth highlighting. The first is Beecroft's deliberately "etic" rather than "emic" approach, which means that his categories are applied to the empirical material "from the outside," rather than derived from within the (or a) tradition or culture itself. This is potentially controversial, for two very different reasons. On the one hand, referring back to our discussion of Apter, untranslatable cultural phenomena risk elision when alien categories do their work. On the other, the supposedly etic could serve to mask ideologically what are in fact emic *Western* categories – the very word "literature" being foremost among these. Beecroft is aware of both these risks, but counters them by underscoring his commitment to comparativism: the critical language that enables comparative study "must be etic to at least one of the cultures under study, if it is not etic to both, or all, of them" (2015, 30). The etic approach is in other words a condition of knowledge, for better or worse – which indicates an inescapable aspect of the comparative undertaking. More importantly, however, a refusal to make the etic leap would reduce comparative literature to what it once used to be: an investigation of the organic and contiguous relationships within Western literature and little besides. There is a line of critique that sees comparatism – in and of itself – as the perpetuation of a Western imperial power matrix (Mufti 2016; Bhattacharya 2016; Slaughter 2018), but those arguments tend to ground themselves in varieties of comparatism. In the choice between two imperfect alternatives, between ethno-cultural isolationism and the misunderstandings that transcultural approaches will risk, it therefore seems preferable to pursue the latter option, even at the cost of devising artificial and defamiliarizing sets of etic concepts.

The second premise is that Beecroft sees not just literature, but more importantly the identification of *a* literature as well as literatures in the plural, as produced through practices of reception. The subtle shift from "literature" to "a literature" is unavoidably etic, since it presupposes a perspective external to the literature. Hence, Beecroft's main focus is not the work "itself," but rather its relation to different constellations of works. Not only can one and the same text at different times be received as vernacular or cosmopolitan or national, but the dominant and legitimate form of circulation in a given context will in turn shape what is written. If we take the case of "English literature," John Milton in the seventeenth century was strongly committed to the *idea* of English literature partly because it was not yet taken for granted. In Milton's day, it was the Greek and Latin classics, the Bible, and the rift between Protestantism and Catholicism, that constituted the dominant cultural horizon in the political turbulence of Cromwell's England and the subsequent Restoration. Milton's writerly production was, accordingly, divided between Latin and English – indeed, his internationally most successful piece was the Latin *Defensio pro Populo Anglicano* (1651), a controversial apology for Cromwell's rule. When, in the eighteenth and nineteenth centuries, "English literature" (identified as a national literature *in the English language*) became an ideological imperative, the Latin texts in Milton's production were, however, quietly forgotten. By the time William Wordsworth penned his lament in the poem "London, 1802" – "Milton! thou shouldst be living at this hour: / England hath need of thee" – this "Englishing" of Milton was in full force, only to be consummated with the belated establishment of English as a nationally defined university discipline in the nineteenth and early twentieth centuries.

Beecroft's wide-angle view of literature is confirmed, then, also by these interrelated methodological premises: "etic" comparatism and literature defined as the grouping of texts. This serves to distinguish the ecologies approach from more interpretive and aesthetically attuned modes of criticism – which is helpful. A method without a limitation is not a method. But if we apply this largely external approach to *A Book of Homage to Shakespeare*, what do we find? One way of putting it would be that the volume is doubly situated in the British national and British imperial circuit. Shakespeare had long been a linchpin of national identity in Britain, which could be exemplified by the chapter in Jane Austen's *Mansfield Park* (1814) where Henry Crawford reads Shakespeare aloud, causing Edmund to extemporize:

> No doubt, one is familiar with Shakespeare in a degree ... from one's earliest years. His celebrated passages are quoted by every body, they are in half the books we open, and we all talk Shakespeare, use his similes, and describe with his descriptions ...
> (Austen 2003, 265)

The "we" and the "every body" here are, of course, unequivocally English and white, at a moment when Englishness was being defined mainly with Frenchness as its foil (foreshadowing Brexit, one might say). A century later, *A Book of Homage* appears when Shakespeare has already become a global figure, partly through translations into numerous European languages, partly through the institutionalization of English literature as an instrument of colonial instruction in British India and through missionary schooling in Africa (Viswanathan 1998; Peterson 2000; Gikandi 2004). Historically, 1916 is at the very apex of British imperial power, and Gollancz's book manifests thereby a crucial shift in the ecological coding of Shakespeare. If during his lifetime, Shakespeare was mainly a *vernacular* writer in Elizabethan England, he gradually transformed into the *national* hero we find in *Mansfield Park* (inspiring other literary nationalisms in Europe, as in Germany or Russia), and then again became produced as a *cosmopolitan* writer on the back of imperial authority. Or, which might be more precise, one could say that throughout all of this, he, the exemplary Elizabethan, became a *cosmopolitanized vernacular* writer.

R. G. Moulton's contribution to *A Book of Homage* supports this account. Moulton was a professor of literary theory and interpretation in Chicago, and his short essay "Shakespeare as the Central Point in World Literature" is fittingly placed in the centre of the book. His definition of world literature – which he had elaborated already in 1911 (Moulton 2013, 28–35) – saw it as "the general literature of the whole world seen in perspective from the English-speaking civilization," and yet, paradoxically, as though "the whole world" could be neatly contained by the English world, he claims that "in the study of World Literature all lines of thought lead to or from Shakespeare" (Moulton 1916, 228). Besides extolling the virtues of his craft, Moulton does, however, make a case for Shakespeare's historically fortunate position in the Renaissance which "brought together three great things in literature: the newly recovered classics of ancient Greece, the mediaeval accumulations of romance, and a universally diffused Bible" (1916, 229). De-emphasizing, by implication, the national aspect of Shakespeare, Moulton points instead to how the "unity of Europe throughout the Middle Ages" formed the cultural precondition for Shakespeare's work. The cultural precondition for Moulton's own take on Shakespeare is, however, a type of *anglophone* cultural unity, produced by the history of British expansionism plus the ascendant power of the United States. This is one indication, as early as 1916, of divergent tendencies in the figuration of "English literature" as either national or cosmopolitan, or both.

Importantly, however, the volume is also replete with world-literary placings of Shakespeare that are *not* reducible to Anglophony. He is most commonly compared to Dante, Homer, Cervantes and Goethe, sometimes with the ancient Greek playwrights, once with Victor Hugo and once with Imru al-Qays. These comparisons (or contrasts) serve to indicate the cosmopolitan pole of the contributors' conception of world literature, but not necessarily from within Moulton's "English-speaking civilization." If Shakespeare is great, the logic goes, then he is as great as these other internationally canonized writers in other languages. Of greater interest, however, are those contributions where, conversely, Shakespeare is placed in relation to other national and vernacular literatures. Karl Warburg's (untranslated) Swedish essay discusses the translation and reception of Shakespeare in Sweden, from the eighteenth century onward. Besides his brief mention of Strindberg, Warburg unapologetically details a very specific reception history without any internationally recognizable names. Similarly, in his article (in English) on Norwegian drama, Christen Collin discusses the details of how Norwegian writers, from Henrik Wergeland to Bjørnsterne Bjørnson have read and made use of Shakespeare. Moving to the margins of the British empire, we find even more striking instances of such a vernacular take on Shakespeare. In "Shakespeare: A Burman's Appreciation," Maung Tin of Rangoon College explains that, in a situation where "literature is religion and religion literature," Shakespeare "very often comes to the Burman Buddhist as a relief – somewhat like the feeling that one experiences at the conclusion of an oppressively long sermon." And yet, he continues, "Shakespearian literature manages to teach the same high standard of ethics as the Buddhist, without a distinct ethical tendency. In spite of his vigorous appreciation of the world, Shakespeare shakes hands with the Buddha, in his utter renunciation of the world" (Tin 1916, 329). Finally, to mention one of the most discussed contributions to *A Book of Homage*, "A South African's Homage," presented (scandalously and inexplicably) as anonymous, but written by the writer, translator, journalist and activist Solomon T. Plaatje, places Shakespeare in an African context, and vernacularizes him by calling him "Tsikinya-Chaka."[2] Plaatje values him not for his greatness in an idealized elsewhere, but because he is recognizably African and on *that* basis universal. "Besides being natural story-tellers," he explains, "the Bechuana are good listeners, and legendary stories seldom fail to impress them" (Plaatje 1916, 338): hence the chief whom Plaatje met at Mafeking asks to hear more about "the white man who spoke so well" – meaning Shakespeare. In his tightly written piece in Setswana, which he summarizes rather than translates fully into English, Plaatje is as firmly positioned in his South African Tswana context as he is in Shakespeare's works, which then enables him to turn this transcultural world literary location against the racist tendencies of contemporary Western culture:

> I once went to see a cinematograph show of the Crucifixion. All the characters in the play, including Pilate, the Priest, and Simon of Cyrene, were white men. According to the pictures, the only black man in the mob was Judas Iscariot. I have since become suspicious of the veracity of the cinema and acquired a scepticism which is not diminished by a gorgeous one now exhibited in London which shows, side by side with the nobility of the white race, a highly coloured exaggeration of the depravity of the blacks. Shakespeare's dramas, on the other hand, show that nobility and valour, like depravity and cowardice, are not the monopoly of any colour.
> (Plaatje 1916, 338–9)

The second film mentioned by Plaatje is most likely D. W. Griffith's infamously racist – yet cinematically innovative – *Birth of a Nation*, which was first screened in 1915 (Willan 1984, 192). It is worth noting that Shakespeare's literary authority enters here as an argument *against* a widely circulated racist narrative in anglophone culture at the time. If R. G. Moulton's piece can be read as a "central" voice in the volume, expressive

Ecologies of literature 59

of an anglophone hegemony, it seems then that the margins of *A Book of Homage* – such as the Swedish, Norwegian, Burmese and South African examples – invite a more flexible consideration of world literature's trajectories. We find here ecologies of literature – national, vernacular, cosmopolitan and even epichoric – that interact dynamically, rather than exclude each other. The power differential in 1916 structuring these interactions is obvious – there are no literature professors in Europe or America at that time eulogizing the qualities of Tswana praise poems. Yet the power differential does not pre-empt, nor fully determine, the *literary* outcome of an engagement with Shakespeare. Plaatje's message to his Western readers could, somewhat irreverently, be summed up as follows: "I'm fine with Shakespeare, please just ditch the racist and imperialist nonsense." In the short term, this appeal was in vain – settler colonial institutions would step by step curtail all of Plaatje's efforts. In the long term, given the South African canonization of Plaatje as a writer, translator, scholar and activist over the last half century, one could argue that he became more successful than he could have anticipated.

A Book of Homage will only take us so far in this discussion – it is a completely idiosyncratic publication. Even so, its didactic purpose in the present chapter will have become clear by now: its many contributions materialize forms of uneven exchange between literatures that are always ongoing but seldom made as graphically visible, and on such a global scale, as here. Besides anthologies in general (which have been much discussed in world literature studies – see Damrosch 2003; and Slaughter 2014), literary magazines – an increasingly important focal point in literary-historical investigations – are an alternative form that lends itself to similar analyses. Whether we choose *La Revue du Monde Noir*, published by black students in Paris in the 1930s, the German Romanticist vehicle *Athenaeum* (ca. 1800), the Brazilian 1940s journal *Clima, Mensagem* in Luanda in the 1950s, Addison's *Spectator* in the early eighteenth century, the *Calcutta Journal* in the 1820s, Mahatma Gandhi's *Indian Opinion* (as will be discussed in Chapter 4), the Cold War internationalist magazine *Lotus, Voorslag* in South Africa in the 1920s, or the contemporary Swedish journal *Karavan*, these journals invariably function – with varying degrees of success – both as connecting nodes between different literary ecologies, and as active participants in shaping a specific ecology. Such an angle on world literature will inform us both of the perception of international canons in a given place and time, but also of what I call the inward trajectory of world literature, namely the gathering of literary resources from elsewhere for the benefit of local literary cultures. As in *A Book of Homage*, the cosmopolitan and vernacular need not stand in opposition to one another. On the contrary, empirical studies will tend to demonstrate that they interact – that vernacular and/or local literatures are sometimes strengthened precisely through a cosmopolitan orientation. Conversely, the unfinished project of cosmopolitanism as a humanism "to come" (Spivak 2012, 461) can only ever realize itself through an ethical attunement towards the vernacular.

Notes

1 This is a complicated argument to make, since national ecologies of English-language literature continue to prevail alongside the global. See the special issue of *Interventions* 20, no. 3 (2018) on the Global Anglophone.
2 The attribution is entirely certain. See Willan 1984, 192.

References

Apter, Emily. 2013. *Against World Literature: On the Politics of Untranslatability*. London: Verso.
Austen, Jane. 2003 [1814]. *Mansfield Park*. Oxford: Oxford University Press.
Beecroft, Alexander. 2015. *An Ecology of World Literature*. London: Verso.
Bhattacharya, Bhaidik. 2016. "On Comparatism in the Colony: Archives, Methods, and the Project of Weltliteratur." *Critical Inquiry* 42: 677–711.
Cheah, Pheng. 2014. "World Against Globe: Toward a Normative Conception of World Literature." *New Literary History* 45, no. 3: 303–329.
Cheah, Pheng. 2016. *What Is a World? On Postcolonial Literature as World Literature*. Durham: Duke University Press.
Damrosch, David. 2003. *What Is World Literature?* Princeton, NJ: Princeton University Press.
Davis, Caroline and David Johnson, eds. 2015. *The Book in Africa: Critical Debates*. New York: Palgrave Macmillan.
Gikandi, Simon. 2004. "African Literature and the Colonial Factor." In *The Cambridge History of African and Caribbean Literature*, vol. 1, edited by Abiola Irele and Simon Gikandi, 379–397. Cambridge: Cambridge University Press.
Gollancz, Israel. 1916. "Preface." In *A Book of Homage to Shakespeare*, edited by Israel Gollancz, vii–x. Oxford: Oxford University Press.
Hayles, N. Katherine. 2004. "Print Is Flat, Code Is Deep." *Poetics Today* 25, no. 1: 67–90.
Heilbron, Johan. 1999. "Book Translation as a Cultural World-System." *European Journal of Social Theory* 2, no. 4: 429–444.
Helgesson, Stefan and Christina Kullberg. 2018. "Translingual Events: World Literature and the Making of Language." *Journal of World Literature* 3, no. 2: 136–152.
Herford, C. H. 1916. "The German Contribution to Shakespeare Criticism." In *A Book of Homage to Shakespeare*, edited by Israel Gollancz, 231–235. Oxford: Oxford University Press.

Kahn, Coppélia. 2001. "Remembering Shakespeare Imperially: The 1916 Tercentenary." *Shakespeare Quarterly* 52, no. 4: 456–478.

Marx, Karl and Friedrich Engels. 2012 [1848]. *The Communist Manifesto: A Modern Edition*. London: Verso.

Moulton, R. G. 1916. "Shakespeare as the Central Point in World Literature." In *A Book of Homage to Shakespeare*, edited by Israel Gollancz, 228–230. Oxford: Oxford University Press.

Moulton, Richard Green. 2013 [1911]. "The Unity of Literature and the Conception of World Literature." In *World Literature: A Reader*, ed. Theo D'haen, César Domínguez and Mads Rosendahl Thomsen, 29–32. New York: Routledge.

Mufti, Aamir. 2016. *Forget English! Orientalisms and World Literatures*. Cambridge: Harvard University Press.

Müller, Jan-Dirk. 1994. "The Body of the Book: The Media Transition from Manuscript to Print." In *Materialities of Communication*, edited by Hans Ulrich Gumbrecht and K. Ludwig Pfeiffer. Stanford, CA: Stanford University Press.

Nauwerck, Malin. 2018. *A World of Myths: World Literature and Storytelling in Canongate's Myths Series*. Uppsala: diss.

Peterson, Bhekizizwe. 2000. *Monarchs, Missionaries and African Intellectuals: African Theater and the Unmaking of Colonial Marginality*. Trenton: Africa World Press.

Plaatje, Solomon T. 1916. "William Tsikinya-Chaka." In *A Book of Homage to Shakespeare*, edited by Israel Gollancz, 336–339. Oxford: Oxford University Press.

Pollock, Sheldon. 2000. "Cosmopolitan and Vernacular in History." *Public Culture* 12, no. 3: 591–625.

Seddon, Deborah. 2004. "Shakespeare's Orality: Solomon Plaatje's Setswana Translations." *English Studies in Africa* 47, no. 2: 77–95.

Slaughter, Joseph. 2014. "World Literature as Property." *Alif* 34: 39–73.

Slaughter, Joseph. 2018. "Locations of Comparison." *Cambridge Journal of Postcolonial Literary Inquiry* 5, no. 2: 209–226.

Spivak, Gayatri. 2003. *Death of a Discipline*. New York: Columbia University Press.

Spivak, Gayatri. 2012. *An Aesthetic Education in the Era of Globalization*. Cambridge: Harvard University Press.

Tihanov, Galin. 2017. "The Location of World Literature." *Canadian Review of Comparative Literature* 44, no. 3: 468–481.

Tin, Maung. 1916. "Shakespeare: A Burman's Appreciation." In *A Book of Homage to Shakespeare*, edited by Israel Gollancz, 329–330. Oxford: Oxford University Press.

Viswanathan, Gauri. 1998. *Masks of Conquest: Literary Study and British Rule in India*. New Delhi: Oxford University Press.

Willan, Brian. 1984. *Sol Plaatje: South African Nationalist 1876–1932*. Berkeley: University of California Press.

3 Genre
Strangeness and familiarity

Mads Rosendahl Thomsen

Non-trivial dichotomies are a strong force for creative thinking. Italo Calvino's *Six Memos for the Next Millennium* is a poetics of literature built on binary couples but with the little twist that he sees opposites as positive. The ability to slow down and speed up, to emphasize lightness as well as heaviness, are to Calvino examples of what literature can do well: "I said at the beginning of my lecture that each value or virtue I chose as the subject for my lectures does not exclude its opposite. Implicit in my tribute to lightness was my respect for weight, and so this apologia for quickness does not presume to deny the pleasures of lingering" (Calvino 1996, 45–6). Literary theory, in particular deconstruction, has excelled in questioning whether things were as simple as they appeared and if there were paradoxical and counterintuitive elements to, for example, the relation between good and evil, or between speech and writing.

In world literature studies, the difference between the familiar and the strange is perhaps the most intriguing. It has, often with some justification, been pointed out that many literary works do not get a foothold in other cultures because they are perceived as being too strange: the world they describe is unfamiliar and does not allow for real engagement from the reader, or the form of verse or the modes of narrative are too unusual to be enjoyed and understood. Conversely, there is a strong impetus to seek the strange, the unfamiliar, and the uncanny in literature. Works of literature should not just bring us the world we know but reveal something different, and not just in terms of representation: it should also challenge the mindset by which we engage with literature and the world. Harold Bloom writes in *The Western Canon* of a fundamental strangeness in canonical literature, which installs a deeply rooted sense that there will always be something that evades the readers and makes it impossible for them to master the text. For all the problems that follow from Bloom's way of canonizing, the focus on strangeness may stand the test of time (Bloom 1994, 3).

The negotiations between the strange and the familiar take on many forms. In Neel Mukherjee's 2014 novel *The Lives of Others*, the consequences that this should have in relation to modes of storytelling is an explicit part of the dialogue. The publisher Bhola Ghosh reacts to a realist story on present-day India – the 1960s in the novel – that does not excite him. Having difficulties to engage with the story,

> Bhola interrupts, "Achchha, this all very well, but ... but isn't this, how should I say, isn't this all a bit familiar?"
> The young man's face falls before he can rearrange it into a mask of defensive contempt. He is still trying when Bhola's colleague seconds his boss, "Yes, yes, right, right, we know all this stuff. So much time to state the obvious ... I'm sure there's a twist coming?"
> The magazine editor begins to defend the writer, "It may be familiar to us, but maybe it's not familiar to a lot of people who have no first-hand or even second-hand experience of *all this stuff*. It's new stuff to them."
> The theatre director says, "It opens up a more philosophical point: should stories be about the familiar world or should they show us something new each time?"
> (Mukherjee 2014, 137–8)

Of course, there is no absolute either-or to the balance of the familiar and the strange, and a range between the two poles is suggested, which for the entirety of a work may be composed of elements that are familiar and unknown. Mukherjee's characters go on to discuss why Kafka is so fascinating, how he is making the ordinary strange, and how they will produce *The Metamorphosis* in Calcutta. Then Bhola drifts away and thinks of Kafka's short story in relation to a meeting he had the day before in a brazen, yet effortless, jump from a classic of world literature and its potential for bringing something new to Indian culture to a quite mundane scene.

Mukherjee's own novel is itself a display of negotiations between the strange and the familiar. First of all, it is a novel that abides by many of the conventions of storytelling and creation of characters in the genre. As I will argue later in this chapter, genres play a key role in mitigating the balance between the strange and the familiar. Against that background, *The Lives of Others* can introduce a world that is not familiar to most readers. A ten-page glossary at the end of the novel as well as an introduction to understanding Bengali family names suggest that the author is well aware that there is a lot that could easily be misunderstood, while also insisting on representing a world with a large degree of authenticity. On the other hand, the stories of two of the most important characters revolve around phenomena that in the end have little specific cultural reference and much universal appeal, namely bodily suffering and mathematics.

The Lives of Others is rife with descriptions of bodies that are suffering under hard labour, violence and sustained torture. The novel opens with a haunting description of hunger, embodied by a man whose family has not eaten for five days. Eventually, it is violence that takes over in the most disturbing scenes of the novel, such as when the young Supranik, who has joined a communist militia, is being tortured:

> The five khaki-clad policemen fall on him in a riot, like a pack of starving dogs, the moment they enter; the dream-like feeling ends. The beating is accompanied by rousing shouts and abuses, all in a continuous stream, drowning out his pitiful mewling. He reacts in the usual human way, by curling up into a ball, but this time there are no niceties observed by his assailants; the blows land everywhere, back, rump, hip, arms, head, shoulders, legs, neck, thighs. He is an open receptacle.
>
> (Mukherjee 2014, 485)

Mukherjee stresses the lack of words to describe the pain, not so much as a writer, but also for the victims of torture that have never experienced anything like this. In *The Body in Pain,* Elaine Scarry writes extensively on the world-destroying effects of intense pain (Scarry 1985, 29), and how "World, self, and voice are lost, or nearly lost, through the intense pain of torture and not through the confession as is wrongly suggested by its connotations of betrayal" (Scarry 1985, 35). Violence can be that which makes the world incomprehensible to everybody, and to Scarry civilization means reconquering the world. This is also the sense one gets when reading Mukherjee: being thrown from trying to envision life in its complexity to completely understanding the absolute horror of being reduced to a body in pain. In a wider perspective, Cathy Caruth has suggested that trauma is taking part in negotiating between cultures (Caruth 1995, 11), and traumatic events bracket the social encodings and customs of ordinary life in a culture and create a space where everybody has a more equal understanding of the centrality of certain events.

At the other end of the spectrum, the fascination with mathematics runs throughout Mukherjee's novel and even includes formulas written in notation that most readers are not able to follow immediately (or at any point), though they would recognize them to be part of an international language of mathematics (Mukherjee 2014, 213). The history of mathematics as a discipline revolves around a purely symbolic world that will keep producing new problems as others are solved, but mathematics also alienates the prodigy Swarnendu from his own community, since no one in Calcutta is able to understand the ventures into advanced mathematics that he is undertaking. The novel's blend of very historically specific conditions with experiences that communicate universalism and states of exception thus makes for an intriguing way of addressing the challenge of the familiar and the strange.

Salman Rushdie's short story "The Courter" pursues a similar strategy by placing chess in the middle of a cultural encounter between Indian expatriates, British people and an Eastern European grandmaster:

> Chess had become their private language. Old Mixed-Up, lost as he was for words, retained, on the chessboard, much of the articulacy and subtlety which had vanished from his speech. As Certainly-Mary gained in skill – and she had learned with astonishing speed, I thought bitterly, for someone who couldn't read or write or pronounce the letter p – she was better able to understand, and respond to, the wit of the reduced maestro with whom she had so unexpectedly forged a bond.
>
> (Rushdie 1996, 194)

Filled with anecdotes and puns and spirited misunderstandings among the many characters, "The Courter" shows how the feeling of not really belonging takes its toll in the long run, making the protagonists face a choice between settling in the United Kingdom or returning to India. Certainly-Mary returns, the young narrator chooses England, and the fate of grandmaster Mecir is unknown. As in Mukherjee's novel, the attention to the responses from different generations is crucial and creates a complex canvas of how change and adaption are or are not possible.

Rushdie has become an emblem of the success of anglophone Indian literature, and he also infamously contributed to the international dominance of Indian literature in English by editing a volume on new Indian fiction which contained only one contribution by a non-English writer. In *Forget English!*, Aamir Mufti criticizes Rushdie for not being sincere about his motives and most of all for trying to "recode this inherently *political* scene of the mutual relations of English and the vernacular languages in the subcontinent in terms of (uniform and supposedly universal) aesthetic *value*" (Mufti 2016, 157) Nonetheless, there can be political value in highlighting the way language functions as a barrier and a medium of understanding and action through aesthetic forms such as fiction, as many works have shown, and sometimes aesthetic values are a precondition for literature's political impact. Graham Huggan, in *The Postcolonial Exotic*, suggests that the exotic can be defined as a relation between the strange and the familiar, while pointing out that this relation is highly complex: "Exoticism, in this context, might be described as a kind of semiotic circuit that oscillates between the opposite poles of strangeness and familiarity. Within this circuit, the strange and the familiar, as well as the relation between them, may be recoded to serve different, even contradictory, political needs and ends" (Huggan 2001, 14). The exotic and the strange can divert attention from political issues, but they have historically also been important elements in bringing attention to politics. By using other means of representation than straightforward discourse, literature runs the risk of being misunderstood and misused, but the alternative of not pushing literary discourse and inventiveness to its limits does not seem inviting.

Local and universal?

The literary historian Georg Brandes argued in the late nineteenth century that what was written directly to be world literature was rarely, if ever, artistically successful. Literary works, he argued, have to be in touch with the fabric of culture and a sense of place (Brandes 2012, 27). But the counter-arguments are also ready at hand and can be backed up by the success of particular genres. What about science fiction? Maybe it only works when it's really about the present? Fantasy is enormously popular, but the genre has never been considered accomplished on the level of the greatest plays, poems and novels, and are the best works of the genre not very reliant on recognizable myths? Absurdist theatre must surely be detached from reality then? Yes, but only to a certain degree when one reads or watches closely. What is perhaps more interesting is how universals and generic elements mix with the particular. Kafka can be read very abstractly, also in an historical context, although in an historical reading, it is difficult to argue that the level of abstraction in his work is not high and that the degree of detachment from an historically recognizable setting is significant (but not complete).

World literature is filled with examples of works that have cut away many layers of cultural references. Atiq Rahimi's short novel on Afghanistan, *The Patience Stone*, takes place in a single room as a monologue, and the intricacies of everyday life are thus set aside and become more of a background noise than the forefront of the novel. A similar focus on one body in one room can be found in the Angolan author José Eduardo

Agualusa's *A General Theory of Oblivion*, where the Portuguese protagonist Ludo takes refuge in her home for 30 years. The world outside is present through recollections but the essential scene is boiled down to a person in a confined space, and that scene becomes a vehicle to address the specific historical conditions. Are these strategies, part of a subgenre of novels with minimal representation of the protagonist's world, also part of the reason why both writers are among the foremost representatives of their place of origin and of their time? Neither writer lays claim to a particular location, yet they have become representatives of Prague at the turn of the century, Afghanistan at the end of the Cold War, and Angola in the process of decolonization.

The question of the strange and the familiar is also related to questions of what reading should provide (which, fortunately, does not have to be just one thing): Stories about what is familiar but maybe with an uncanny side to it? Or worlds of which we have little experience ourselves, but where we recognize something that seems to be universal? Or maybe an encounter with something strange that cannot and should not be assimilated or explained as a variation of what one's own identity is? In *A Common Strangeness*, Jacob Edmond has written extensively on the relationship between strangeness and commonness across Eastern and Western literatures. He also points to some of the paradoxes or trade-offs that exist for the role of strangeness in a transnational literature:

> During the late twentieth century, avant-garde poetry took a transnational turn that was caught between poetic, personal, and collective assertions of strangeness and commonness and that shared with comparative literature a desire to avoid either radical nominalism or abstracted globalism. Building on the search for a poetics that traverses the boundaries of nation and culture, which had been a major driver of avant-garde poetry for the past one hundred years, many writers had a powerful if ill-defined dream of an imagined transnational poetic community whose shared sense of location was based, paradoxically, on its dislocation. Dislocation here means not just separation or estrangement from home and nation, but an aesthetic that questions the solidity of the relationship between word and world through writing that foregrounds its own strangeness. These forms of textual strangeness derived from diverse modernist and avantgarde practices and were intertwined with imaginings of other places and times, but poets gave them increasing emphasis in response to the period of change at the end of the twentieth century. They articulated renewed international affiliations and a heightened sense of location and difference. Like many transnational

movements, they adopted an ambivalent position between participating in and resisting globalization and its homogenizing forms.

(Edmond 2012, 6)

This ambivalence can be seen as an important element that any theory of transnational or world literature has to address. Particular historical situations and the futures that can be envisioned affect the configurations of international and national preferences, and ideas about what the role of literature should be. Edmond describes a bold programme that nevertheless found a durable place in criticism. The discussion of what should be local and what should be universal is perhaps the most stable element in discussions of world literature, but changes, however slight, may be the most important historical aspect.

In *What Is World Literature?*, David Damrosch argues that there has been a shift in the way works are selected as representatives of world literature (Damrosch 2003, 133). Formerly, there was a tendency to focus either on works that displayed the maximum distance in form and theme from the critics' own literary culture in order to show maximum diversity, or works that in many ways resembled genres and themes that were also known to their literary culture, to underscore a sense of universality. Damrosch argues that this sharp divide has been replaced with a more compromising approach, a balance between the familiar and the unfamiliar. These three positions – with, in practice, many degrees of intermixture – provide very different ideals of what an engagement with world literature should bring about. Few scholars, if any, would be bold enough to argue that there is an optimal balance between diversity and universality, but can one avoid having a sense of the ideal between the extremes? In a later article, Damrosch has repeated his pragmatic approach to the balance between the strange and the familiar and the role of the reader:

> For all its theoretical extent, in practice world literature is what an individual reader experiences in reading works written outside the reader's own home tradition. For the nonspecialist reader of a foreign work, reading takes place in what can be described as an elliptical space bounded by the work's culture of origin and the reader's own culture. Inevitably, the reader's understanding of the foreign work will be conditioned by prior experience, first and foremost the fund of knowledge and expectations developed within the home tradition, but often also the expectations generated by previous reading of other works from the foreign culture. If we pick up a new novel by Murakami Haruki, or a previously unread classic by

Gogol, we will read these books with certain expectations as to what "a Japanese novel" or "a Russian novel" will be like, if we already know other books by Kawabata and Tanizaki, or by Tolstoy and Dostoevsky. The new work will interact with these expectations, potentially destabilizing them even as it takes a new shape and significance from these relations.

(Damrosch 2018, 110)

As we sketched in the Introduction to this volume, Chinua Achebe's *Things Fall Apart* is in many ways a work of balance: among forms, languages, themes, and historical contexts, and in meetings of cultural impressions and multiple perspectives. The impact of his work could be tied to the way that the work creates balances among all of these elements, perhaps because it evades being pigeonholed and mixes different genres and references freely. But what about works whose genre characteristics are reproduced and become dominant in the conception of the genre, whose international success also ends up limiting the literary space that they can explore? I will explore three effects of this genre transformation in the rest of this chapter: productive misconceptions, the lure of banality, and the ways in which genres can be used to write back from minor literatures.

Spirited misconceptions

The Japanese haiku is an example of a genre that has been very influential in many literary cultures, both in translation and in local appropriations. In many respects, the haiku is an example of a successful cultural transfer of a literary form and heritage, but also a flawed and limiting one. It has become part of popular culture and writing your own haiku has become a handy exercise for teachers to give to their students, while remaining a difficult task for serious translation of original Japanese poetry. The haiku outside Japan has strong cultural significance as an expression of a certain Eastern demeanour and stoic view of life, but that is only part of the story of haiku. The dominant perception of haiku is as a medium to capture situations with a certain calm and non-judgemental stance. It thus comes to represent a desirable trait that one can find missing in, for example, Western cultures with all their emphasis on individuals, subjectivity, and action.

The haiku, which like the sonnet has had an influence that seems contrary to the brevity of its form (but is perhaps due to its brevity), owes some of its success to the two very different elements of its definition. One is the very simple formal feature of three verses of five, seven and five syllables, which is simple to replicate, no matter that this count of syllables does not make sense across Japanese and Indo-European languages:

> Many Western authors have fallen into the simplistic trap of saying that the haiku is a seventeen-syllable poem in three lines of five, seven, and five syllables. This has led to whole classrooms of teachers and children counting English syllables as they attempt to write haiku. But Japanese haiku are written in Japanese, which is quite different from English or other Western languages.
> (Higginson 1985, 101)

For all the problems of the five-seven-five schema, it sets a very low bar for participating in the genre, which has undoubtedly contributed to its wide success. The other element is the much more elusive spirit of haiku: of the way objects should be represented, the affects that should be conveyed, and the judgements that should be avoided. Established authors who write haiku in Indo-European languages often eschew the metric requirements and instead use haiku as a part of the paratext that prepares the reader for a particular engagement with the genre. Such genre demarcations include by default a collective understanding of what a haiku is supposed to convey, and that the Western tradition may have to find other ways to let the haiku do what it is supposed to do. The wit and humour of haikus are not a part of this narrative, but rather a sense of mysticism, which is not representative of either the genre or the culture of origin: "Japanese literature as a whole, and haiku in particular, has no mysticism in it" (Blyth 1963, 10). The haiku is thus highly successful in upholding a particular exoticizing image of Far Eastern philosophy of life and a poetry that matches it, while also excluding other versions of this strong image. The lure of a genre that can represent a particular view of the world, which is perceived as desirable but perhaps also truly unreachable to the foreign reader is not just an important element of the haiku, but could also be said to be integral to magical realism in all its forms and varieties. Just as with haiku, basic definitions of magical realism are not difficult to come by, and they are backed up by a number of internationally widely read novels and short stories. However, the technique itself has become a problematic and outworn part of South American literary culture, where new generations of writers have distanced themselves from the modes and often the clichés of an enchanted perspective on the world.

The paradox of the haiku is that it thrives on the banality of an all too recognizable and reproducible genre, while defying the idea that it can be mastered. It is read with a promise of strangeness, even when it dangles the banality of a mundane scene in front of the reader. There is certainly orientalism in the reception of the haiku, but without condescension. Haikus are read with the ambition of getting a bit closer to a genuinely different way of perceiving the world, and if there is a comical element to some Western haikus, it is because they fail so clearly in delivering that sense of being in touch with a different world.

Best-selling enchantment

The haiku may be a special case of the canonization of a potentially marginal genre by way of a projection of a cultural otherness. However, one need only look at lists of best-selling books in world literature over the past 50 years to see the role played by the strange and enchanted.[1] Such lists are typically filled with works that have a strong relationship with modes of enchantment. Some lists have *The Bible* as number one, followed by *Quotations from the Works of Mao Zedong*, the sales of both supported by their mandatory reading for large groups of people, while at the same time they promise different futures for mankind. Three works that have been sold in more than 50 million copies based entirely on market demand are J. K. Rowling's *Harry Potter*, J. R. R. Tolkien's *The Lord of the Rings* series, and Paulo Coelho's *The Alchemist*, all works that very much depend on different types of enchantment or magic. Dan Brown's *The Da Vinci Code* and Stephenie Meyer's *Twilight Saga* are also high on the list, as well as Lewis Carroll's *Alice's Adventures in Wonderland* and Antoine de Saint-Exupéry's *The Little Prince*. These works also engage in narratives that re-enchant the world in different ways and make claims that are difficult to believe. Some of the best-selling historically-based works are Margaret Mitchell's *Gone With the Wind* and *The Diary of Anne Frank*, which both feature an interesting relation between trauma and enchantment.

The success of tales of enchantment is not welcomed by all. In a review article of Henrik Pontoppidan's *Lucky-Per*, Fredric Jameson questions this formula for success:

> The formal result, for the novel, is strange and paradoxical, yet momentous: all successes grow to be alike, they lose their specificity and indeed their interest. Success sinks to the level of emergent mass culture – which is to say, fantasy and wish-fulfilment. Only the failures remain interesting, only the failures offer genuine literary raw material, both in their variety and in the quality of their experience.
>
> (Jameson 2011)

Of course, this is not only pessimistic but also inaccurate. All successes are not alike, even if they thrive on fantasy. But no matter what one thinks of fantasy, wonder, wish-fulfilment and enchantment, one has to accept these as part of what is driving the circulation of works in world literature. It is quite likely that the only Brazilian author to be found in a bookstore in a mid-sized European city would be Paulo Coelho (although one could hope for Clarice Lispector to be there as well), just as the only decent-sized windows into contemporary Japanese literary culture consist of *manga* and the works of Haruki Murakami. There is nothing wrong with either, except the feeling that one is missing the whole picture and that there must be some method in this madness of literary influence. Some genre traits end up being so strong that they throw a significant shadow on the rest of a country's or a region's literature. The success of magical realism in South America was well-deserved and important, but in the long run, its popularity has also made it difficult for the next generation of writers to become part of a new story and to form a new international canon (Siskind 2014, 54).

Thriving on mystery rather than the mysterious, crime fiction is a genre that is frequently frowned upon, often rightfully, for the at times questionable quality of writing and the way the novels obey the conventions of the genre. But genre conventions are also challenged: they inspire new characters and the novels are sometimes driven by crime plots that also involve societal affairs, critique of inequality at all levels, or engagement with cultural history and art, as the editor of *Crime Fictions as World Literature* notes. Opera, jazz, painting, or poetry can all be part of the universe in highly successful writers of crime fiction (Nilsson 2017, 4). Conversely, there have been numerous "serious" writers who did not shy away from writing crime fiction. And it is hard to argue with the way that genres can appeal across cultures, making the boom in Scandinavian crime fiction, for example, a strange case of fascination with a semi-peripheral place in the world that is not exactly known for crime (but maybe that is what is so fascinating). The banality of a strong plot, of the twists and turns that the author employs to misguide his readers, and the eventual gratification in solving the crime, could be said to function as beacons that allow the reader to absorb unusual names: Kurt Wallander, Carl Mørck and Patrick Hedström.

But for all the critique of the banality of crime fiction, it has also been pivotal as a device for complex writers such as Jorge Luis Borges or Orhan Pamuk, who each in their own way adopted the crime fiction format and retooled it for their own purposes. Umberto Eco's *The Name of the Rose* is also unthinkable without crime fiction and the work of Jorge Luis Borges, while Peter Høeg's *Smilla's Sense of Snow* begins in the mode of the learned encyclopaedic novel but eventually reads more like an Alastair McLean thriller, playing both on elements of Nordic Noir and a vision of Greenland as an enchanted space. Perhaps the most decisive use of crime fiction in ways that both embrace and mock the genre can be found in Roberto Bolaño's work. Both *The Savage Detectives* and *2666* are built on the crime fiction genre, but use it for their own purposes in sprawling narratives and deliberate disappointments of the reader's expectations for clarity.

A more general question that emerges from the fascination of crime fiction plots, which is rarely, if ever asked, is whether there is a contemporary Western mysticism. Is there a strangeness in Western cultures that can be presented as something that outsiders can comprehend but not share a belief in? History abounds with examples: witch hunts, seeking contact with dead spirits, miracles by saints, and many more instances of practices that are less than rational and secular in the way that modernity is usually conceived. For sure, monotheistic religion could count. Except that none of these examples is particularly contemporary Western but part of a history where the historical roots of an enchanted world are seen as something distinctly different from present culture rather than an element that lives on, despite how it can be playfully reinvoked in stories and movies. What would then count as the incomprehensible West? By way of anecdote, a Chinese translator thought that the hardest thing to translate in a novel was a portrait of a disrespectful son, since how could he not honour his parents? Would Protestant work ethics count as a mystery? Or are theories of modern physics in themselves an expression of Western mysticism? The relativity of time! Particle and wave! The question of Western authentic strangeness may not be that important, but it is worth pointing out, also in relation to the differences between cultures that are either portrayed as being in a continuous relationship with an enchanted past and those that are given a free pass to claim clear-sightedness, while taking an interest in the enchanted abroad.

Writing back through genre

By focusing on authenticity and enchantment, we acquire a different version of the geography of literature from the "centre to periphery" model for which Franco Moretti has argued. Moretti has convincingly demonstrated how the first waves of the novel spread out in this way, but he does not pay much attention to movements from the periphery to traditional centres of world literature. He touches upon this in *Modern Epic*, with Gabriel García Márquez as a prime example, although Márquez's work is still very reliant on European precursors (Moretti 1994, 238). Rather than successive waves, there are often connections between more or less scattered works, which I have called "lonely canonicals" (Thomsen 2008, 44). Borges, Coelho, Rushdie, Okri, Díaz, Mo Yan, Høeg, and Murakami form part of such diffuse constellations rather than waves, writers of a literature dependent on places where new visions of authenticity and enchantment can be found for all kinds of readers. Enchantment seems to be literary capital, and, given its huge influence on the dynamics of translation, it is a phenomenon beyond good and evil, even if a certain idealist vision of world literature would beg to differ. As long as there is enough diversity in what gets translated, there should be little to worry about. The windows onto the major literatures of the world are sufficiently large, but, with less diversity, the discrepancy between the canonized and the non-canonized becomes visible, as described in a number of examples here.

Of course, this does not imply that realism and complete sobriety should be hailed as the foremost literary value, or that nineteenth-century ideas of national spirit should again be brought forward. In *The Argentine Writer and Tradition*, Jorge Luis Borges criticizes the idea of an authentic Argentine literature by showing that the prime example of a national epic, *Martín Fierro*, relies on imported traditions (Borges 2000, 421). In his beautiful short story, *The South*, Borges also debunks the idea of finding authentic expressions of a continuous identity, but nevertheless acknowledges the desire for experiencing such a feeling of authenticity. Sadly, the desire of Borges's protagonist Johann Dahlmann for authentic roots not only leads him to a version of the Argentine South that is just as composite as his own background, but also to his presumed violent death:

> From out of a corner, the motionless old gaucho in whom Dahlmann had seen a symbol of the South (the South that belonged to him) tossed him a naked dagger – it came to rest at Dahlmann's feet. It was as though the South itself had decided that Dahlmann should accept the challenge. Dahlmann bent to pick up the dagger, and as he did he sensed two things: first, that that virtually instinctive action committed him to fight, and second, that in his clumsy hand the weapon would serve less to defend him than to justify the other man's killing him.
>
> (Borges 1999, 179)

Dahlmann is caught between a fantasy of the authentic South and the incapacity to embody what follows from it. The desire is real, but on closer inspection, reality cannot live up to the hopes. Instead, literature can, as the emblematic reference to the *Arabian Nights* as Dahlmann's favourite book in Borges's story makes clear, help bring about such moments of re-enchantment. Hans Ulrich Gumbrecht presents a similar argument concerning the longing for authenticity in his book *In 1926: Living at the Edge of Time*. He writes that during the 1920s there was a longing for authentic expression that contrasted with everyday life in the big cities of Europe and North America. Instead, the periphery of Europe, both North and South, South America, and Africa became locations to which authenticity could be attributed (Gumbrecht 1997, 267). This kind of attribution continues to this day as part of the dynamics of world literature, for better or for worse.

The lure of the authentic can be a prerequisite for attention in the big pond beyond the small lakes of national literature, where it is possible to make an impact, but also possible to present a false impression of cultures. However, if the authentic and the enchanted are the means to make a mark, this could also open doors for smaller literatures into world literature, as well as making us aware of what we sometimes, though not always, seek in another culture's literary work. Junot Díaz in a footnote at the beginning of *The Brief Wondrous Life of Oscar Wao*, addresses "those of you who missed your mandatory two seconds of Dominican history": the writer can assume little knowledge ahead of reading the novel, but its readers probably know a great deal more about the Trujillo regime after reading it, even though it means figuring out whether the magical "fukú" spell has anything to do with the whole story or not (Díaz 2007, 2).

Over the past two centuries, the novel has become a more and more dominant genre, so much so that even students of literature sometimes express discomfort at reading poetry. The novelization of the literary world can be seen as both a positive and a negative development. Being an essentially open form, never finished and able to include elements from other genres, the novel is very adaptable to new cultures and well-suited for depicting vernacular language and ordinary life in ways that are more difficult for other genres. Following Georg Lukács's dictum that novels are essentially biographical in form, the underlying form is also universal, namely the idea of a human life. The spread of the novel, which began to speed up at the time Goethe wrote about world literature, but which in some cultures is still more recent, could be seen as the creation of world literature through a global genre. And it is not just the spread of the genre from a perceived centre of origin that is important, but that the novel is the form in which texts from both older and younger literatures circulate internationally. Readers around the world are more likely to read a lengthy account of Afghanistan, Egypt, Japan or China in novelistic form rather than in any other genre. The flip side of the success of the novel is that it narrows down the multitude of literary forms to fewer expressions. But that is a process that is not only related to the international circulation of literature but to the shift in the status of genres, which decisively moved around 1970 away from poetry towards prose, according to references in books and news media. This means that the circulation and reception of literature has been increasingly focused on a main genre that is not representative of the long history of most literary cultures around the world. This raises the question of whether it is better for a particular cultural tradition to be represented in the canon of world literature, even if the works that make it into the canon are neither the most typical nor the most accomplished works of that tradition, or not to be represented at all if representation distorts the tradition.

There seems to be a fine balance between productive and meaningless strangeness that can also be a battlefield for recognition. When Goethe mentions that he has read a Chinese novel and Eckermann first asks incredulously whether the Chinese have novels, and later remarks that their novels must be very strange, it is worth noting that it is the idea of the novel that frames the discussion. The notion of genre is thus very important in Goethe's reading as a common ground for spotting similarities and differences. The novel is, following Bakhtin, defined by being a genre that has not come to an end but continues to evolve. Goethe anticipates this notion and suggests that world literature is a rhizomatic and ever-changing complex of relations. Yet he cannot escape the idea that the ancient Greeks should have a privileged place:

> National literature means little now, the age of Weltliteratur has begun; and everyone should further its course. But this esteem for foreign productions should not stop with specific characteristics and declare them models. We should not think that the truth is in Chinese or Serbian literature, Calderón or the Nibelungen. In our pursuit of models, we ought always to return to the Greeks of antiquity in whose works beautiful man is represented. The rest we contemplate historically and assimilate from it the best as far as we can.
> (Goethe 2012, 11)

If it were not for the reliance on Antiquity as an unsurpassable pinnacle of human achievement, Goethe's idea seems refreshingly modern. Rather than a system of centre and periphery, he envisions a rhizomatic network of influences and role models. If there is some irony in his perspective on the Greeks, it would be that the absence of novels from the Greek canon makes them slightly odd as role models for a literary culture that relies so heavily on that genre.

In *Postcolonial Poetics*, Elleke Boehmer reflects on the functions of strangeness as a mode of fascination which is also troubling in its ability to disclose the reality it is concerned with:

> [T]he element of the strange, irregular, or inexplicable functions as a narrative device is designed to pique the reader's interest and lead them further into the story. In this sense of course it hardly merits further comment. Yet the aspect of this initial strangeness that does demand attention is how it combines with the narrator's evident concern to give a full report, usually from a first-person perspective, including on that precise experience of strangeness – a concern that is also reflected in the overriding commitment to realism across anthologies. Whether the story tells of immigration or displacement, of war memory, relationship breakdown, bereavement, or family disagreement, it opens a window onto a significant event or moment in the individual's or their community's life that they are motivated to narrate, yet ultimately without full disclosure. What I am calling strangeness (a catchall term to make my argument – the unknown would be equally appropriate) appears to impose certain limits on their realist commitment.
>
> (Boehmer 2018, 187)

Boehmer's account presents the central dilemma addressed in this chapter and extends the question of the strange to a more general way of making sense of the unknown. One has to recognise the benefits of strangeness as a driver of narratives, and more philosophically as a way of accepting that one will never be able to completely understand the world. But the aspiration to present a particular cultural world to others in a way that will make them understand something new is at odds with this. Magical realism is emblematic of this division as a highly influential genre that has undoubtedly been a primary source for many readers to find out about historical conditions and events that they would otherwise never have learned much about, but it has also come with the risk of distorting an historical world.

The question of strangeness is important in world literature studies as it accentuates a general quality of literature. In Hans Georg Gadamer's seminal work on hermeneutics, *Truth and Method*, he writes at length on literature in general and the concept of world literature in particular. In his general theory of understanding as a process of overcoming the distance to a different horizon of understanding, texts generate more difficulty than any other form of communication, as well as more fascination:

> The mode of being of a text has something unique and incomparable about it. Nothing is so strange, and at the same time so

demanding, as the written word. Not even meeting speakers of a foreign language can be compared with this strangeness, since the language of gesture and of sound is always in part immediately intelligible. The written word and what partakes of it – literature – is the intelligibility of mind transferred to the most alien medium. Nothing is so purely the trace of the mind as writing, but nothing is so dependent on the understanding mind either. In deciphering and interpreting it, a miracle takes place: the transformation of something alien and dead into total contemporaneity and familiarity.

(Gadamer 2013, 163)

Against this background, Gadamer struggles to define exactly what world literature is and brings about. A wide and lasting influence is a pragmatic definition that Gadamer stands by, but he also suggests much more ambitious ways of thinking of world literature. First of all, it is literature that belongs to the world at large, and thus is not confined to its cultural origin but speaks to people everywhere, although in different ways, depending on their local world and its horizon. Secondly, Gadamer suggests that the idea of literature is historically tied to the possibility of belonging to world literature, because writing is part of "human sciences as a whole" (Gadamer 2013, 162). Thirdly, Gadamer likens literature to science and the quest for uncovering truths about the world, even though it seeks these in a different way. He rejects the idea that the formal achievements of literary work distinguish it categorically from other texts since content and meaning are essential for all texts (Gadamer 2013, 162). While this could be disputed, Gadamer's reflections are also filled with questions that show a genuine doubt about the potential of literature for disclosing truths about the world, a hope that may seem too ambitious for the more pragmatically inclined. What remains, though, is strangeness as a unique quality, a resistance that readers seek out, and which exercises strong influence on world literature, historically and in the present day.

Note

1 For example: https://en.wikipedia.org/wiki/List_of_best-selling_books. Accessed on 19 November 2018.

References

Achebe, Chinua. 1994. *Things Fall Apart*. New York: Anchor Books.
Agualusa, José Eduardo. 2016. *A General Theory of Oblivion*. London: Vintage.

Bloom, Harold. 1994. *The Western Canon: The Books and School of the Age.* New York: Harcourt Brace.
Blyth, R. H. 1963. *A History of Haiku: From the Beginnings up to Issa* vol. 1. Tokyo: Hokuseido.
Boehmer, Elleke. 2018. *Postcolonial Poetics.* Cham: Palgrave Macmillan.
Bolaño, Roberto. 2007. *The Savage Detectives.* New York: Farrar, Strauss and Giroux.
Bolaño, Roberto. 2008. *2666.* New York: Farrar, Strauss and Giroux.
Borges, Jorge Luis. 1999. *Collected Fictions.* New York: Penguin Books.
Borges, Jorge Luis. 2000. *Collected Non-Fictions.* New York: Penguin Books.
Brandes, Georg. 2012. "World Literature." In *World Literature: A Reader*, edited by Theo D'haen et al. London: Routledge.
Calvino, Italo. 1996. *Six Memos for the Next Millennium.* New York: Vintage.
Caruth, Cathy. 1995. *Trauma: Explorations in Memory.* Baltimore, MD: Johns Hopkins University Press.
Coelho, Paulo. 1993. *The Alchemist.* New York: HarperCollins.
Damrosch, David. 2003. *What Is World Literature?* Princeton, NJ: Princeton University Press.
Damrosch, David. 2018. "Frames for World Literature." In *Tensions in World Literature*, edited in W. Fang. London: Palgrave Macmillan.
Díaz, Junot. 2007. *The Brief Wondrous Life of Oscar Wao.* New York: Riverhead Books.
Eco, Umberto. 1980. *The Name of the Rose.* New York: Harcourt Brace.
Edmond, Jacob. 2012. *A Common Strangeness.* New York: Fordham University Press.
Gadamer, Hans-Georg. 2013. *Truth and Method.* London: Bloomsbury.
Goethe, Johann Wolfgang von. 2012. "On World Literature." In *World Literature: A Reader*, edited by Theo D'haen, César Domingúez and Mads Rosendahl Thomsen. London: Routledge.
Gumbrecht, Hans Ulrich. 1997. *In 1926: Living at the Edge of Time.* Cambridge: Harvard University Press.
Higginson, William J. 1985. *The Haiku Handbook: How to Write, Share, and Teach Haiku.* New York: Kodansha.
Høeg, Peter. 1993. *Smilla's Sense of Snow.* New York: Farrar Straus and Giroux.
Huggan, Graeme. 2001. *The Postcolonial Exotic: Marketing the Margins.* New York: Routledge.
Jameson, Fredric. 2011. "Cosmic Neutrality." *London Review of Books*, 20 October.
Moretti, Franco. 1994. *Modern Epic.* London: Verso.
Mufti, Aamir. 2016. *Forget English! Orientalisms and World Literature.* Cambridge: Harvard University Press.
Mukherjee, Neel. 2014. *The Lives of Others.* London: Chatto & Windus.
Nilsson, Louise, Theo D'haen and David Damrosch. 2017. "Introduction." In *Crime Fiction as World Literature.* London: Bloomsbury.
Rahimi, Atiq. 2011. *The Patience Stone.* London: Vintage.
Rushdie, Salman. 1996. *East-West.* London: Vintage.

Scarry, Elaine. 1985. *The Body in Pain: The Making and the Unmaking of the World*. Oxford: Oxford University Press.
Siskind, Mariano. 2014. *Cosmopolitan Desires: Global Modernity and World Literature in Latin America*. Chicago, IL: Northwestern University Press.
Thomsen, Mads Rosendahl. 2008. *Mapping World Literature: International Canonization and World Literature*. London: Continuum.

4 Geographies
Reading the oceans

Stefan Helgesson

In 1560, mid-way between Goa and Mozambique Island, the renegade Jesuit priest Manuel Antunes spends a night among the slaves in the hold. He sleeps fitfully, but descends eventually into "his interior labyrinths." Previously, his superior Dom Gonçalo da Silveira had been talking about the souls of the blacks that he so wished to whiten, but that night,

> Father Antunes, who was white and the son of white parents, became uncertain of the colour of his soul. He dreamed he was travelling on a luminous ship, made of flames rather than wood. On this vessel there were no covered quarters, no hold. There was only the deck, exposed to the sun. There were no slaves, no starved seamen. Everyone shared bread and water among themselves. And water was so plentiful that it seemed to flow from inside him, as if he had been transformed into a spring and all those who were thirsty could drink from him.

(My translation)

> naquela noite, o padre Antunes, branco e filho de brancos, duvidou da cor da sua alma. E sonhou que seguia numa nau luminosa, feita mais de exalações do que de madeira. Nessa embarcação não havia cobertura, não havia porão. Tudo era convés, aberto ao sol. Não havia escravos, não havia grumetes famintos. Todos partilhavam do pão e da água. E a água era tanta que parecia jorrar dentro dele, como se se houvesse convertido em fonte e nele bebessem os sedentos todos do mundo.

(Couto 2006, 236)

The negations affirm the actual conditions in which the young priest Antunes finds himself, conditions marked by slavery, hunger and hierarchy. Yet his dream also allows for the possibility of transformation. The ship is a microcosm of its own, detached for the duration of its five-week passage from the constraints and rigours of land-based society (albeit with constraints and rigours of its own). Antunes himself transforms during the passage – upon arrival in Mozambique, he renounces his Catholic faith – and the relationships among seamen, slaves, clergy and passengers on board ship are, just like the outcome of the voyage itself, less than fully predictable.

The narrator points out that *A Nossa Senhora de Ajuda* ("Our Lady of Succour") is not a slave ship. It is a caravel, built for cargo. The slaves on board are brought along for labour, not as commodities to be sold. Rather, the ship's voyage, which is one of the two main narratives in the Mozambican writer Mia Couto's novel *O outro pé da sereia* (2006; "The Other Foot of the Mermaid"), occurs during the short century of Portugal's dominance of the Indian Ocean and belongs to the traffic necessary both for the extraction of wealth through trade and the administration of the empire.

There are both commercial and symbolic goods on board. Spices, silk and benzoin share the cramped spaces with a wooden figure of the Virgin Mary – the "mermaid" of the title. For Dom Gonçalo da Silveira – an historical figure who also makes an appearance as José da Silvestra in H. Rider Haggard's *King Solomon's Mines* (1885) – it is an essential component in his endeavour to convert the Emperor Monomotapa in the African inland. One of the ship's trusted slaves, Nimi Nsundi, also reveres the sculpture, however. In his eyes, it does not represent Mary, but the Congolese water spirit Kianda. Hence, symbolic authority is in flux; the signs of Catholicism (the moral and spiritual justification for imperial rule) become susceptible to reappropriation. This syncretic "Africanization" then recurs in the other, contemporary narrative strand of the novel, in which the sculpture is rediscovered in northern Mozambique.

Even in that moment of sixteenth-century Portuguese dominance, we can see how the novel claims the Indian Ocean as a liminal, transformative and transgressive space. Father Antunes's dream is of water and blackness, the "realism" of which derives from the spilling of his drinking water. The scene's lyrical force as an affirmation of cultural and spiritual fluidity – despite imperial domination – is all the more evident, and also supported by much current scholarship on the Indian Ocean.

The history of contacts across the Indian Ocean goes back a long way. There is evidence of trade between the Indian subcontinent and ancient Egypt, and for many centuries during what is known as "the Middle Ages" in Europe ships sailed between India, the Arab world and East

Africa. The sea, in all its vastness, has been a means of connection and communication as much as conquest and conflict. Indeed, it might even be the case that "conquest," the ambition to rule the waves by force, only enters the Indian Ocean with the Portuguese and subsequent state-backed European empires. Before then, trade routes hadn't been exclusive to any state or polity. The voyage of *A Nossa Senhora de Ajuda* in Couto's novel is in that sense still something of a novelty, crossing waters rife with a different and decidedly non-European history.

In recent years, these long and layered histories of the Indian Ocean have attracted increasing attention from literary scholars. For Gaurav Desai, the Indian Ocean offers "possibilities of engaging in a postcolonial form of critique that doesn't unduly prioritize the West or its inherited modes of academic disciplinary knowledge" (2013, 11). Similarly, Isabel Hofmeyr has argued that "at every turn the Indian Ocean complicates binaries, moving us away from the simplicities of the resistant local and dominating global," prompting in this way the development of more flexible categories of analysis than the ones canonized by the early phase of postcolonial studies, inscribed as they were in the metropole-colony dynamic (2010, 722).

But this discussion doesn't begin and end with the Indian Ocean. Rather, as the present chapter sets out to demonstrate, oceans as such have emerged as an increasingly compelling macro-context for literary studies. Two sets of interventions have been particularly consequential for this development. The first was Paul Gilroy's seminal book *The Black Atlantic: Modernity and Double Consciousness* (1993) and the ensuing debates that it generated. The second was the emergence of the Indian Ocean as a framework for cultural and literary studies, spearheaded by historians such as Chaudhuri (1985), Subrahmanyam (1997a), Pearson (2003) and Bose (2005), reconfigured by literary scholars such as Hofmeyr and Desai, and further developed by (among others) Meg Samuelson (2017) and Pamila Gupta (2014). In both cases, my account must be strictly selective – but what I wish to show is the resonance between these alternative geographies (and histories) and the concerns of world literature. Indeed, if the "world" risks being too big and vague a concept to handle, the expansive yet comparatively bounded oceanic spaces provide a productive metageographical limitation to the ways in which connectivity across time and space can be understood in world literature. Even more to the point, the oceanic context presents us with a strong combination of what has been called "connected histories" (Subrahmanyam 1997b) and "significant geographies." If Subrahmanyam's notion is offered as an alternative to "comparative histories," then Karima Laachir, Sara Marzagora and Francesca Orsini's concept refers to "trajectories and imaginaries that are *recurrent* and/or that *matter* to actors and texts" (2018, 294; emphasis in the original). The term significant geographies combines in this way conceptual, imaginative and real aspects of geography and "underlines how 'the world' is not a given but is produced by different, embodied, and located actors" (294). Addressing a number of examples, mainly but not only textual, I will explore one at a time some of the significant literary geographies of the Atlantic and the Indian Ocean. In the conclusion, I also connect the oceanic paradigm to Beecroft's literary ecologies (as discussed in Chapter 2) to see how the two perspectives can illuminate one another.

Adopting oceans as a framework for reading means privileging geography and history, yet the implications for literature are far-reaching. If connection is a minimal condition for world literature – connection across literary cultures, languages, spaces – then oceans present us with one of the maximal conditions for connection. If world literature has its focus on what moves across, beneath and beyond nations, then oceans are one of the most significant trans- and non-national arenas. And if the modern world of ultramarine empires and capitalist trade took shape through the emergence of long-distance ocean travel, then, as Margaret Cohen has argued, this must be understood as having a formative influence on literature and literary genres. "Only using the scale of the Atlantic," she writes, "can we grasp the importance of sea adventure fiction as one of the major narrative genres of the nineteenth century" (2010, 658), a genre which subsequently had a tremendous impact on the development of the novel through writers such as Herman Melville and Joseph Conrad. Moreover, if we recognize that the prime means of long-distance travel in the *ancient* world were sea-borne, then this sheds light not only on a foundational text such as Homer's *Odyssey* but also, for example, in the multilingual and multiscriptal collections gathered in the Hellenic library of Alexandria that included texts from as far afield as the Indian subcontinent (McGann 2013, 243).

These few remarks already show, however, that "the ocean" can never be reduced to a single method or perspective. It invites, rather, a range of approaches functioning at various scales and with different combinations of intra- and extratextual foci. What they have in common is a sense of historical density, or what Elizabeth DeLoughrey – following Bachelard – has termed "heavy waters" (2010, 7). The oceans are not empty. The unimaginably vast "Great Pacific garbage patch" in our day is just one of the most scandalous and distressing oceanic traces of human activity; literature, in its capacity to address the forgotten, the repressed, the invisible, the barely conceivable, speaks to many more such traces on an oceanic and world-historical level. This is the domain of the "abyss" and the "poetics of Relation" of which, as we shall see, the Martinican philosopher Édouard Glissant has written so evocatively and which unsettles a number of national, land-based assumptions of literary history. But it is also the domain of less conflictual connected histories that can inspire nostalgic retrievals, as in Amitav Ghosh's *In an Antique Land*.

Besides providing a selective overview of Black Atlantic and Indian Ocean studies, the main aim of this chapter is in other words to demonstrate how the oceanic paradigm can function as *a mode of world-literary reading* on a scale one notch below the potentially problematic notions of "globe" and "planet" (see Introduction), yet decisively larger and less containable than nations. Such a reading can be understood in two ways: either text-immanently, focusing on how the literary work constructs maritime worlds, or as a way of grouping and contextualizing texts. This chapter will attempt to look at both aspects.

The Black Atlantic (the abyss)

Although the pioneering historian of the Atlantic, Marcus Rediker, has long lamented what he saw as the "terracentric" bias of historical studies (Bloch-Lainé 2017), the poets were there before him. Derek Walcott's famous poem "The Sea Is History," from 1979, made explicit what Walcott's lyrical labour had already long demonstrated:

> Where are your monuments, your battles, martyrs?
> Where is your tribal memory? Sirs,
> in that grey vault. The sea. The sea
> has locked them up. The sea is History.
> (Walcott 1986, 364)

This was hardly news to the long succession of writers and storytellers who had textualized and narrated the sea, and Walcott is never less than acutely aware of literary inheritances when he articulates this history. In his later, monumental work *Omeros*, where he superimposes the Mediterranean of Homer onto the Caribbean, he speaks of how "I followed a sea-swift to both sides of this text; / her hyphen stitched its seam, like the interlocking / basins of a globe in which one half fits the next" (1990, 319). Combining worlds in his writing, Walcott brings the formal and literary-historical resources at his disposal to bear on the Caribbean experience. Homer and a host of European texts and images are in this way appropriated in his lyrical endeavour.

This is inevitably an ambiguous undertaking. The long reception of Shakespeare's *The Tempest* (1611), nominally set in the Mediterranean but typically read as an allegory of trans-Atlantic colonization, has established a paradigm for this two-way mode of reading (Hulme and Sherman 2000). If the play apparently sides with Prospero, the expelled duke of Milan who asserts his dominion over the island and his two slaves Ariel and Caliban, the dialogic complexity of the play nonetheless grants voice to the degraded figure of Caliban, who derides Prospero and Miranda for having "taught me language, and my profit on 't / is I know how to curse. The red plague rid you / For learning me your language!" (Act 1, scene 2). This has been reread and appropriated innumerable times, perhaps with the greatest literary sophistication in Aimé Césaire's play *A Tempest* (*Une tempête*, 1969). By making Ariel and Caliban embody, respectively, the principles of accommodation and rebellion, and by turning Prospero into a colonizer (rather than a banished ruler), Césaire makes his play speak directly to the concerns of twentieth-century decolonization.

An even more ambivalent case would be Luís de Camões's epic *The Lusiads* (*Os Lusíadas*, 1572). A masterpiece of the Portuguese language, composed in the same era in which Dom Gonçalo da Silveira was active, the epic achieves an unashamedly partisan conceptual capture of the Atlantic and Indian Oceans, extolling the grandeur of the Portuguese-Catholic imperial endeavour and textualizing the oceans with the full arsenal of European classical mythology. It is also the most maritime of poems, providing unparalleled images of billowing sails and treacherous currents. The epic's undeniably imperial framing notwithstanding, however, the density of its motifs and symbolism allows for multiple and alternative readings. Perhaps the most famous of alternative readings concerns a mythical creature of Camões's own invention, Adamastor, a giant banished to the Cape of Good Hope for his rebelliousness (and more particularly for falling in love with the sea nymph Thetis). When prompted in Canto V by Vasco da Gama to tell his story, the dreadful Adamastor is humanized and even becomes a figure of pity. Portrayed as the ruler of the treacherous currents around the Cape of Good Hope, and threatening the Portuguese with destruction, Adamastor is so moved by the opportunity to tell his story that he lays himself to rest (transforming into Table Mountain) and calms the waters to allow the Portuguese their passage into the Indian Ocean.

Wedding in this way the historical experience of Portuguese mariners to the mythological episteme of classical (European) learning, Camões casts Adamastor as an allegory of the African subcontinent's natural forces. But he can also be read as a Portuguese projection of the Africans themselves: cowed into submission, whilst at the same time constituting a colossus of frightful powers and tender passions. In a paradigmatic case of world literary transfer and transformation, this polysemy of Adamastor as the repressed element in the colonizing consciousness has inspired numerous literary responses in South Africa, beginning with Roy Campbell's poems in the 1920s and continuing with, among others, André Brink's ludic *Cape of Storms: The First Life of Adamastor* (1993), which reimagines Adamastor as a man from the indigenous Khoikhoi community, one among the first to come into direct contact with Portuguese seafarers. Adopting the established "writing back" mode of postcolonial literature, this fictional conceit plays havoc with Camões's narrative and reverses the perspective.

What Caliban, Ariel and Adamastor all *mean* is, in other words, susceptible to continuing renegotiation. Historically, it is impossible to ignore the European and imperial conditions of possibility for both *The Tempest* and *The Lusiads*. In this regard, they could be accused of locking up history in the "grey vault" of Walcott's sea. *Unlocking* the vault requires instead an active retrieval of alternative and silenced perspectives in order not to reproduce, be it naïvely or wilfully, the imperial gaze on the Atlantic. As Césaire's rewriting of Ariel and Caliban indicates, the history of slavery, and the effort to refocalize the historical narrative from within the experience of slavery looms large in this labour of retrieval. Here is one influential attempt, by Édouard Glissant, to articulate the foundational rupture of the Middle Passage:

> The first dark shadow was cast by being wrenched from their everyday, familiar land, away from protecting gods and a tutelary community. But that is nothing yet. Exile can be borne, even when it comes as a bolt from the blue. The second dark of night fell as tortures and the deterioration of person, the result of so many incredible Gehennas. Imagine two hundred human beings crammed into a space barely capable of containing a third of them. Imagine vomit, naked flesh, swarming lice, the dead slumped, the dying crouched. Imagine, if you can, the swirling red of mounting to the deck, the ramp they climbed, the black sun on the horizon, vertigo, this dizzying sky plastered to the waves. ... But that is nothing yet.
>
> (Glissant 1997, 5–6)

This is, in Glissant's account, what produced "the abyss" of Atlantic history, a foundationless foundation for subsequent constructions of subjectivity and community. In the long human history of slavery, the trans-Atlantic trade – first enabled by those early Portuguese voyages around Africa – produced an experience of rupture, alienation and creolization on an unprecedented scale and level. As Achille Mbembe has memorably described it, the African slaves became imprisoned in "the dungeon of appearance," belonging "to others who hated them. They were deprived of their own names and their own languages. Their lives and their work were from then on controlled by the others with whom they were condemned to live, and who denied them recognition as cohumans" (2017, 2).

Yet it is precisely from within this extreme negation that an alternative, transnational and potentially universal humanism evolves and can be traced as a counterpoint to the history allegorically contained by *The Tempest* and *The Lusiads*. In *The Black Atlantic*, the book that established the concept, Paul Gilroy's key argument was that the legacy of trans-Atlantic slavery had fostered a "counterculture of modernity." This counterculture is not confined to any specific locality in the Atlantic world, but should rather be understood as a communicative network, mediated by music and literature, reaching across the shores of Africa, Europe, the Americas and even beyond. Indeed, for Gilroy, the chronotope best suited to capture the functional logic of the Black Atlantic was the ship itself, "in motion across the spaces between Europe, America, Africa, and the Caribbean" (1993, 4). As a "living, micro-cultural, micro-political system in motion," the image of the ship connects synecdochally not just with the Middle Passage and various initiatives for returning to an African homeland, but also with "the circulation of ideas and activists as well as the movement of key cultural and political artefacts: tracts, books, gramophone records, and choirs" (1993, 4).

Within this communicative network we can locate individuals such as the eighteenth-century abolitionist (and erstwhile slave) Olaudah Equiano, the early twentieth-century South African writer and activist Solomon Plaatje, the Jamaican activist Marcus Garvey, the US poet Langston Hughes, the Cuban poet Nicolas Guillén, the Martinican poet Aimé Césaire, the Guadeloupe author Maryse Condé, the Jamaican writer and philosopher Sylvia Wynter, the Mozambican poets José Craveirinha and Noémia de Sousa – the list goes on. This is not a grouping or network that speaks with one voice; these names are also, with few exceptions, different from the ones discussed by Gilroy. The three African examples – Plaatje, Craveirinha and de Sousa – are moreover not directly linked to the history of trans-Atlantic slavery: it was rather that they found analogies to their experiences of settler colonialism, racism and dispossession within the Black Atlantic communicative context. "Billie Holiday, my American sister," the half-Goan Mozambican Noémia de Sousa would write in Maputo (then Lourenço Marques) in 1949, "keep singing in that bruised way of yours / the eternal 'blues' of our disgraced people" ("Billie Holiday, minha irmã americana, / continua cantando sempre, no seu jeito magoado / os 'blues' eternos do nosso povo desgraçado"; 2001, 135; my translation). With no direct connection to the black experience in the United States, except through music and texts, de Sousa's pathos illustrates also the force of this particular oceanic perspective. The enduring point is that the Black Atlantic has given rise to exceptionally powerful articulations of the ambiguities of modernity – articulations which are not restricted to any exclusionary community, but which circulated with increasing frequency in the twentieth century through journals, records, books, newspapers and films, sparking recognition among colonized communities. In this way, if the slaves on the Atlantic can be thought of as the first fully alienated, rootless subjects of modernity, they and their descendants ultimately shaped a critical counterpoint to a Western modernity that at one and the same time had created them and excluded them.

The most influential articulation of this inside/outside position is found in the American sociologist W. E. B. Du Bois's *The Souls of Black Folk* (1903), where he speaks of the African-Americans' "double consciousness":

> It is a peculiar sensation, this double-consciousness, this sense of always looking at one's self through the eyes of others, of measuring one's soul by the tape of a world that looks on in amused contempt and pity. One ever feels his two-ness, an American, a Negro; two souls, two thoughts, two unreconciled strivings; two warring ideals in one dark body, whose dogged strength alone keeps it from being torn asunder.
>
> (Du Bois 2000, 3)

Produced through the sinister logic of racism, it is such doubleness that for Gilroy informs the culture of the Black Atlantic. Shaped by people who both belong and do not belong, this is an inherently transitive culture which resists, constitutively, containment by national, ethnic and racial categories, but is instead always on the move, connecting one thing to another. In the words of Glissant, this has enabled a "Poetics of Relation, in which each and every identity is extended through a relationship with the Other" (1997, 11).

Equiano's *Interesting Narrative of the Life of Olaudah Equiano* (1789) stands here as a paradigmatic precursor. This life story, parts of which should be read as a novel rather than a direct account of Equiano's experiences – if Vincent Carretta's claim that the author was born in South Carolina rather than West Africa holds – is mostly sea-borne. Drawn into the so-called Seven Years War (which lasted nine years, from 1754 until 1763) at an early age, and subsequently criss-crossing the

Atlantic for many years – first as a slave, later as a free seaman – Equiano became quintessentially an "Atlantic creole" (Carretta 2007, 47), shaped by the experience of mobility rather than any particular place. Indeed, by travelling also to the Arctic as well the Constantinople of the Ottoman empire, he saw far more of the world than most of his contemporaries.

The significance of *Interesting Narrative* lies, nonetheless, in its manifestation of double consciousness. Towards the end of the seventh edition Equiano writes:

> My life and fortune have been extremely chequered, and my adventures various. [...] I early accustomed myself to look at the hand of God in the minutest occurrence, and to learn from it a lesson of morality and religion; and in the light every circumstance I have related was to me of importance. After all, what makes any event important, unless by it's [sic] observation we become better and wiser, and learn "to do justly, to love mercy, and to walk humbly before God!"
>
> (360)

The juxtaposition of his "chequered" and "various" experiences with what he identifies as the consistent presence of God alerts us to how a spiritual vocabulary typical of his time allows Equiano rhetorically to transcend the divisions internal both to the Atlantic and to his speaking position. If the life journey presented in the narrative is consistently marked by the dualism of both belonging to and being excluded from an imperial Atlantic world order, this is precisely what explains both the narrative's urgency and its rhetorical strategy to adopt the vocabulary of conversion and humanitarianism (sometimes with a patronizing tone towards his "African brethren"). Shaped as *Interesting Narrative*'s narrator was by the contradictions of the Atlantic world, the account of a "life" passing through sharply divergent positions in that world made it possible for Equiano's English readers to relativize their own positions (to a greater or smaller extent as beneficiaries of slave labour) and commit to the cause of abolitionism. In this way, by literary means, Equiano became one of Britain's most influential abolitionists – alongside names such Thomas Clarkson and Granville Sharp.

If, as I am claiming here, the work of writers from Equiano to Condé, from de Sousa to Césaire, can meaningfully be brought together under the rubric of the "Black Atlantic," then this is an excellent example of how concepts can function productively. Since the publication of Gilroy's book, an entire sub-field of cultural studies has emerged out of that intervention. Important criticism has been voiced – concerning, for instance, Gilroy's lack of attention to Africa (Masilela 1996; Chrisman 2000) – and other scholars have presented alternative angles on the Atlantic – the hispanophone Black Atlantic, for example, or the Green (meaning Irish) Atlantic (Whelan 2004) – but this adds to rather than detracts from the heuristic value of viewing the ocean as a conflicted, culturally dense space of connectivity.

Indeed, to underscore this, I will in closing indicate how the Black Atlantic perspective can be relevant also to work coming from another "racial" and social angle. Published in 1869, Castro Alves's "The Slave Ship" ("Tragédia no mar: o navio negreiro") counts as Brazil's most famous abolitionist poem. It is clearly written from the humanitarian viewpoint of a white Brazilian, yet provides lyrically unsettling images of the very preconditions for the emergence of the Black Atlantic (and here one should remember that Brazil was the single largest recipient of African slave populations during the long era of the slave trade):

> As in a vision of Dante,
> I saw the quarterdeck, slippery with blood,
> The skylight washed with crimson.
> The clanking irons ... the crack of a whip ...
> Legions of men black as the night,
> Dancing their horrible death-dance ...
> Black-mouthed and listless children
> Hang at their black mothers' exhausted breasts
> Spattered with blood
> Shivering and naked girls,
> A crowd of ghosts dragging
> Their wretched bodies ...
> The ironic chorus laughs at itself
> As the dark serpent coils
> Its mad and spiralling dance ...
> If an old man gasps for breath ... falls to the ground,
> There are screams, the cracking of whips ...
> And their feet move on and on ...
>   (Alves 1990, 15–7)[1]

> Era um sonho dantesco ... o tombadilho
> Que das luzernas avermelha o brilho.
> Em sangue a se banhar.
> Tinir de ferros ... estalar do açoite ...
> Legiões de homens negros como a noite,

> Horrendos a dançar ...
> Negras mulheres, suspendendo às tetas
> Magras crianças, cujas bocas pretas
> Rega o sangue das mães:
> Outras môças ... mas nuas, espantadas,
> No turbilhão de espectros arrastadas,
> Em ânsia e mágoa vãs.
> E ri-se a orquestra, irônica, estridente ...
> E da ronda fantástica a serpente
> Faz doudas espirais ...
> Se o velho arqueja ... se no chão resvala,
> Ouvem-se gritos ... o chicote estala.
> E voam mais e mais ...
> (Alves 1960, 280)

Strikingly, this vision of hell, this floating prison suspended between the sea and the sky, is populated not just by African captives, but by seamen from Greece, England, Italy, France and Spain – all of them destined for Brazil. Alves's slave ship becomes in this way also an image of a racially divided world-system in the nineteenth century, in which profit is produced at unfathomable human cost. The sense of immobility produced by the poem, caught as the ship is between the sky and the sea, brings to mind Elizabeth DeLoughrey's claim that engaging the violence of Atlantic history leads "not to a liberating mobility, but to the cessation of movement across space, an immersion" (2010, 704). A more optimistic reading, along the lines of Glissant's poetics of Relation, would insist rather on the potential for literature to act in the world and transform the apparent rigidity of racialized and reified human relations. The canonization of Alves's poem, his radical manifestation – in his time and social circles – of slavery and Africans as topics fit for poetry, and Alves's inscription in the belated history of Brazilian abolition (achieved only in 1888) would all seem to speak in favour of Glissant's transformative vision.

Indian Ocean narratives

The literary version of Indian Ocean studies has taken shape under inspiration from the Black Atlantic, but also challenges this concept's basic parameters. In a field-defining article in 2007, Isabel Hofmeyr argued for the distinctiveness of cultural and political relations in the Indian Ocean. To begin with, if trans-Atlantic sea travel is essentially a modern phenomenon (give or take a few excursions by Vikings and others), transoceanic voyages in the Indian Ocean stretch back to antiquity. Understood as a space for commerce and cultural hybridization, it has a deeper and more layered history than the Atlantic. The development of Swahili along the African east coast, and the subsequent emergence of Swahili poetry – under strong influence from Arabic – possibly as far back as the twelfth or thirteenth centuries, provides one example of a literary development separate from the history of European expansionism, yet with an obvious world literary dimension.

Because of this longer history, and because of the number of sovereignties and empires that have acted upon it, the Indian Ocean is less amenable to the more binary paradigm of the Black Atlantic. Slavery, Hofmeyr and many other scholars argue, has a less definite meaning in the history of the Indian Ocean. There were many categories of slaves, and the boundary between slavery and freedom could be porous. Above all, it didn't have the singularly racialized meaning that we find in the Atlantic. This exposes a limitation in what Hofmeyr sees as the normative model of the Atlantic, as does the long presence of contending religions and polities. Taken together, these differences produce, as Hofmeyr phrases it, "a view of colonialism less as an encounter of the local and the global than as a contestation of different universalisms" (2007, 8). The implications of this claim are far-reaching. If the Black Atlantic produces a counterculture to a singular (Western) modernity – as encapsulated in the notion of "double consciousness" – the contestation of different universalisms invites a more pluricultural reading of the Indian Ocean through deep time. This raises the stakes for world literature quite dramatically, given that it moves far beyond the "Eurochronology" (Prendergast 2004) of the world republic of letters and necessitates a multi-perspectival approach to the Indian Ocean. In practice, such studies remain unusual, although there are a number of literary works as well as critical investigations (within the ambit of my own linguistic and scholarly reach) that demonstrate the rewards of such multi-perspectivism. I will first discuss three novels – Amitav Ghosh's *In an Antique Land*, Couto's *O outro pé* and Abdulrazak Gurnah's *Paradise* – and then Isabel Hofmeyr's account of the journal *Indian Opinion* (published by Mahatma Gandhi in Durban in the early twentieth century) to demonstrate this. Gurnah's *Paradise* will also allow me to elaborate on the history of Swahili literature as an Indian Ocean literature.

As illustrated by the motley crew aboard *A Nossa Senhora de Ajuda* in Mia Couto's novel, the Indian Ocean has never been the exclusive dominion of any single group, ethnicity or indeed religion, even under conditions of imperial rule. Within this multi-ethnic panorama, it can be illustrative to explore the fate of Indians – or South Asians, rather – traversing the Indian Ocean and occupying a range of positions in this oceanic world. From the humble slaves and *lascars* – Muslim seamen – that Amitav Ghosh's historical fictions have rendered visible, to the labourers, farmers, merchants and craftsmen we encounter in, for example, work by Moyez Vassanji, Imraan Coovadia, Mia Couto, Shailja Patel, J. M. G. Le Clézio and João Paulo Borges Coelho, the hybridized Indian presences across the seaboard consistently confound binaries and neat categorizations. South Asians in East Africa have typically been compelled to occupy "in-between" positions that elude easy, binaristic social and racial pinpointing, and have in that way also been susceptible to exclusionary policies. As Shailja Patel, a transnational poet of Kenyan origin, puts it in "Shilling Love":

> I learn / like a stone in my gut / that third-generation
> Asian Kenyan / will never / be Kenyan enough / that all
> my patriotic fervour / will not / turn my skin / black
> (2010, 38)

This should not be taken as a blanket statement – Patel's work is *also* thoroughly Kenyan – but it indicates an experience of racial anxiety and unbelonging produced, in a more extended analysis, within a history of Indian Ocean peregrinations. The in-betweenness of diasporic South Asians in Africa emerges in fact as a dominant theme in, say, Moyez Vassanji's *The Gunny Sack* (1989), Imraan Coovadia's *The Wedding* (2001), and also in V. S. Naipaul's more controversial novels *A Bend in the River* (1973) and *Half a Life* (2004). Shailja Patel's own term for this in-betweenness, echoing "negritude," is *migritude*. For her, it is not just an arbitrary, idiosyncratic experience, nor is it essentially "Indian," but rather a problematic category of being, produced within the crucible of imperialism, shared by millions and extended into our contemporary moment of globalized hyper-mobility and US military dominance.

Taking a somewhat more optimistic view of in-betweenness, Gaurav Desai emphasizes the productively syncretic and hybridizing dimensions of the encounters between groups. Amitav Ghosh's canonized novel *In an Antique Land* (1992) is here a central point of reference. Offering a compelling vision of how syncretism pervades the Indian Ocean, also long before the rise of Western, transoceanic empires, the novel painstakingly weaves together two separate narratives. The first is based on Ghosh's own experience, as a young Indian student, of conducting anthropological research in a rural Egyptian village. The focus is on how the narrator – apparently Ghosh himself – very gradually adapts to village life and builds relationships with the local inhabitants. As a stranger from India, culturally a Hindu, and struggling to master the colloquial

Arabic of his new environment, the narrator undergoes an emotionally demanding transition, often presented in a comical vein and at the narrator's own expense. Co-existence is not in any way presented as frictionless: embedded in their Islamic life-world, the villagers question what they perceive as the Hindu barbarism of the narrator. Do you burn your dead? Do you worship cows? Aren't you circumcised? The strong friendships that develop between the narrator and several villagers should therefore be seen as an *overcoming* of cultural differences, rather than a straightforward accommodation of the other.

It is this complicated experience that then motivates the novel's second storyline, which concerns the narrator's enquiry into the life of a twelfth-century Jewish merchant in Cairo, Abraham Ben Yiju, and his slave, Bomma. One part of this enquiry is philological and historical, another part is fictional (the name "Bomma," for example, is conjecture). Following the trail of documents originally found in a Geniza in Cairo, Ghosh pieces together the few details he can find concerning Ben Yiju's itinerant life, and resurrects in this way the memory of a thriving twelfth-century Indian Ocean cosmopolis in which geographically distant places such as Cairo, Aden and Mangalore (in India) were connected through trade and human relationships.

The Geniza serves here as a compelling image of the fragility of cultural memory and, by extension, of alternative conceptions of world literature. An enclosed space within a synagogue, the Geniza became a repository for virtually any scrap of writing. As Ghosh explains it, each synagogue across the Middle East once had its own Geniza, the purpose of which was "to prevent the accidental desecration of any written form of God's name" (1992, 39). Since God was routinely invoked in most genres of writing among the Jewish population, this meant that the Geniza, over time, became a disorganized library of Babel in its own right, comprising both sacred and profane texts. Indeed, as Desai explains, "what was meant to be a practice related to documents of a religious nature was extended to almost all documents written in the Hebrew script, which came to be considered holy in itself" (2013, 22).

Contrary to the common practice of eventually emptying the Geniza and disposing of the texts through an appropriate ritual, the Cairo Geniza accumulated instead writings throughout eight centuries. The earliest document dated from the eleventh century. The most recent, "a divorce settlement written in Bombay" (Ghosh 1992, 40), had been composed in 1875 – not long before the Geniza was torn down in 1890. This massive jumble of texts, both sacred and profane, began to attract the attention of European scholars in the 1860s, and once the documents were acquired by various collectors, they would find their sinuous way into various research libraries in Europe and the United States. This, of course, is the *starting point* for Ghosh's own enquiry into the lives of Ben Yiju and Bomma. The gradual unravelling of how he came to discover the traces of these two individuals and their Indian Ocean life world is a riveting story within the story. In this way, the story within the story addresses the conditions of possibility for the project resulting in *In an Antique Land*. In the conjunction of knowledge and power prevailing when Ghosh wrote his novel, there was no way for him to work his way around the mediation of this knowledge via Western institutions of philology. (Today, two decades after the breakthrough of the Internet, access has changed dramatically, the distribution of centres of knowledge less so.)

The question is what one makes of this epistemological double bind, and how it reflects both on Ghosh's novel and on iterations of world literature. There is by now a long line of thinkers, counting from Edward Said of *Orientalism* (1978), to Aamir Mufti (2016) and Siraj Ahmed (2018), who argue that philological knowledge production is not only intimately tied to the exercise of Western colonial power, but has also come to shape postcolonial projects of recovery or nation-building. On this reading, there is a systemic logic to this way of constructing knowledge that holds each participant hostage to a particular Western, "Orientalist" perspective. Without denying the historical validity of such an analysis, an alternative approach would highlight the contingent nature of knowledge. In Desai's estimation, Ghosh's act of recovery "is based on an extraordinary triumph of chance over will, of luck over intent" (Desai 2013, 22). Ben Yiju and Bomma could easily have slipped into the abyss of oblivion. Indeed, nothing else should have been expected. Yet, through an infinitely thin thread stretching from the twelfth century to our day, held barely intact through the vicissitudes of different orders of textual circulation and archiving, the fading traces of these two individuals were salvaged – not forever, this no one can say, but for us, as readers in the present.

Such an approach, without denying the asymmetries and injustices of knowledge-power relations, emphasizes the unfinished and malleable nature of knowledge production. Importantly, it also resists the temptation to reduce the "West" and the "East" to monoliths. In Ghosh's novel, this temptation is always latent, breaking out in full force at the most conflictual moment in the story, when the narrator and an Imam in the village have a shouting match over which country – Egypt or India – is more advanced and powerful. At this moment, the West is reduced to the sheer power of "science and tanks and guns and bombs," and the Imam and the narrator turn themselves into "delegates from two superseded civilizations, vying with each other to establish a prior claim to the technology of modern violence" (Ghosh 1992, 193–4). This could be compared to Mia Couto's take on globalization in *O outro pé da sereia*, written more than a decade after *In an Antique Land*. As we have seen, both novels develop a deep-time view of the embattled present by combining two separate narratives – an approach that, arguably, speaks to the specificity of Indian Ocean history as "a contestation of different universalisms," to refer once again to Hofmeyr, but also to the impossibility to uphold rigid Orientalist and colonial separations between cultures and groups. Exercising the imagination on the distant past becomes in this way a means to challenge entrenched patterns of thinking in the present. By juxtaposing two time-periods and making protagonists from five continents converge on the same small region of northern Mozambique, *O outro pé da sereia* is a novel that consistently asks the reader to move outside the neat boxes of nation, territory, race and religion, so as to confront a vision of history marked by a protean and messy particularity. The sea becomes in the process a protagonist in its own right, a catalyst both of imperial rule and its undoing.

In the contemporary narrative strand of *O outro pé da sereia*, it is air travel rather than sea voyages that jostle people together. Funded by a non-governmental organization whose mission it is to combat "afro-pessimism," the academic African-American couple Benjamin and Rosie Southman descend upon the small town of Vila Longe ("longe" meaning "far away"). The portrayal of the historian Ben Southman is satirical: animated by his desire to connect with an authentic Africa and to confirm his preconceptions of the history of slavery, Vila Longe both confounds and complies with his desire. The entrepreneur Casuarino strictly instructs the inhabitants of Vila Longe to give the Americans what they want. He enthusiastically interjects that "This is globalization, my friends! Worldwide globalization! Vila Longe is the capital of the global village!" (Couto 2006, 168). What such globalization entails for Casuarino is that Vila Longe should suppress the ambiguities of its own history, so that the Americans (Rosie actually originates from Brazil) will be happy to share of their wealth. When the postman Zeca Matambira starts talking about how people in the region once had been enslaved by another African tribe, the Vanguni, he is quickly admonished by Casuarino to shut up and toe the line: Ben Southman is only interested in the enslavement of Africans by Europeans.

All differences between the two novels aside, we see here how both *O outro pé da sereia* and *In an Antique Land* challenge the consistent pull towards binary modes of thinking produced both by intellectual habit and objective – and extreme – imbalances in the distribution of economic and political power. The genre of the novel and the qualified freedom of the literary writing intervene in this way in the contemporary world imaginary. Given their success – their high level of "visibility" in discrete literary networks – both Couto and Ghosh have entered contemporary world literature in so far as world literature refers to literature in circulation. More importantly, however, their novels *world* literature (if "world" is understood as a verb) by creating narratives of and around the Indian Ocean that run counter to other contemporary discourses. They could be invoked in this way as strong examples of what Debjani Ganguly identifies as the contemporary "global novel," emerging at the conjuncture of three phenomena: "the geopolitics of war and violence since the end of the cold war; hyperconnectivity through advances in information technology; and the emergence of a new humanitarian sensibility" (2016, 1). Seen from this angle, *O outro pé* and *In an Antique Land* participate in literature's active production and critique of world-conceptions – of an imaginative "making" of a totality that could be named "the world."

Adulrazak Gurnah's novel *Paradise* (1994) is equally exemplary in its Indian Ocean orientation, yet its formal approach to history differs from Ghosh's and Couto's. Set in German East Africa (Tanganyika) before the First World War, the novel follows the young and exceptionally beautiful Yusuf who at an early age is taken into the custody of his "uncle" Aziz – in actual fact a wealthy and powerful Arab-African trader based on the Tanganyikan coast. Aziz appropriates Yusuf as payment for a debt incurred by Yusuf's father. In other words: Yusuf becomes a *rehani*, a domestic slave. In the long middle section of the novel, Yusuf accompanies Aziz and his entire entourage of bearers and interpreters and negotiators on a trading expedition to the inland. Historically, this occurs precisely at the transition between two regional orders of power. If the coastal Swahili traders had become increasingly powerful throughout the nineteenth century, with their cultural, religious and economic influence extending far into the continent, German colonial authority was becoming more keenly felt around 1900. Aziz's fictional expedition traces in this way the waning of an Arab-African world that saw itself just as self-evidently central and civilized as the Germans imagined themselves to be.

Hussein, a Zanzibari storekeeper they meet on their way through the interior, provides some clear coordinates of this civilizational world: "Those mountains on the other side of the lake are the edge of the world we know ... The east and the north are known to us, as far as the land of China in the farthest east and the ramparts of Gog and Magog in the north. But the west is the land of darkness, the land of jinns and monsters" (Gurnah 1994, 83). Islam and the Arabic language are here the touchstones of civilization; non-Islamic Africans are heathens and savages. As for Europeans, they are seen as crude and bizarre. A traveller recently returned from Russia talks to Aziz about their barbaric customs – "[t]he Rusi people were not civilized" (Gurnah 1994, 105) – but also about his surprise at discovering fellow Muslims in that far-off region. The Germans, more than anything else, instil fear: "The more severe the punishment, the more firm and unforgiving he [the German] is. And his punishment is always severe. I think they like giving punishment" (1994, 115), Aziz's overseer Simba Mwene explains.

Contrary to Couto's and Ghosh's novels, the narrative discourse in *Paradise* remains contained within a single historical moment. This allows Gurnah to draw the reader more fully into Yusuf's world, without recourse to a "knowing" position external to it – even though structurally, of course, the knowing position after colonialism and after postcolonial disillusionment is the novel's condition of possibility. As James Hodapp (2015) and Fawzia Mustafa (2015) both have shown, the building of this fictional world is based on a highly specific set of texts, namely Swahili travel narratives and biographies written around 1900. The most famous of these is the 1902 "autobiography" of Tippu Tip, one of the most powerful of the nineteenth-century traders – an account which really was a transcribed version of his oral testimony. Another is Salim bin Abakari's *Safari Yangu ya Urusi nay a Siberia* ("My Travels through Russia and Siberia," 1901), and a third is Selemani bin Mwenye Chande's *Safari Yangu ya Bara Afrika* ("My Travels to the Interior of Africa," 1901). As with Ghosh's excavation of Ben Yiju's history, these texts are doubly and triply mediated. The very fact that they were published at this time – and in Latin rather than Arabic script – is a consequence of European colonial presence, initiated and/or facilitated by German and British ethnographers. They were then frequently translated into English or German, with European reading audiences in mind. Their reinscription in the novel, in turn, is the outcome of Gurnah's intervention not just as an author, but also as a translator. As he explains in an interview:

> I read one story of travel that had been translated into English – and it didn't "sound right" – it sounded like Swahili translated into English. My novel is full of these moments when people don't understand each other. I tried to find a narrative voice which would show this kind of guesswork, moving between different registers.
>
> (quoted in Deckard 2010, 110)

It is this translational and inscriptional labour that leads Mustafa to assess that "while the Swahili accounts of either life experiences or local customs solicited by German collectors [...] were composed on order with a specific non-local audience in mind, one which enjoyed unprecedented power over the authors, they also signified of different (less transparent) registers, the power of which Gurnah's novel captures and redeploys so brilliantly" (2015, 23).

It is important, however, not to limit one's understanding of Swahili to the colonial era. Its earlier written form evolved rather in the centuries when Arabic was a lingua franca of the Indian Ocean and Islam its hegemonic religion – the history from which Gurnah's protagonists emerge. European colonization and the advent of print technology would shift the coordinates drastically, but well into the nineteenth century the Arabic influence prevailed. As Clarissa Vierke describes it, Swahili's absorption of Arabic culture should first be conceived of in terms of translation: "poems have metamorphosed from Arabic into Swahili and have found their way into new genres, local song lyrics, Friday sermons, and newspaper pages. At a time before print and digital media, poetry traveled in manuscripts, and the technique of writing was soon adapted to produce a large number of written Swahili translations" (2017, 321). But the transfer, she argues, also had a sensual element to it. Rejecting the dualism of imitation vs. originality, she demonstrates instead how the eighteenth- and nineteenth-century *utendi* in Swahili also cultivated a sense of proximity to the "other side" of the ocean. *Utendi* (*tendi* in plural) could be defined as a didactic, often narrative poem, the oldest surviving Swahili example of which dates to 1728. Motifs and entire narratives in the *tendi* were derived from what could be described as an Islamic-Arabic cultural commons eulogizing the deeds and achievements of the Prophet. As Vierke and others argue, however, this is never just a straightforward transfer but an active appropriation in which Arabic narratives become Africanized even as the East African communities become culturally Arabized. "Swahili poets and musicians," Vierke writes, "have been found to integrate texts and images into the flexible texture of their own poetry or music, whereby the alien other is transformed into a marker of one's own identity, becoming part of the culture's system of reference" (326). When assessing *Paradise*, this deep-time view of Swahili literature evolving within a non-Western literary ecology must also be taken into account.

"Circulation" in *In an Antique Land* and *Paradise* is in other words not a seamless phenomenon. Rather, it is all about how texts change function, shift genre, and are remediated, recontextualized and translated. The work of authors such as Gurnah and Ghosh could in this respect be seen just as one episode in a long chain of textual events, demonstrating the processual nature of "entextualisation" in Karin Barber's sense (2007) and the irreducibly social nature of what Jerome McGann calls "the textual condition" (1991).

This view finds further support in yet another textual level at which *Paradise* operates. The structure of the story, and in particular its denouement, is patterned on the Quranic (and Old Testament) story of Yusuf/Joseph and the wife of Potiphar (see Sura 12 and Gen 39). Here, the novel acquires an almost mythical stature as a repetition of a timeless story of frustrated desire and asymmetrical power relationships. Potiphar is called by the honorific title "Aziz" in the Quran, which makes the connection to the novel's narrative evident. It is his wife who first acts on her forbidden desire for Yusuf and then accuses him of attempted rape when he resists her designs. This complexly rendered episode would merit further comment, but the point I wish to convey concerns a significant contrast between this mode of intertextuality and the novel's reworking of the Swahili texts. With the Biblical/Quranic intertext, Gurnah taps into the extensive and much older communities shaped by religion. Here, authority and mediation are (almost) entirely separate from the textual production and dissemination enabled by European colonialism. If we read the story as mainly Quranic, it locates itself in the deep time of the Islamic, Indian Ocean life-world of the protagonists. In this way, Gurnah mobilizes two distinct dimensions of textual circulation in his novel, providing in this way a temporal and cultural layering to the lost Indian Ocean world evoked by the story.

The Indian Ocean as a public sphere

My final example in this chapter looks at how the oceanic approach can group texts and organize literary study along significantly different lines than nation-based and monolingual modes of investigation. The operative term in Isabel Hofmeyr's book *Gandhi's Printing Press* is "print culture" rather than "text" or "literature." By looking at Mahatma Gandhi's early years of activism in South Africa – specifically the production and textual content of his journal *Indian Opinion* – Hofmeyr explores the dynamics of a "colonial born" transnational public sphere with the Indian Ocean as its main arena. Her use of the term "colonial born" indicates the historical peculiarity of Gandhi's position and that of his widely dispersed reading community. Coined originally to designate Indians born elsewhere in the British empire, Hofmeyr sees it as a more precise label – in this historical context – than the blanket term "diaspora," allowing for a polycentric conception of the empire circa 1900.

By ambiguously fudging the fact that India itself was a colony, the term "colonial born" enables a double vision in which "centre" and "periphery" are "one integrated space *both* to a metropole/colony axis *and* to India's subimperial relations with its indentured peripheries" (Hofmeyr 2013, 12). It thereby helps to make visible the complex entanglement of "colonial, semicolonial, para-colonial, and anticolonial formations" within which Gandhi developed his philosophy and political strategies.

The establishment of the International Printing Press (IPP) in Durban in 1898 lends support to this complex view of empire. Vociferously resisted by white workers at first, it nonetheless succeeded in establishing itself as an Indian-run enterprise that for a period – especially from 1906 until 1914 – became the key facilitator for Gandhi's experiments with print formats in *Indian Opinion* as well as a variety of pamphlets and booklets. In this respect, the IPP was hardly anomalous but of a piece with contemporary developments around the Indian Ocean: modest commercial printing ventures were emerging at the time in a number of similarly multi-diasporic, multilingual and multi-faith environments in Mombasa, Beira, Bombay, Cairo, Zanzibar, and so on. Their mission, frequently, was to produce material on behalf of "grand transoceanic schemes, whether Hindu reformist, Sikh transnationalist, African nationalist, pan-Islamic, or white laborist," thereby facilitating the dissemination of vast amounts of "periodicals, pamphlets, leaflets, and tracts" around Indian Ocean port cities and beyond (Hofmeyr 2013, 33).

In this macro-context, the journal *Indian Opinion* represented a utopian attempt at not only bridging the divide between discrete readerships, but also at cultivating an ethos of reading that resisted the accelerated, standardizing rhythms of imperial capitalism. As the first vehicle for Gandhi's notion of satyagraha, which was as much a spiritual as a political principle of non-violent self-possession and "self-rule," *Indian Opinion* became something of a laboratory for print-experimentation. The IPP itself boasted that it could produce material in ten languages (and seven scripts); *Indian Opinion* was slightly less adventurous, but would in its early phase nevertheless conjoin texts in Tamil, Hindi, Gujarati and English on its pages – the considerable technical obstacles to pursuing such multilingualism notwithstanding.

Authorship is not a focus in Hofmeyr's study, but rather form and readership – the form of the journal, and the types of publics rhetorically convened by the journal. Given such a disclaimer, however, the sceptical question might well be asked: does a print-culture focus on *Indian Opinion* and the transnational public sphere retain any link with literary matters, or is it a full turn towards sociohistorical enquiry? There are two ways to approach this question. One is – as Hofmeyr does – to further elaborate the analysis of the journal as an ephemeral, collage-like, small-scale form. In characteristic fashion at the time, much of *Indian Opinion* consisted of clippings that were gathered from across the world, but particularly from India and South Africa. The periodical became in this way a relay station for snippets and reports that had already been published elsewhere, but combined and juxtaposed in a fashion unique to *Indian Opinion*. Reinforced by the multilingual make-up of the journal, this practice of remediation created a textual time-space in which India and South Africa were brought into imaginative proximity and animated political aspirations among readerships on both sides of the ocean.

Considering that the primary political purpose of *Indian Opinion* was to champion the rights of Indians in South Africa, this in itself would also affect the periodical's form. When the crackdowns on Gandhi's satyagraha campaign in South Africa disrupted the production of the journal, this led him in 1913 to make a virtue of necessity:

> It is our intention to continue providing the same [reading] matter [as before], but in as short a form as possible. By so doing we will be able to fit in more material within the same space or even less. Beginning this time, we have reduced the number of Gujarati and English pages, but we wish to provide more information, though not more words within these pages.
> (Gandhi qtd. in Hofmeyr 2013, 69–70)

This is one instance where Hofmeyr identifies Gandhi's shaping of a "less-is-more" ethos of reading and writing running counter to the tendency towards acceleration and consumerist abundance. Instead, reduction in volume and size should be seen as concentration, and a call for concentrated reading, rather than a diminishment.

An alternative "literary" approach to *Indian Opinion* would be to look at how more conventional literary genres figure on its pages. Gandhi's own appreciation of Tolstoy, Ruskin and Emerson becomes evident on the "book pages" of the journal, which offered titles for sale via the IPP – alongside numerous titles with a syncretic religious or spiritual profile. The form of the poem also carries a premium, as in so many other periodicals in the Indian Ocean sphere, as a genre that could "free itself from the textual relay of the exchanges" by being unmediated by other publications, but at the same time highly detachable, always presented "as itself" and not as a quotation or paraphrase (Hofmeyr 2013, 78). A striking example would be the almost simultaneous publication in India and South Africa in 1910 of the poem "The Cry of Transvaal."

Indian Opinion, as with so many other journals (points of comparison could be, for example, the Mozambican journal *Itinerário*, which ran from 1942 to 1954, or *Voorslag* in Durban in 1926), becomes in this way a focal point for certain literary investments that encourage its subscribers to tailor their own readerly itineraries beyond the covers of the journal in a particular fashion. In the case of *Indian Opinion*, this would spill over into other publishing ventures by the IPP. Versions of the Bagavadghita, the Ramayana and the Mahabharata were published piecemeal in the journal, and then in more extended form in pamphlets. Other pamphlets contained adaptations of Plato and Ruskin as well as – surprisingly – an English-language summary of the Indian epics by the Boer commandant J. L. P. Erasmus. A further example is Tolstoy's *Letter to a Hindoo*, also (re)published by the IPP. The IPP's most ground-breaking publication in 1909 – namely, of Gandhi's anticolonial treatise *Hind Swaraj* ("Indian Home Rule") – was obviously political rather than literary, yet its philosophical approach to its topic testifies to the accommodation of, and traffic between, numerous genres established in the short-lived, intensive, transoceanic and transnational print culture established by *Indian Opinion* and the IPP.

By way of conclusion: oceans and ecologies of world literature

This potted history and deliberately capacious account of oceanic texts and modes of reading is not meant to issue in a neat conclusion. That would be to traduce the complexity of what is at stake in these diverse historical contexts and literary forms. Mobility – be it forced or desired, human or textual, actual or fictional – does, however, present itself as a common feature. Even if the heaviness of the waters, in DeLoughrey's sense, apparently sets itself against movement, this heaviness, too, results *from* histories of movement, confrontation, and entanglement.

The communicative network of the Black Atlantic, producing its counterculture of modernity, could in this regard be seen as just one instance of many comparable networks made possible (prior to mass aviation) by sea travel. Approaching these networks from a world literary angle will direct our attention to the transfer of texts, both in a material, physical sense, but perhaps even more importantly in terms of historically determinate forms of generic transformation. If the Christian Virgin transforms into the Congolese Kianda in Couto's rewriting of Dom Gonçalo da Silveira's correspondence, and if Ghosh's and Gurnah's fictions present us with the literary recoding of texts that had served entirely different purposes (as personal correspondence, as sacred scriptures, as ethnographic information), then *Indian Opinion* similarly hosts and distributes texts with previous histories and different generic functions.

These modes of transfer and circulation could then be tested against the "ecologies" perspective discussed in Chapter 2. As mentioned, Beecroft hypothesizes six quite distinct modes of circulation: epichoric, panchoric, cosmopolitan, vernacular, national, and global. The cases discussed in this chapter would, by contrast, mostly point towards circulation between, or an entanglement of, ecologies. If the Black Atlantic could cautiously be labelled a panchoric ecology – creating a strong sense of (counter)cultural community across discrete polities – it is also the case that when Noémia de Sousa in the 1940s hears Billie Holiday's recorded voice in Lourenço Marques, then this feeds directly into the anti-colonial creation of a national literary ecology in Mozambique. Or if we locate Camões's *Os Lusíadas* in the cosmopolitan ecology established by the Portuguese empire, then it is equally evident that it – or Canto V, to be precise – is absorbed into a national South African circuit. The case of Césaire and Shakespeare's *The Tempest* is slightly different: reaching Césaire by dint of British literature's cosmopolitan authority, his own play *Une Tempête* enters rather the Black Atlantic and pan-African literary ecologies. Equiano's *Narrative*, which does not accord with the high-canonical model of Camões or Shakespeare, has two distinct reception histories – one as a highly successful intervention in the British struggle to abolish the slave trade, and another beginning in the twentieth century, when his book is seen as an inaugural text not just of the slave narrative genre, but of modern African literature (Irele 2001, 46–9). Here, too, the range of literary ecologies is notable: from national British print culture in the eighteenth century to the slave narrative which in the nineteenth century evolved into a distinctly American (US) genre, to the continental category of "African literature," which is predicated less on national boundaries and more on the historical processes of colonization and decolonization. Gurnah's *Paradise*, finally, fictionally revives an East African and Indian Ocean Muslim cosmopolis, yet at the same time incorporates through translation historical Swahili texts (some of which started as oral texts). It draws in this way on both cosmopolitan and vernacular ecologies, even as the published novel itself is arguably part of the emergent global ecology of anglophone world literature.

The challenge, as always with world literary studies, is to find what balance between scales of reading – between distant and close modes – provides the best explanatory value. Oceanic reading, understood as a macro-context, does not in itself prescribe any particular mode. The question is rather what the oceanic view might offer that other approaches do not. Most importantly, by unsettling nation- and language-based categories of literary inquiry, and by concretizing a crucial and historically specific means of transcontinental mobility, it makes other types and combinations of material and themes in literary history visible.

Note

1 It should be noted that this is a domesticating translation that smoothens the syntax and disambiguates Alves's elusive imagery.

References

Ahmed, Siraj. 2018. *Archaeology of Babel: The Colonial Foundation of the Humanities*. Stanford, CA: Stanford University Press.
Barber, Karin. 2007. *The Anthropology of Texts, Persons and Publics: Oral and Written Culture in Africa and Beyond*. Cambridge: Cambridge University Press.
Bloch-Lainé, Virginie. 2017. "Marcus Rediker: 'I Took an Interest in Pirates and Sailors because They Were Poor.'" www.versobooks.com/blogs/3349-marcus-rediker-i-took-an-interest-in-pirates-and-sailors-because-they-were-poor.
Bose, Sugata. 2005. *A Hundred Horizons: The Indian Ocean in an Age of Global Imperialism*. Cambridge: Harvard University Press.
Brink, André. 1993. *Cape of Storms: The First Life of Adamastor*. New York: Simon and Schuster.
Bystrom, Kerry and Isabel Hofmeyr. 2017. "Oceanic Routes: (Post-It) Notes on Hydro-Colonialism." *Comparative Literature*, 69, no. 1: 1–6.
Carretta, Vincent. 2007. "Olaudah Equiano: African British Abolitionist and Founder of the African American Slave Narrative." In *The Cambridge Companion to the African American Slave Narrative*, edited by Audrey Fisch, 44–60. Cambridge: Cambridge University Press.
Castro Alves, Antonio de. 1960. *Obra completa*. Rio de Janeiro: José de Aguilar.
Castro Alves, Antonio de. 1990. *The Major Abolitionist Poems*, edited and translated by Amy A. Peterson. New York: Garland Publishing.
Chaudhuri, K. N. 1985. *Trade and Civilisation in the Indian Ocean: An Economic History from the Rise of Islam to 1750*. Cambridge: Cambridge University Press.
Chrisman, Laura. 2000. "Rethinking Black Atlanticism." *The Black Scholar* 30, no. 3–4: 12–17.
Cohen, Margaret. 2010. "Literary Studies and the Terraqueous Globe." *PMLA* 125, no. 3: 657–662.
Couto, Mia. 2006. *O outro pé da sereia*. Lisbon: Editorial Caminho.
Deckard, Sharae. 2010. *Paradise Discourse, Imperialism and Globalization*. London: Routledge.
DeLoughrey, Elizabeth. 2010. "Heavy Waters: Waste and Atlantic Modernity." *PMLA* 125, no. 3: 703–712.
Desai, Gaurav. 2013. *Commerce with the Universe: Africa, India, and the Afrasian Imagination*. New York: Columbia University Press.

De Sousa, Noémia. 2001. *Sangue Negro*. Maputo: Associação dos Escritores Moçambicanos.
Du Bois, W. E. B. 2000 [1903]. *The Souls of Black Folk*. Chicago, IL: Lushena Books.
Equiano, Olaudah. 1793 [1789]. *The Interesting Narrative of the Life of Olaudah Equiano, or Gustavus Vassa, the African*, 7th edition. London.
Ganguly, Debjani. 2016. *This Thing Called the World: The Contemporary Novel as Global Form*. Durham: Duke University Press.
Ghosh, Amitav. 1992. *In an Antique Land*. New Delhi: Ravi Dayal.
Gilroy, Paul. 1993. *The Black Atlantic: Modernity and Double Consciousness*. London: Verso.
Glissant, Édouard. 1997. *Poetics of Relation*, translated by Betsy Wing. Ann Arbor: University of Michigan Press.
Gupta, Pamila. 2014. "Some (Not So) Lost Aquatic Traditions: Goans Going Fishing in the Indian Ocean." *Interventions* 16, no. 6: 854–876.
Gurnah, Abdulrazak. 1994. *Paradise*. London: Hamish Hamilton.
Hodapp, James. 2015. "Imagining Unmediated Early Swahili Narratives in Abdulrazak Gurnah's Paradise." *English in Africa* 42, no. 2: 89–108.
Hofmeyr, Isabel. 2007. "The Black Atlantic Meets the Indian Ocean: Forging New Paradigms of Transnationalism for the Global South – Literary and Cultural Perspectives." *Social Dynamics* 33, no. 2: 3–32.
Hofmeyr, Isabel. 2010. "Universalizing the Indian Ocean." *PMLA* 125, no. 3: 722–729.
Hofmeyr, Isabel. 2013. *Gandhi's Printing Press: Experiments in Slow Reading*. Cambridge, MA: Harvard University Press.
Hulme, Peter and William H. Sherman, eds. 2000. *The Tempest and Its Travels*. London: Reaktion.
Irele, Abiola 2001. *The African Imagination: Literature in Africa and the Diaspora.*. Oxford: Oxford University Press.
Laachir, Karima, Sara Marzagora and Francesca Orsini. 2018. "Significant Geographies: In Lieu of World Literature." *Journal of World Literature* 3: 290–310.
Masilela, Ntongela. 1996. "The 'Black Atlantic' and African Modernity in South Africa." *Research in African Literatures* 27, no. 4: 88–96.
Mbembe, Achille. 2017. *Critique of Black Reason*. Translated by Larent Dubois. Durham: Duke University Press.
McGann, Jerome. 1991. *The Textual Condition*. Princeton, NJ: Princeton University Press.
McGann, Jerome. 2013. "Philology in a New Key." *Critical Inquiry* 39: 327–346.
Mufti, Aamir. 2016. *Forget English! Orientalisms and World Literatures*. Cambridge, MA: Harvard University Press.
Mustafa, Fawzia. 2015. "Swahili Histories and Texts in Abdulrazak Gurnah's Paradise." *English Studies in Africa* 58, no. 1: 14–29.
Patel, Shailja. 2010. *Migritude*. New York: Kaya Press.
Pearson, Michael. 2003. *The Indian Ocean*. London: Routledge.
Prendergast, Christopher, ed. 2004. *Debating World Literature*. London: Verso.

Samuelson, Meg. 2017. "Coastal Form: Amphibian Positions, Wider Worlds, and Planetary Horizons on the African Indian Littoral." *Comparative Literaure* 69, no. 1: 16–24.

Subrahmanyam, Sanjay. 1997a. *The Career and Legend of Vasco da Gama*. Cambridge: Cambridge University Press.

Subrahmanyam, Sanjay. 1997b. "Connected Histories: Notes Towards a Reconfiguration of Early Modern Eurasia." *Modern Asian Studies* 31, no. 3: 735–762.

Vierke, Clarissa. 2017. "Poetic Links Across the Ocean: On Poetic Translation as Mimetic Practice at the Swahili Coast." *Comparative Studies of South Asia, Africa and the Middle East* 37, no. 2: 321–335.

Vink, Marcus P. M. 2007. "Indian Ocean Studies and the 'New Thalassology'." *Journal of Global History* 2, no. 1: 41–62.

Walcott, Derek. 1986. *Collected Poems 1948–1984*. London: Faber & Faber.

Walcott, Derek. 1990. *Omeros*. London: Faber & Faber.

Whelan, Kevin. 2004. "The Green Atlantic: Radical Reciprocities between Ireland and America in the Long Eighteenth Century." In *A New Imperial History: Culture, Identity and Modernity in Britain and the Empire, 1660–1840*, edited by Kathleen Wilson, 216–238. Cambridge: Cambridge University Press.

5 Media and method
The digitized library of Babel

Mads Rosendahl Thomsen

Jorge Luis Borges's famed short story "The Library of Babel" from 1941 presents a library that contains an immense but finite number of books, each of about 400 pages and no two identical. Together these volumes would contain all possible combinations of letters. Even if a few volumes should be missing in the mind-blowingly large tower with hexagonal floors, there would always be almost similar duplicates. All possible stories would be there, all novels and poems that could ever be written, as well as every story about any possible existence. All accurate accounts of history, as well as all false accounts of history, in all kinds of languages, both historically existing, marginally recognizable and new languages that have never been imagined by humans. And most of it would be a mess of unintelligible collections of letters. As a footnote to the end of his story, Borges suggests that a single volume with infinitely thin pages would also do the trick and present the reader with a sense of completion and totality, although the pages would be impossible to handle (Borges 1999, 112).

Now, more than seven decades later, there is a website that can generate the volumes Borges envisioned and deliver them to your screen, holding the promise of showing something brilliant and new, even though the chances are that it will probably be unreadable. This virtual version of the books is somehow not as exciting as envisioning a walk on the floors of Borges's imagined library, reaching out for a volume, searching for meaning, putting the volume back and hoping that the next dusty book will reveal something of interest.

It was in the years just after Borges wrote his story, a quintessential and emblematic narrative in world literature, that computing took off. Soon short-lived metaphors such as "electronic brain" became part of language, although that one may be revitalized in some form in the years to come as General Artificial Intelligence is being developed, magnitudes more powerful than the early computers of the 1950s. Now it is almost impossible to imagine a world without computing and digital interfaces as one of the primary ways by which we produce, access, and study text. When interest in world literature was renewed in the late 1990s, texts were increasingly written on computers, but that was a quite recent phenomenon. Photocopies were the backbone of much education and the printed book was still unrivalled. While David Lodge, in his 1984 campus novel *Small World*, already poked fun at a computational approach to literary studies by mocking a linguist who analysed word frequencies in an author's work (Lodge 2012, 183), the idea of computational approaches did not matter much at the time. However, this changed throughout the 2000s, and today most humanities disciplines are figuring out how to come to terms with the plethora of ways that digitization can influence a subject. Ignoring that the media landscape, not least for text, has changed is hardly the way forward, but there is also much to be lost if the core interests and values of a discipline do not guide the new approaches.

Franco Moretti's highly influential article "Conjectures on World Literature" from 2000 has been used both by world literature scholars as a point of reference for setting new goals and conceptual frameworks for comparative literature studies, and more widely by humanities scholars. The notion of distant reading has become a shorthand in digital humanities for analysing larger corpora with computational approaches. What is often overlooked is that Moretti's article does not mention any digital approaches to literature but refers to ways of compiling the results of other researchers. Later on, the Stanford Literary Lab and the consortium NovelTM, led by Andrew Piper of McGill University, went on to develop, along with numerous other research environments, methods for analysing bigger corpora of literature, often drawing on research from linguistics. But the initial interest in formulating a foundation for distant reading was a challenge for being able to produce knowledge about the hypercomplex subject of world literature. It is not the digital approach for its own sake that is interesting, but its potential for creating new knowledge.

This chapter will address some of the key issues wherein world literature studies are influenced by the digital revolution. The first section discusses how access to literature has changed and how machine translation is providing a new perspective on linguistic barriers. This is followed by a section on the improved understanding of the circulation of literature, which better access to data and the creation of new types of data has brought about. Finally, we will discuss new methodologies for studying literary works with computational approaches across borders and how they may be suited for the study of world literature. Or how they may not be suited: the critique of computational approaches to literary studies is an essential element of developing the field.

World literature in your pocket

One of the chief instruments for connecting people in an unprecedented way, the Internet, is for most people something they learned about a little more than two decades ago, yet it already seems like a very mature and almost old-hat phenomenon. The digitization of communication has had a huge impact, not least in generating new senses of belonging that defy the boundaries set by national borders and their accompanying media ecologies. The simple fact that billions of people have begun to use similar instruments for communication is also creating new ways of identification across borders, just by way of the interface that a computer or a phone presents with few variations across the globe (Thomsen 2016).

New opportunities for studying world literature have opened up with the digital accessibility of texts and data on the larger realm of literature. It is also easier to publish than ever before, enabling anyone to make her or his work accessible globally (however, that is by no means the same as finding readers). Even more importantly, it has become easier to circumvent censorship and bring forbidden literature into countries where it is difficult to possess certain books and risky if done (Leberknight 2010). Censorship has become much more difficult to exercise as the Internet has opened up the world and made it possible to "smuggle" illegal books across borders in new and more discreet ways (yet, surveillance has also changed and the control of electronic information in, for example, China has increased). On the other hand, new media habits are challenging the practices of reading of literature, although the print medium has not gone out of fashion as had been predicted (Bershidsky 2017). The fear that new media will kill the book and reading is not new. Television, film, radio, and records were also seen as threats against the virtues of reading (Ong 1982; Hayles 2007). This threat should not be downplayed, but the picture is quite muddled, and if there is one thing that digital communication has brought about, it is a renewed reliance on written communication.

A banal but important consequence of the new means of communication is that literature has become much more widely available for readers everywhere. Enormous collections of texts can be accessed by almost the 3 billion people and counting who are on the Internet, many of the texts for free, for example at Project Gutenberg, which holds more than 50,000 texts. Getting hold of literary works from far away is easier than ever, and the threshold is not so much a question of economy and infrastructure as it is a question of motivation and the time and capacity to read. Online bookstores are also contributing to a new sense of accessibility of literature, and these new marketplaces bring attention to two competing narratives of world literature: with the prominence they give to best-selling books, they create a structure that narrows down what is visible and support the idea of world literature as the widest circulating works (as well as the newest). On the other hand, their vast searchable inventories and suggestions for similar books underscore the diversity of literature. The inclusion of user reviews has also generated a new forum for publishing opinions on works, which was formerly the exclusive domain of critics with access to mass media.

Many resources are invested in making the literary cultural heritage accessible in digital form. There are numerous projects, with Google Books the most significant, that digitize literature and make it machine readable and accessible. The Norwegian state has sponsored a complete digitization of all Norwegian books and made them freely available (if you are physically in Norway or have a licence). Around the world, the works of seminal authors are put online in carefully edited versions with commentary, but books are also being put out in more or less accurate versions, within or outside the laws of copyright. Libraries are lending digital editions of works, and there has been a surprisingly strong comeback of the audiobook as people commute more and have devices at hand that can hold what seems like a lifetime of recorded books (Rowe 2018). As such there has never been a time when literature has been available in so many media and so much literature can be read freely. The history of literature has in part been determined by the cost of book production, which was lowered significantly first with the printing press in the sixteenth century, then with industrialized print in the early nineteenth century. Now, the cost of obtaining new text is practically zero for almost half of the world's population, and it is not hard to imagine that this shift will look even more significant in retrospect.

However, the copyrights of authors are also being challenged by digitization projects as well as illegal copying. The potential for a new book utopia where everything is accessible for everybody in an instant of time is getting closer, but as with all utopias there are unwanted consequences. If readers more and more expect texts to be freely accessible, how will writers make a living? Currently new models of subscription that are also known from the music industry appear as one way to pay producers, but it is doubtful that they will be able to produce even a fraction of the income that book sales deliver. While electronic book sales have stagnated, the market for print books has remained steady. And even if things should change, it is worth noting that book sales have for many authors already been a minor or even tiny part of their incomes (Cole 2018).

Read everything?

Beyond access to books, digitization also opens up new perspectives on translation. Machine translation has created new ways of accessing text, at least on the level of being able to grasp what a work is about, though at present certainly not as a work of literature. In many ways, it can be seen as uplifting that the task of the translator of literature seems to be quite some way from being taken over by computers in an age when predictions of jobs that will be taken over by machines are in no short supply. Bringing style and meaning together in a consistent way across languages is a highly difficult task which is not easily formalized in a way that machines can emulate. There is some comic relief attached to this inadequacy, yet also a sense that the machines may not be that far off from being able to provide a fairly good translation. Here are the opening lines of *Ulysses* by James Joyce:

> Stately, plump Buck Mulligan came from the stairhead, bearing a bowl of lather on which a mirror and a razor lay crossed. A yellow dressinggown, ungirdled, was sustained gently behind him on the mild morning air. He held the bowl aloft and intoned:
> – Introibo ad altare Dei.
> Halted, he peered down the dark winding stairs and called out coarsely:
> – Come up, Kinch! Come up, you fearful jesuit!
>
> (Joyce 1992, 1)

Using Google Translate (on 12 March 2018), first translating the English original into German and then back into English (a two-fold task which is not completely fair to the machine), the new version reads:

> Tall, stout Buck Mulligan came out of the staircase and carried a bowl of foam with a mirror and a razor. A curly morning dress, unstretched, was gently held behind him in the mild morning air. He held up the bowl and intoned:
> – Introibo ad altare Dei.
> Holding it, he peered down the dark spiral staircase and shouted roughly:
> – Come on, Kinch! Come up, you frightened Jesuit!

This is no longer Joyce, and the cliché of literature being what is lost in translation certainly holds in this case. And it is even more pronounced when translating into Turkish and then back to English (on 21 November 2018):

> The majestic, fuller Buck Mulligan came from a staircase carrying a dish and a mirror and a shaker standing on a shaver. A spooky, yellow gown, gently behind in the soft morning air. The cabin was held in the air and covered with:
> – Introibo ad altare Dei.
> Halted looked down the dark winding stairs and called to the rude:
> – Come, Kinch! Come on up, fearless lifeguard!

Meanings are distorted, sentences do not make sense, the elegance of the prose is not what it used to be, and its value for scholarly work focused on the connection of style and meaning is close to zero. But maybe "fearless lifeguard" will live on. Still, had this been a little-known Danish or Vietnamese novel, it would certainly have been useful for some purposes to have a version similar to the English-German-English translation – not as a version that one would read, publish or use for critical purposes, but as a document that could give information about themes, narratives and even stylistic elements of a literary work. As machine translation becomes more and more used in many non-literary genres, it is worth observing how it will influence literature, both in terms of enabling interested readers to get a sense of works that would otherwise be inaccessible to them, and as a tool that may be developed well enough to be adopted by translators alongside their dictionary. Here is another example, the famous opening lines of Franz Kafka's *Der Prozess*:

> Jemand mußte Josef K. verleumdet haben, denn ohne daß er etwas Böses getan hätte, wurde er eines Morgens verhaftet. Die Köchin der Frau Grubach, seiner Zimmervermieterin, die ihm jeden Tag gegen acht Uhr früh das Frühstück brachte, kam diesmal nicht. Das war noch niemals geschehen. K. wartete noch ein Weilchen, sah von seinem Kopfkissen aus die alte Frau, die ihm gegenüber wohnte und die ihn mit einer an ihr ganz ungewöhnlichen Neugierde beobachtete, dann aber, gleichzeitig befremdet und hungrig, läutete er. Sofort klopfte es und ein Mann, den er in dieser Wohnung noch niemals gesehen hatte, trat ein.
>
> (Kafka 1998a, 7)

Google Translate (on 8 November 2018) turns this passage into a readable but error-prone text ("the wife of Mrs. Grubach" for example):

> Someone must have slandered Josef K., because without his doing anything, he was arrested one morning. The wife of Mrs. Grubach, his landlady, who brought him breakfast at eight o'clock in the morning, did not come this time. That never happened before. K. waited a while longer, saw from his pillow the old woman who lived opposite him and who watched him with a strange curiosity, but then, alienated and hungry, he rang the bell. Immediately there was a knock and a man he had never seen in this apartment entered.

The syntax is not far off from what Breon Mitchell's translation, widely regarded as the best version in English, produced:

> Someone must have slandered Josef K., for one morning, without having done anything wrong, he was arrested. His landlady, Frau Grubach, had a cook who brought him breakfast each day around eight, but this time she didn't appear. That had never happened before. K. waited a while longer, watching from his pillow the old woman who lived across the way, who was peering at him with a curiosity quite unusual for her; then, both put out and hungry, he rang. There was an immediate knock at the door and a man he'd never seen before in these lodgings entered.
>
> (Kafka 1998b, 3)

Another translation by a human, David Wyllie, is in some ways further away from both Mitchell and Google Translate:

> Someone must have been telling lies about Josef K., he knew he had done nothing wrong but, one morning, he was arrested. Every day at eight in the morning he was brought his breakfast by Mrs. Grubach's cook – Mrs. Grubach was his landlady – but today she didn't come. That had never happened before. K. waited a little while, looked from his pillow at the old woman who lived opposite and who was watching him with an inquisitiveness quite unusual for her, and finally, both hungry and disconcerted, rang the bell. There was immediately a knock at the door and a man entered. He had never seen the man in this house before.
>
> (Kafka 2012, 2)

Some of the decisions by Wyllie are questionable, for example "Mrs. Grubach was his landlady" which repeats the name in a way that seems unnecessary. Whereas the human translation has domesticated Kafka through its grammar, up to a point, the automated translation has kept closer to Kafka's original.

Another service for machine translation, DeepL, takes the liberty of turning Josef into Joseph, but otherwise produces a readable version of Kafka (translated on 5 November 2018):

> Someone must have slandered Joseph K., because one morning he was arrested without doing anything wrong. The cook of Mrs Grubach, his landlord, who brought him breakfast every day around eight o'clock in the morning, did not come this time. That had never happened before. K. waited a little while, saw from his pillow the old woman who lived opposite him and who watched him with an unusual curiosity, but then, at the same time alienated and hungry, he rang. Immediately there was a knock and a man, whom he had never seen before in this apartment, entered.

A study by Pierre Isabelle and Roland Kuhn showed that DeepL generally performs better than Google Translate, but also that both services had made significant improvements in the span of the three months between their tests in 2017 and 2018 (Isabelle 2018, 8). While not fit to print, these examples are getting closer to passing a Turing test for translation. Machine translation is thus important in relation to world literature in both its usefulness and its limitations. It is now possible to get a sense of what a work is about, what the words mean (roughly) in languages for which there may not even be qualified translators in one's own native language. Getting a sense of the objects, the actions, the dialogue, the setting, and so on, is within reach for everyone with an interest, but it will ultimately also be frustrating as the quality of the translations is not what one would expect of a human translation of literature. This may change sooner than expected (or feared, depending on one's expectations), given the progress in the development of machine translation. The cooperation between humans and machines on translation, which already takes place in many sectors, could also become a part of the literary world, provided that it will be able to improve translation. At the moment, this would be widely frowned upon and the shift towards a new form of agency in translation would certainly be a seismic shift in the way that literature is produced. At a minimum, the sense that the majority of the world's literature is unreachable because of linguistic as well as economic barriers is being transformed, which at the end of the day seems like a step forward, and as David Bellos predicted in 2011, machine translation will advance far beyond what we know now (Bellos 2011, 256).

Circulation

It is up for debate how much international circulation should matter in world literature studies, but it is hard to ignore completely whether a work has been picked up by readers in other cultures or if it did not get a following. Similarly, the flows of translations and the patterns that can be found in the genres of works that are made available by publishers are also pivotal to understanding what works have a chance of becoming world literature in the sense of being widely read outside their cultures of origin. Literary sociology is by no means a new discipline, but the amount of data that are available has grown in recent years and become easier to access, making it possible to stitch together a more accurate picture of where literature circulates and what readers think about it. The study of canonization has been given new tools that can replace vaguer notions of influence and unsatisfactory back-of-the-envelope calculations of translations and sales. It is also possible to paint a more interesting picture of the diversity in literary interest, not least thanks to the way social media have become part of the literary public.

The sources are manifold and all add up to a larger picture. Library records and many other sources cannot be trusted completely, but they are good enough to indicate overall tendencies. Translations published since 1980 have been recorded by UNESCO's Index Translationum, which enables many detailed searches of genres, source and target languages, and much more. The database also provides a sense of the overwhelming diversity of the languages and literatures of the world, not to speak of the, at first glance, strange routes certain works have taken across the world. It is also transparent all the way down to the single volumes that are included in the statistics. Supplementing UNESCO's records, the www.worldcat.org website makes it possible to find records of library holdings across the world and apply filters such as language, genres, publication date and format, which can be used to compile the numbers of editions by an author as well as the holdings of works. Again, this is not a complete record of all library holdings, but it has a significant reach and it is useful as a tool to compile translated editions of works.

In principle, translations and library holdings could have been calculated before digitization, but in practice it makes a significant difference that UNESCO's database gives access to the data. With social media, a number of services have emerged to make sense of what readers are interested in, which obviously did not exist two decades ago. The website Goodreads has built a community with millions of readers who can grade works and write reviews of them. This both creates a wealth of data about which works get attention from present-day readers and opinions from non-professional critics who express their views on works across all genres, including lengthy one-star reviews of *Hamlet* and five-star reviews of dubious self-help and business books. But more importantly, it gives an idea of which books are actively being read, at least by the kind of readers who will also voice their opinions on books. As with all collections of data in the field, it is not complete and there will be obvious biases, not least towards literature in English. Yet, among comparable authors and within the works of one author, there is much to be learned from the attention given to particular works and the relative oblivion of others. It may not be surprising but telling that Albert Camus's *The Stranger* has ten times as many ratings as *The Fall*, although they are rated almost equally high; no surprise either that Salman Rushdie's most-rated books are *Midnight's Children* and *The Satanic Verses*. Similar indications of what readers actually care about can be found through Amazon's Sales Ranks, which give a good indication of which books are selling steadily and those that rarely get picked up. The results for Camus and Rushdie are quite similar to those from Goodreads, displaying a clear difference in the impact of these authors' various works. These figures are not the final truth about the works but they are a vast improvement over prior vague guesses about how literature circulates.

The study of attention in criticism has also been changed. Research databases such as the MLA (Modern Language Association) bibliography are not new but very useful in combination with other sources. Google Books Ngram Viewer covers references in books better than any other available source, although the corpus is not complete and only "surveys" about 4 per cent of all books ever published. Nevertheless, it gives a good indication of trend lines that can show, for example, when interest in Emily Dickinson's authorship emerged (around 1920), or when a critical term such as "postcolonial" was being used regularly (since the 1960s, but with a significant rise in the late 1980s).

A number of other approaches have been taken to show how the world and the books are connected. A study of authors described in 15 different language versions of Wikipedia – which has grown from being an easy target for the fallacies of user-generated content to a less than perfect but fairly trustworthy source with an enormous range – uses a number of different measurements for calculating impact in culture. Some simple measures track which authors users are searching for or how long the articles are, and more complicated rankings are based on the number of links to the author's page and their weighted importance, which is measured both for links to all articles and to those of other authors, giving an impression of who is the author's author. In a world literature perspective, it is interesting to observe how native and international writers mix in the different versions of the encyclopedia (Hube 2016): how decadent writers feature prominently in the Italian edition, how French writers are prominent in the Romanian one, or how J. R. R. Tolkien has a significant presence in the Korean, Portuguese, Chinese and a number of other Wikipedia versions (http://data.weltliteratur.net/ranking.html).

Google's tool for analysing tendencies in search queries, Google Trends, allows for a nuanced perspective on the reach of authors. One typical discovery is that authors who seem to be universally interesting may not really have crossed language barriers. On the other hand, the search interest in some places leads one to wonder why there is a surprisingly large interest in a particular author. The relative search interest in Haruki Murakami, for example, is very high in Serbia and Lithuania, far higher than in Sweden and Germany. Hans Christian Andersen is being searched a lot in Moldova, relatively more than in Norway.

Another benefit of getting more information on literary circulation is the ability to discover a second tier of recognized works, which can counter the tendency for very few works to represent nations' contributions to world literature. Rather than "winner takes it all," it is possible to show that there is a long tail of works and authors that may not have had a big breakthrough internationally, but which still have been picked up, translated and published. This puts the idea of lonely canonicals into perspective without ignoring that some literatures are mostly represented to a wider international audience, lay as well as academic, by a few writers.

One of the key problems of all these data is to put them together. They provide indications, sometimes robust signals of a particular and sustained influence, but there is no gold standard for combining the findings. There is no way of getting it exactly right as the data are not perfect themselves, but there is certainly more to do in terms of making the different sources comparable, not least in order to show how general popularity and critical acclaim are distributed.

The study of literary circulation is in some respects a low-hanging fruit for a digital approach to world literature. It is difficult to deny the relevance of circulation to literary culture; the bar for accessing data has been lowered significantly, and the methodologies for processing the data are much less challenging than working with the content of texts, which requires a leap into unstructured data. This is, however, also an important aspect of the new opportunities for world literature studies.

Reading the great unread

While world literature is linked to canons and debates over what counts as the best and more refined works of literature, it also involves the task of understanding the enormous field of literary production across cultures. Machine-readable texts and computational analysis have changed the potential for studying what could be called "the great unread," works of literature that are not and probably will not be part of literary canons, but which are part of a literary culture that can be studied. Computational approaches can help to include works that would otherwise not be objects of research, but which can help to develop a better picture of the context of the active canon and to show developments in literature over time.

The field of computational literary studies is still relatively young and the development of methods does not always yield interesting results, as is the case with any other expansion of approaches in literary studies. But there is a growing number of cases that both provide methods that can be replicated on other materials and give striking examples of insights that could not have been produced without machine-readable texts.

One such example is found at the end of Ted Underwood's *Why Literary Periods Mattered* (2013), where he shows the development of the vocabulary in an English corpus of prose fiction, non-fiction and poetry from 1600 to 1900. Underwood's approach is not complicated: using a database of the date of the origin of words and calculating the frequency of words that entered the English language before 1150, he is able to demonstrate how the language of poetry as well as prose fiction became more archaic, while the overall tendency of non-fiction was to use fewer old words (Figure 5.1). Of course, this makes sense given the themes of Romantic literature but there is a long way from that intuition to actually showing, as Underwood has done, how this affected the vocabulary of literature itself.

One of the problems with computational approaches is that some of the questions that one would like to answer, such as "How are protagonists characterized in early twentieth-century fiction across the world?," are difficult to formalize in such a way that they can be used in automated analyses of texts. And some questions that are easy to formalize, such as "What is the average length of sentences in fiction in the nineteenth century?," may not contribute much to research. But there is a middle ground, where relatively simple investigations can provide an important part of the larger puzzle, as Underwood's example demonstrates, or where more advanced models are able to cluster works in ways that are not

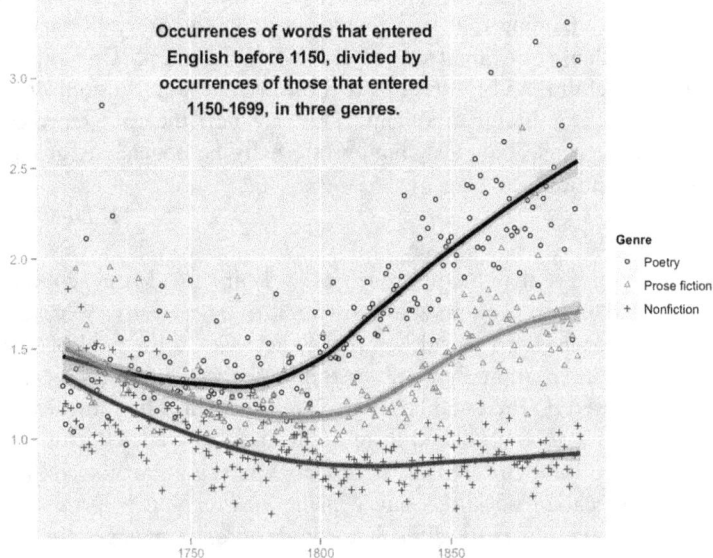

Figure 5.1 Ted Underwood, *Why Literary Periods Mattered*

trivial and where the models' underlying parameters help to understand strong currents in literary history, as Jodie Archer and Matthew Jockers's (2016) work on best-sellers shows. A study on American fiction by Matthew Wilkens, "Genre, Computation, and the Varieties of Twentieth-Century U.S. Fiction," also works with multiple parameters that take theme, style and geography into account. What is interesting about such attempts to find meaningful clusters is not just how a computational model can reproduce the conventional wisdom of which works should be lumped together, but also how lesser-known writers fit in and how some canonical works may not appear as close to the context in which they would usually be placed. Wilkens comments on his large canvas of American texts:

> [O]ne might emphasize the specifically *generic* coherence of the texts in cluster 8, a coherence that argues against the anti-generic interpretation of literary fiction. On this reading, the remarkable, utterly surprising generic affinity of a large group of highly respected and seriously studied (mostly) dead (mostly) white men suggests the need for a reconsideration of variety and diversity as purported hallmarks of contemporary literary fiction. Critics and scholars, this view

argues, would no more limit their professional purview to detective fiction by claiming that it is the core of contemporary literary production than they ought to go on treating Steinbeck, Updike, Vonnegut, DeLillo, and O'Brien as if those writers were, indeed, figures typical of our literary moment. They are not; they are representatives of a single, atypical, highly internally homogeneous group of writers and texts.

(Wilkens 2016)

Wilkens's point is that his approach allows him to identify coherence within a field and to show how it is surrounded by diversity. What could such an approach do to world literary studies? Could the field of works that circulate internationally be ordered differently? Could new works be discovered based on their similarity to classics of world literature? Could theses of influence be grounded in more precise analysis? A lot of this is easier to hope for than actually be done. Whereas literary sociology is relatively detached from direct engagement with texts, it is more technically demanding and more difficult to work across languages. Is it, for example, possible to compare levels of complexity in different languages? Maybe within European languages, but the methodology and research on comparison between East Asian languages and European languages, for example, have not been sufficiently developed.

World literature studies is limited by some of the demands computational approaches create, in particular with respect to the limited resources that minor languages have, not just in terms of having digitized works at hand but also the proper tools that can work with languages, for example part of speech taggers and sentiment analysis packages. But given that some of these obstacles have been overcome, new comparison projects across languages have become possible. A research project led by Jianbo Gao and Kristoffer L. Nielbo is one among several groups that are working on the internal coherence of texts based on sentiment analysis (Nielbo 2018). Jianbo and Nielbo's work is focused on describing levels of predictability in narrative fiction, and having analysed a corpus of more than 20,000 books, the approach appears interesting for a number of reasons. It can work with literature from several languages because the sentiment score – the foundation of this research – has been generated by linguists across a number of languages. It is also a method that is simple enough in its core objective to generate comparable results across a large corpus. And the ability to apply it to thousands of books enables analyses that are impossible without a computational approach.

One of the theses of the researchers is that there is an optimal range of complexity in texts. The preliminary results are promising, showing for example how Hans Christian Andersen's very popular fairy tales are lumped in a range higher of unpredictability than most texts, however much more coherent than highly avant-gardist experiments. The development of the *Harry Potter* series shows a move away from the zone that in the tentative results seems to produce works that are both critically acclaimed and popular towards a more and more predictable plot. Taken out of context such an approach is very reductive, essentially assigning one number to each work. But as a means to understand the characteristics of literary works that one might have a general idea about but cannot systematize, let alone document across thousands of works, such approaches do create a new kind of knowledge about literature. Without a context the raw numbers do not constitute new knowledge, but they can be the condition for discovering new facets of literature. Jianbo and Nielbo's research turns simplicity and reductiveness into a strength when the method is put to scale and applied across languages. A measure for narrative complexity is obviously not the end of discussion about a work, but rather an insight that can be difficult to ignore when it is put in perspective by thousands of other texts. Simplicity is also important for being able to use it across languages, where it draws on the sentiment dictionaries that have been compiled based on the same methodology.

Another approach to large-scale corpora that works across linguistic barriers can be found in Matthew Wilkens's project "Textual Geographies" (http://txtgeo.net), which makes it possible to see which locations literary works as well as non-fiction publications mention. The corpus consists of more than 10 million volumes from which each named entity has been extracted and assigned a geolocation. In a world literature context this tool is particularly interesting in that it sheds light on the geographical horizons of a particular period, region, genre, and so on. It is possible to formulate queries that are focused on single authors as well as carry out a massive search of the literature of whole nations. "Textual Geographies" is not a perfect tool for world literary studies because it only comprises four, albeit major, languages – English, Spanish, German and Chinese – but it does create many opportunities for understanding the relation between literature and geography in ways that would not have been possible if one relied on traditional methods. It is possible to see trend lines in how a nation is being mentioned in these four other languages, or one can zoom in on the geography of cities and get insights into what parts of a city are actually referred to in a given period. The possibilities are manifold, but they will only garner results if there are meaningful research questions that guide them.

Computational approaches have recently produced studies that are both counterintuitive and politically important. Ted Underwood, David

Bamman and Sabrina Lee's study "The Transformation of Gender in English-Language Fiction" is based on a, for all practical purposes, humanly unreadable corpus of more than 100,000 books. The authors show that contrary to what would be a reasonable hypothesis, namely that women would be better represented in novels, given more dialogue, as time progressed and women's liberation became more and more certain, the opposite has actually happened.

> Some forms of gender differentiation (associated for instance with domestic space and subjectivity) are declining while other forms (associated for instance with the body and clothes) are on the rise. If you add them all together, we may be able to say generally that gender is less insistently marked by the end of the twentieth century than it was in the 1840s. But that slow increase in blurriness could be less important than the churn we have seen along the way: the rise and fall of different forms of gender differentiation. Although the opposition of *he* and *she* remains grammatically the same, gender is actually a different thing by 2007 than it had been in 1840.
> (Underwood, Bamman and Lee 2018)

The project has "only" been carried out on English-language works, but the distinction between male and female would be possible to process in other languages and will certainly be meaningful in a comparative approach to gender in literary history (even though gender has increasingly been recognized as a much more complicated distinction than the binary male/female). The results generated by Underwood, Bamman and Lee are obviously important, and their article made the news in a number of mainstream media across the world. Methodologically it also shows how a computational approach can be the only way to garner results like this.

In "Toward a Computational Archaeology of Fictional Space," Dennis Yi Tenen has also approached a corpus of works with the intent to look at a very specific element, namely the representation of spaces and objects in works. This is again an example of a project that would not make sense if it was performed on just a few works, but scaled up to hundreds of works, it conveys insights that would otherwise not be attainable. Tenen's study is based on one language, including literature in English translation, but its underlying reliance on grammatical concepts could make it possible to transfer the methodological approach to other Indo-European languages.

In the computational approach to literary studies, the task of building models for analysis pushes the researcher to rethink the categories of text. Tenen notes that:

> The methodological difficulty of modeling fictional space presents several interesting theoretical problems. We intuit that any account of high-level systemic changes in the quality of narrative space must rest on a quantity of low-level linguistic observations. Unlike real spaces, however, fictional spaces defy conventional notions of size or magnitude. For this reason, defining space in terms of explicit magnitudes, settings, or frames – as is often done in narratological theory – is insufficient for our purposes.
>
> (Tenen 2018, 125)

The research presented here by Wilkens, Jianbo and Nielbo, Tenen, and Underwood, Bamman and Lee have in common that they approach literature with categories that are both relevant to the experience of a literary work and which are not heavily dependent on culture. Representations of gender, objects, and places as well as narrative coherence can be compared more robustly than more culturally encoded phenomena and stylistic traits and they could therefore be particularly valuable in the study of literature globally.

Critical perspectives

It is a common, sometimes wilful, misconception about computational approaches to literature that they implicitly or explicitly argue that all literary studies should rely on distant rather than close reading. In practice, scholars mix close and distant reading in order to find better answers to research questions: for example, how canonical works differ from the large archive of less prominent texts, as Matthew Jockers has also pointed out in *Macroanalysis* (Jockers 2013, 19). Is it their narrative, their complexity, their mix of themes, their vocabulary? We may have intuitions about this question, but they will remain largely unfounded until investigations engage with larger corpora. Ted Underwood has commented on the critique of distant reading as being inconsequential:

> But first I want to point out that distant readers are presented with two alternative critiques that cannot be advanced at the same time. On the one hand, we commonly confront the objection that our results are too transparent: they are things a reader might have guessed intuitively from diffuse recollection. If that turns out not to

be true, we immediately confront the opposite objection: any pattern that isn't transparently legible in a reader's memory is rejected, as too subtle to matter.

(Underwood 2018, 12–3)

It is also a strawman that computational approaches should be one-size-fits-all or that distant reading should become the only kind of reading. Like all other methods and approaches, they should be used when appropriate. And a different argument could also be made: is it not irresponsible *not* to consult other kinds of knowledge about a text, rather than relying only on one's own reading and imperfect recollection? Ignoring dimensions such as word frequencies or narrative complexity is just as problematic as an exclusive reliance on distant reading. Reading more is always good, as Franco Moretti wrote in "Conjectures on World Literature," but not really an option when it comes to world literature. A proposal for a graduate scholarship would mostly likely be turned down if it suggested analysing 50 novels through close reading, but analysing thousands of novels as part of a computational project may be feasible in ways that have not been seen before.

While there are obvious benefits to the new possibilities opened up by digital tools, there are also drawbacks, some of them due to the larger context. Easier access to translation and instant machine translations could be blamed for eroding the incentive to learn other languages. On the other hand, translation tools can assist readers who may want to work on languages that they have not mastered but can work on with some assistance. Easy access to books could erode the publishing industry and the earnings of writers, but the Internet also gives everybody a chance to publish. The lure of distant reading or an interest in "the great unread" could threaten the practices of close reading. Yet, this is not a question of either-or but how to create the best mix of methods. One should also notice that close reading as a genre has been going in and out of style throughout the history of literary criticism. The heydays of theory in the 1980s were not primarily occupied with uncovering the finer details of literary texts.

Although there is really no drawback to being better informed about literary circulation, there should be a continued debate about what literary criticism and history should do and how they should accomplish it. The orientation towards facts, figures and big data that is becoming more and more important across disciplines and in public communication should not become the dominant mode in literary criticism. In earlier periods of the discipline there was enthusiasm about turning criticism into a science, which in most cases ended up producing little of lasting value. Walter Benjamin warned against this in the 1920s:

> Rarely has a word that has been so much abused displayed so much nobility as the word "poetry." And with all that, this science throws its weight around while simultaneously betraying itself through the "breadth" of its object and through its "synthesizing" comportment. The profligate drive toward totalities is its misfortune.
>
> (Benjamin 1999, 461)

There is an inherent risk in computational criticism of turning the complexities (and joys) of literary works into easily comparable numbers. The most obvious but wrong response would be to shy away from computational work and the desire to grasp the great unread. First of all, the discipline is already making claims about genres and periods in ways that need to be investigated, perhaps to be expressed with more accuracy or to be proven more nuanced or different from conventional wisdom. Secondly, there is no reason why different modes of investigation, close and distant reading, should not be part of methods for research. Computational criticism not only leads to new knowledge and conclusive evidence, but also generates new theses and turns up information that is challenging and needs to be processed. This heuristic side is not so different in form from interpreting a metaphor, which can be both frustrating and rewarding. Ted Underwood also points to the critical potential of reading more broadly through computational methods:

> Even scholars who are interested strictly in canonical writers will sometimes need to measure questions of degree across a long timeline. Otherwise we can end up giving Joyce and Proust credit for changes that actually sprawled across several centuries.
>
> (Underwood 2018, 363)

And even a single work may be too complex to observe certain details. An example of a discovery that would probably not have been made without digital tools is the use of the word "like" in Joyce's *Ulysses*. Using Voyant Tools to disclose word frequencies and their distribution throughout the novel, "like" comes up as one of the most used words, more than 700 times out of the almost 270,000 words of the novel. A graph of the distribution also reveals that the use of the word drops to almost zero towards the end of the novel, before skyrocketing at the very end. A closer examination of the text itself shows that "like" is used extremely sparsely in the lengthy "Ithaca" chapter, where the concise style of question and answer promotes facts rather than simile, feelings, and the like (so to speak). In contrast, Molly's soliloquy in the final "Penelope" chapter has "like" scattered all over it, including in the first and the last ten words. It is by far the most used term with 209 instances, compared to merely 91 examples of "yes" in second place, taking up about 1 per cent of the word count in this chapter. What does it mean – except that it is hard to ignore once one knows this? It highlights a stylistic element, and it raises the question of whether Joyce used other strategies, besides the obvious differences in narration and the use of central words, to mark significant contrasts between different chapters. And it underscores a particular epistemological stance, reminiscent of Hamlet, that will not tolerate approximation: "'Seems,' madam? Nay, it is. I know not 'seems'." Whereas Hamlet's struggles with uncertainty are fraught, the discovery of unusual patterns should be seen as a welcome element in literary criticism that calls for attention, interpretation and explanation. It is also a humbling element, pointing to all the things that we cannot grasp as close readers.

Another example of this lack of insight concerns culture at large and literature: the idea of an epiphany is often related to Joyce, but it could be useful to put the use of the term in perspective. A search on the nouns that appear most frequently along with "epiphany" in books in English since 1920 turns up a number of unsurprising terms such as "revelation." But the most interesting observation (see Figure 5.2) is that "God" and "Joyce" seem to battle among the only proper names that are highly related with the term. Joyce even had the lead at some point, but then lost out.

The digital age is still maturing, but it has provided new opportunities in world literature studies that demand both care and creativity in order

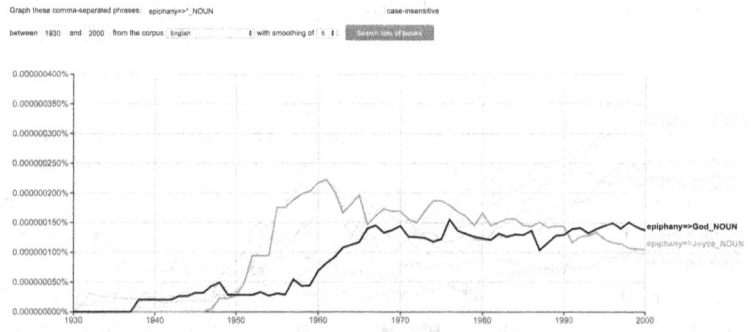

Figure 5.2 Nouns that most typically occur with the concept "epiphany" on Google Books Ngram Viewer

to generate valuable knowledge. Eventually, the success of a digital approach would be that it is not thought of as a particular mode, but just as one of the many tools that are needed to make sense of the world's text. In the computational approaches to literary studies, there is also an inherent critique of the way literary studies goes about some of the core conceptions and the foundation they rest upon. There are many commonly held ideas that have been established unsystematically on the collective efforts of critics and students but often resting on quite different conceptions, approaches and goals. What do notions of genres, currents, periods and so on actually rest upon? Can literary studies sit easily knowing that many of its assumptions are based on parts representing the whole?

References

Archer, Jodie and Matthew Jockers. 2016. *The Bestseller Code: Anatomy of the Blockbuster Novel*. New York: St Martin's Press.
Bellos, David. 2011. *Is That a Fish in Your Ear? Translation and the Meaning of Everything*. New York: Farrar, Strauss and Giroux.
Benjamin, Walter. 1999. *Selected Writings* vol. 2. Cambridge: Harvard University Press.
Bershidsky, Leonid. 2017. "How print beat digital in the book world." *Sydney Morning Herald*, 27 January.
Borges, Jorge Luis. 1999. *Collected Fictions*. New York: Penguin.
Cole, Nicolas. 2018. "7 Skills You Need to Practice to Become a Successful Writer in the Digital Age." *Inc*. Available at: www.inc.com/nicolas-cole/the-7-skills-you-need-to-practice-to-become-a-successful-writer-in-digital-age.html. Accessed 15 November 2018.
Hayles, N. K. 2007. *Electronic Literature: New Horizons for the Literary*. Notre Dame: University of Notre Dame.
Hube, Christoph et al. 2016. "World Literature According to Wikipedia: Introduction to a DBpedia-Based Framework." Available at: https://arxiv.org/abs/1701.00991. Accessed 15 November 2018.
Isabelle, Pierre and Roland Kuhn. 2018. "A Challenge Set for French → English Machine Translation." Available at: https://arxiv.org/abs/1806.02725v2. Accessed 15 November 2018.
Jockers, Matthew. 2013. *Macroanalysis: Digital Methods and Literary History*. Champaign: University of Illinois Press.
Joyce, James. 1992. *Ulysses*. London: Penguin.
Kafka, Franz. 1998a. *Der Prozess*. Stuttgart: Reclam.
Kafka, Franz. 1998b. *The Trial*. Tr. Breon Mitchell. New York: Schocken.
Kafka, Franz. 2012. *The Trial*. Tr. David Wyllie. Mineola: Dover Thrift.

Leberknight, Christopher et al. 2010. *A Taxonomy of Internet Censorship and Anti-Censorship*. Available at: www.princeton.edu/~chiangm/anticensorship. pdf. Accessed 15 November 2018.

Lodge, David. 2012. *Small World*. London: Vintage.

Moretti, Franco. 2000. "Conjectures on World Literature." *New Left Review* no. 1: 54–68.

Nielbo, Kristoffer et al. 2018. "Dynamic evolution of sentiments in Never Let Me Go: 2 Insights from multifractal theory and its implications for literary analysis" (manuscript under review).

Ong, Walter J. 1982. *Orality and Literacy: The Technologizing of the Word*. London: Methuen.

Rowe, Adam. 2018. "The Rising Popularity of Audiobooks Highlights The Industry's Backwards Pay Scale." *Forbes*, 27 March.

Tenen, Dennis. 2018. "Toward a Computational Archaeology of Fictional Space." *New Literary History* 49, no. 1: 119–147.

Thomsen, Mads Rosendahl. 2016. "Grand Challenges! Great Literature? Topics of the Future and Their Consequences for the Past." *Journal of World Literature* 1, no. 1: 97–106.

Underwood, Ted. 2013. *Why Literary Periods Mattered: Historical Contrast and the Prestige of English Studies*. Stanford, CA: Stanford University Press.

Underwood, Ted. 2018. "Why literary time is measured in minutes." *ELH* 85, no. 2: 341–365.

Underwood, Ted. 2019. *Distant Horizons: Digital Evidence and Literary Change*. Chicago, IL: University of Chicago Press.

Underwood, Ted, David Bamman and Sabrina Lee. 2018. "The Transformation of Gender in English-Language Fiction." *Cultural Analytics*, 13 February.

Wilkens, Matthew. 2016. "Genre, Computation, and the Varieties of Twentieth-Century U.S. Fiction." *Cultural Analytics*, 11 January.

6 Translation

Duration and cosmopolitan reading

Stefan Helgesson

Translation is the paradoxical condition of possibility for connecting different speech communities and literary cultures. If, on the one hand, translation might be defined as the *transfer* of a text from one language to another, it equally involves a dramatic *transformation*. With literature, after all, one can argue that the materiality of its form and the materiality of its mediation are one and the same. This distinguishes literature from non-verbal art. An art object such as Marcel Duchamp's iconic bottle-dryer will *signify* differently if placed in a museum or in a restaurant kitchen, or if it is exhibited in Paris or in Delhi – but the molecules of its metal structure remain the same. Or, to take a different example, experiencing a live performance by the dancer Yuan Yuan Tan is different from viewing a recording of that performance, yet her dance movements remain the same. Not so with a work of literature. Change the medium of Nikolai Gogol's Шинель (*The Overcoat*) from Russian to Tamil, and the material of the form will also have changed.

But why should this be paradoxical? Because media theory teaches us that texts "must always be embodied to exist in the world" (Hayles 2004, 69). Even the shortest narrative, such as "For sale: baby shoes. Never worn" (anecdotally attributed to Ernest Hemingway), requires speech, writing, print or screen to become perceptible. Accordingly, with translation, the recognizable material characteristics of those six words – their shape, their sound – will change. Here is my attempt at a Swedish translation: "Till salu: barnskor. Aldrig använda." Obviously different. And yet – the same? This is what translation scholars recognize as the problem of the *tertium comparationis*. We could spot it already in the machine translations performed in Chapter 5. What is "it" that remains the same if each and every word has been replaced?

Sameness, in this instance, could be located at other levels than the strictly linguistic one. The minimal narrative assumes familiarity with classified ads in newspapers, or at least with a market economy where goods are freely bought and sold. It also takes the existence of shoes manufactured for babies for granted. These are not universal phenomena, but historically specific. "For sale" would make little sense in a community without monetary economy – and would, accordingly, require a translation (perhaps with an explanatory note) that makes it comprehensible in its new context. This helps us to set the deeper philosophical implications of the *tertium comparationis* to one side, and instead recognize that translation involves different *degrees* of transformation. Translating an Ibsen play from Norwegian to Swedish is almost (but not quite) pointless, since the two languages and cultures are so proximate. In such an instance, the transformation is limited – depending as much on the translator's approach as on the linguistic conditions. (An empirical case could be made here out of comparing Herbert Grevenius's and Klas Östergren's two Swedish translations of *Hedda Gabler*, the former from 1964, the latter from 2003.) Translating Ibsen into Mandarin or Japanese – as has frequently been done – is another matter. The grammar and the lexicon of these languages are radically different from Norwegian, their script and print systems are based on other principles than the Latin alphabet and, last but not least, the cultural and social contexts are self-evidently different (even if it is not self-evident just *how* they are different).

Thinking in terms of degrees of transformation – conditional on language, function and context – can accommodate the two extreme positions on translation that otherwise present themselves. The first is the pragmatic position that translation is a mere repackaging of semantic content. The second is the incommensurability position which dwells only on difference – or on untranslatability, to use the term developed by Emily Apter (2013). Degrees of transformation may instead account for how literary cultures connect (or fail to connect), as well as for the range of versions that a literary work might assume in its travels across languages and through time. By the same token, such an approach enables a differentiated account of power relations between literatures and languages. In some cases, more drastic transformations are needed to make a work acceptable in the new language. This is what Lawrence Venuti (following Schleiermacher) has dubbed *domestication* (1995; see also Chapter 1). Under other circumstances, a translation is allowed to sound awkward, supposedly retaining more of the literary work's initial qualities. In Venuti's vocabulary, this is called *foreignization*. When, where and why either mode becomes operational is a complicated question, to say the least, but the question can be identified more generally as a relational one.[1] High-prestige works from high-prestige languages (say, James Joyce's *Ulysses*) are allowed to sound stranger in translation than unknown works from minor languages. By extension, this indicates how world literature evolves through shifts in what I will call cosmopolitan reading desires.

In this chapter, the fate of Brazilian literature in other languages and literary markets – particularly Euclides da Cunha's *Os sertões* (1902) – will serve as the main case through which these questions will be explored. Each language and national context has its own peculiarities with respect to translation, depending on its relative position in the exchanges among print-based literatures. A "major" literary language such as French will confer value on writers from "minor" literatures if they are translated into French. A "minor" literary language such as Estonian will boost its own literary capital by translating works from "major" literatures – but the international consecrating effect of an Estonian translation is minimal compared to a French or English translation. It is these relations that motivate the *descriptive* account of centres and peripheries in world literature. As Moretti summarizes it, "movement from one periphery to another (without passing through the centre) is almost unheard of […] movement from the periphery to the centre is less rare, but still quite unusual, while that from the centre to the periphery is by far the most frequent" (2003, 75–76; see also Lindqvist 2018). The first point is in fact debatable – but Moretti sums up a general *logic* of centrality and peripherality within a given system, a logic that can then be tested empirically.

What makes Brazil intriguing is the asymmetry between the sheer magnitude of its own literary production and its relative invisibility in other languages (with Clarice Lispector and Paulo Coelho as two recent, completely different exceptions). It is, on its own, a major literature, yet minor abroad. Observed also by Casanova (2004, 227, 277–8), the problem is an old one, as can be seen in a 1939 essay – poignantly entitled "Made in France" – by the São Paulo modernist Mario de Andrade. After perceptively dissecting the logic of translation and reception in what Casanova much later would call the world republic of letters, Andrade notes with surprise how some Brazilian authors he had always considered mediocre suddenly seem brilliant in French translation. "Oh, the prestige of that language!," he laments:

> The truth is that not only do we suffer from the bane of a language that the world doesn't even know exists, what's worse is that this language, be it written with the pen of the Portuguese, or shooting forth from our coarser [Brazilian] lips, will never manage to constitute itself as a literary language.
>
> (1948, 32; my translation)

He blames this state of affairs on Brazilian individualism, social disorder, and nostalgia. Compared to French, the Portuguese language has no "normalized clarity of expression." Conversely, however, French condemns everyone to write well. The stylistic idiosyncrasies and personalized diction of Brazilian writers such as Euclides da Cunha and Gilberto Freyre would not be possible to achieve in French. And once Machado de Assis arrived at his clear late style, this proved that Portuguese could comprise all registers of the literary. The social and historical obscurity of Portuguese, in other words, turns out to be a literary strength and a source of renewal; the loser wins. This is Andrade's inverse logic of vernacularism, both apologetic and defiant. Its defence of the "untranslatable," however, is premised on the prior fact of translation. It was, after all, Andrade's uncanny experience of reading his Brazilian colleagues in French that made him reassess the value of Portuguese. In the terms of translation theory, one could say that Andrade experienced a high degree of (French) domestication in the translations, which indicated not just the inherent qualities of the French language, but rather the asymmetrical power relations between the French and Brazilian literatures.

Andrade's self-discovery by way of translation illustrates the necessary link between translation and world literature. Or rather: *world literature* has a necessary connection to translation, whereas the opposite need not be true. Translation studies has its own intellectual history, famously instituting itself academically at a conference in Copenhagen in 1972, when James S. Holmes (1988) gave a paper entitled "The Name and Nature of Translation Studies," but also with a much older intellectual pedigree, stretching (at least) back to St Jerome. In recent years, it has secured its place as a central discipline in the humanities. It deals, however, not just with literature, but with all forms of translation. Hence, some branches of translation studies are more relevant to our current discussion than others. There is first of all the quantitative approach of the sociology of translation, as developed by Johan Heilbron (1999), Gisèle Sapiro (2008), Yvonne Lindqvist (2018) and others. Rather than gesture broadly towards "circulation," their work painstakingly maps the frequency and volume of literary translation between languages and countries – providing thereby the empirical evidence needed to support or contest statements such as the one by Moretti quoted above. Also within the sociological domain is the actor-oriented approach to translation: by following the output of specific publishers or the work of specific translators, this can achieve a fine-grained account of specific translation exchanges. Sapiro (2015) is again an important name here, but also Lawrence Venuti, Susan Bassnett, Theo Hermans (2007) and others.

Many of these scholars are equally involved in investigating translation history (Pym 2009). Finally, there are various text-based approaches to literary translation that deal with textual transformation and recontextualization. These can address highly technical aspects of literary translation, ideological angles (Meylaerts 2011; Munday 2008; Bassnett and Trivedi 1999; Niranjana 1992), as well as more theoretical perspectives on what enables translation (Alvstad 2014). At the more philosophical end of the spectrum, one finds also a fundamental questioning of boundaries between languages and the complicity of translation in maintaining these boundaries (Sakai 2009).

Within translation studies proper, the shift that occurred in the 1980s from a normative to a descriptive approach to translation was crucial: instead of analysing how a given translation was true to its original (the problem of fidelity or equivalence), attention shifted – with the work of scholars such as Gideon Toury, André Lefevere, Antoine Berman, Bassnett and Venuti – to the function of the translation in its new context. To use translation terminology, the interest shifted from the source text to the target text, and above all to the *target culture*, as summed up in Toury's paradigmatic statement: "translations are facts of target cultures" (1995, 29). In Berman's more hermeneutic vocabulary, translation was conceived as an *épreuve de l'étranger* (1984), the trial or proof of the foreign. This referred to the relationship between the self and the foreign that translation sets up, but also to the trials that the foreign text undergoes when resituated. Again, as we can see, it is the target context that is in focus here.

In more recent world literature studies, the very distinction between source and target has come to be questioned. Rebecca Walkowitz's influential notion of "born-translated" literature (2015) has instead drawn attention to the increasingly common phenomenon of writing that is not only published simultaneously (more or less) in numerous languages, but that inscribes a cosmopolitan, multilingual homelessness in its very form. This can be ascribed both to the transnational corporatization of trade publishing (dominated globally by companies such as Pearson, Hachette, HarperCollins, Penguin Random House and Grupo Planeta), and to Internet publication, which makes national provenance less important and sometimes irrelevant. Nonetheless, most literary works produced globally remain confined to one language and to one field of publication. Arguably, then, it is the threshold cases – those works that almost, or only after repeated attempts, manage to break through the barrier of obscurity that Mario de Andrade lamented – that are the richest sources of information on the changeable constructions of international literary value.

Consider, for example, Brazil's Euclides da Cunha. One of Cunha's famous translators, Samuel Putnam, begins his introduction to *Rebellion in the Backlands* with a flourish: "There can be no doubt that Euclides da Cunha's *Os Sertões* is a work that is unique not only in Brazilian literature but in world literature as well" (1995, v). This is in 1944, towards the end of the Second World War and just as the United States is embarking on its 60-odd years as global hegemon. It is also the moment when Brazil, virtually unscathed by the war, is poised to flourish both culturally and economically, up until the military coup in 1964. The decision to translate *Os sertões* – a monumental war documentary first published in 1902 and almost instantly canonized as a national Brazilian classic – into American English was particularly apt, given these changing dynamics of inter-American and global relations (which would soon slip into the destructive logic of the Cold War).

"[N]ot only in Brazilian literature but in world literature as well": Putnam, of course, does not only speak of world literature. Instead, he oscillates in his introduction between the national and transnational levels, drawing on both to convince his North American audience of the exceptional qualities of this work that he has rewritten in English:

> In no other instance, probably, has there been such unanimity on the part of critics of all shades of opinion in acclaiming a book as the greatest and most distinctive which a people has produced, the most deeply expressive of that people's spirit. On this the native and the foreign critic are in agreement.
>
> (v)

To substantiate this claim, he cites the Brazilian critic Agrippino Grieco, on the one hand, and Stefan Zweig, the ill-fated Austrian author who spent his last years in Brazil, on the other. The rhetorical operation at work here is characteristic of the moment when a hitherto unknown, "obscure" work is translated and presented to a new interpretive community. The challenge is to appeal to a cosmopolitan desire in the target reader. This reader must be convinced that the obscurity in question is a shortcoming on her or his part, and not justified on the grounds that the work is flawed according to target standards. Putnam the translator is doing his utmost to mediate between Brazil and the United States, in order to make the work accepted – indeed, acceptable – in the latter. But as discussed above, the juxtaposition of nation and world also has a particular poignancy with respect to Brazilian literature and its relatively weak international reputation.

Two questions arise out of this reflection. The first concerns the nature of cosmopolitan desire in readerships – the urge not just to read, but to extend one's reading beyond a given (if always more or less porous) cultural, linguistic or national community. Such a cosmopolitan desire is by no means a constant in history, nor is it evenly distributed across societies or readerships within any given society (see also Siskind 2014). This relates directly to the question of "strangeness" discussed in Chapter 3. One might hypothetically suggest that the strength of a cosmopolitan desire is proportional to a greater acceptance of strangeness in literature. If that is the case, the wide disparity in translation flows indicates rather dramatic differences between the cosmopolitan inclinations of readerships. According to post-millennial figures, 2–3 per cent of the books published in the United States were translations, compared to 35–40 per cent in Portugal (Sapiro 2008). The volume of book publishing in the United States is of course many times greater than in Portugal, but the relative difference remains striking. However, cosmopolitan reading, as it plays itself out in myriad practices, need not be a superior ethical practice. It is equally a marker of privilege and serves, at worst, to reinforce power disparities. The world literary resonance of Euclides da Cunha's work, steeped as it is in social Darwinist racial thinking, is a challenging case in point. Cunha himself was exceptionally cosmopolitan in his reading habits, which led him, at the outset at least, to use an objectifying, racist vocabulary when describing the *sertanejos* of the backlands. The "acceptance" by foreign readerships of *Os sertões* could in other words just as well point to an acceptance of a Eurocentric, racist outlook – whereas today, "cosmopolitanism" necessarily entails anti-racism and a non-Eurocentric outlook. Cunha is fortunately not quite so easy to pin down (as we shall see), but the question of the content and substance of cosmopolitan reading needs always to be asked.

This leads me to the second question, which has more specifically to do with *Os sertões* and its translations. Being a quirky combination of a geological treatise, an ethnography and a war documentary, this work is an ideal test case for my claim about Brazilian literature and its difficulties in reaching beyond its borders. We have here a work of exceptional *national* specificity that has *not* been translated into a number of languages with strong translation cultures such as Polish, Hebrew, or Norwegian.[2] It has, on the other hand, been translated, sometimes twice, into a number of other European languages, including Dutch, Danish, Italian, French, German, etc. More than that, *Os sertões* provides the basis for the Nobel Prize-winning author Mario Vargas Llosa's novel *La guerra del fin del mundo* (*The War of the End of the World*, 1981), whose global reach is linked to another moment in translation history, namely the North American construction of the Latin American "boom" in the 1960s and 1970s, as discussed by, among others, Jeremy Munday (2008). As companion pieces to Vargas Llosa's fiction, one could also mention the Hungarian author Sándor Márai's novel *Itelet Canudosban* from 1970, or, for that matter, the Frenchman Lucien Marchal's 1952 novel *Le Mage du sertão*, both of them adaptations of *Os sertões*, but without the impact of *The War of the End of the World*.[3] The global reach of *Os sertões* is in other words far from uniform. Putnam's rhetorically high-handed claims have been vindicated retroactively, perhaps, but the paths that *Os sertões* has taken into other languages and continents have seldom been straightforward.

What I intend to do in this chapter is to approach my first question by way of the second: that is to say, by reflecting on three different translations of Cunha – I have no possibility of presenting a full reception history here – and how they relate to what I call the time of translation and the differentiated production of cosmopolitan reading.

Of the three versions under discussion, two are anglophone: Samuel Putnam's 1944 *Rebellion in the Backlands*, and Elizabeth Lowe's recent *Backlands*, published in 2010. It is in fact Lowe's version that more correctly can be called "anglophone," marketed globally as it was by Penguin. Putnam's earlier translation, by contrast, is clearly *American*, published in the United States for a US readership. This already tells us a great deal about the different times of translation and different world literary moments. The third translation is anomalous, but intriguing for that very reason. I refer to Thomas Warburton's *Markerna brinna*, published in Sweden in 1945. This seems to be the first European translation of *Os sertões*. The hispanophone version *Los sertones* by Benjamin de Garay appeared in 1938, but that was an Argentine publication, not a Spanish one. The first French translation entitled *Les terres de Canudos* by Sereth Neu – which, surprisingly, was a joint French-Brazilian publication venture – would not appear until 1947, and it was in the following years that Danish (1948), Italian (1953) and Dutch (1954) versions were produced. Berthold Zilly's *Krieg im Sertão*, the first German translation, would not appear until 1994.

These external facts – dates, languages, places of publication – do tell us something about *Os sertões* as circulating world literature. It is, for instance, notable that the Dutch 1954 edition was published in a series known as the "Wereldbibliotheek," or the world library, thereby including Cunha in a local Dutch construction of world literature. The external facts tell us far from everything, however, and we need to ask just how much they can tell us of the textual and literary qualities of the disseminated, repeatedly rewritten and serially reproduced work itself. It is necessary but also insufficient in the ambit of world literature studies to attend to dates, languages and places of publication. A more trenchant account of how world literature is created needs therefore to be complemented by a stronger conception of translation's two temporalities: translation as event and translation as duration.

I have hitherto been talking mainly about the event of translation, i.e. publication, which presents its own methodological challenges.[4] The sequencing of translational events shows how more influential target languages enable translation into smaller target languages (Heilbron 1999). It is not by chance that the English and French translations are early in Cunha's sequence, followed by smaller languages. The Swedish translation may look like an exception, but proves this point instead: Warburton's is a second-hand translation, translated from Putnam's version, not Cunha's original. Portuguese, being the more obscure language – as Andrade lamented – needed the centrality of English to reach out to a peripheral language such as Swedish. Putnam's invocation of world literature could in other words be read as performative and optative rather than descriptive: it is the very fact of *his* translation of Cunha into English that helps produce *Os sertões* as world literature.

Translation, however, also entails a particular mode of *duration* that has far-reaching implications for how we conceive of world literature. In its simpler form, this duration has to do with how a particular translation endures over time. Through rereading and republication it may accumulate authority as the preferred version of a work, much like certain Bible translations. More complicated than this, however, is the accumulation of translations over time and hence the gradual, staggered construction of what is thought of as "a" work of literature as a work of world literature in Damrosch's sense, a work that moves beyond its context of origin and gains in stature the more it is translated (2003, 6). This form of duration, which involves numerous translations and editions of the same work, is baffling in so far as it both strengthens and dissolves the identity of a given work. Take 14 different translations of Ferdinand Oyono's *Une vie de boy* (as is done in Moore et al. 2013): will the real *Une vie de boy* please stand up? The question returns us to my initial remarks about the *tertium comparationis*. What, exactly, is it that endures? What enables us, from a world literary perspective, to speak of "a" *Une vie de boy* that somehow remains the same in all the different instantiations of it?

One possible approach to the duration of a work is to think of world literature in terms of collective labour and an expandable "textual zone" (Helgesson 2018). A "work" is thereby constituted not just by an author, but by what I have elsewhere called a serial collective of readers, publishers, translators, etc., who may know nothing about each other but all relate in changing ways to the work in question (Helgesson 2010). Such a perspective connects with Hans Robert Jauss's claim that "[a] literary work is not an object that stands by itself and that offers the same view to each reader in each period. It is not a monument that monologically reveals its timeless essence. It is much more like an orchestration that strikes ever new resonances among its readers" (1982, 21). This, in turn, recalls the argument developed by J. M. Coetzee in his essay "What Is a Classic?" (2002), where he uses the example of Bach and the performances of his music throughout the centuries to provide a non-idealistic explanation of the durability of literary classics. They endure not because of some essential quality, but because they are, in effect, tested, "performed," and found to be worth continued testing. The duration that Jauss and Coetzee are talking about, then, is entirely dependent on actual readers (including readers who are practitioners of criticism, creative writing, etc.) that test the viability of a given work. This is a time – a duration, a *durée* – that is *made*, and made collectively; it thins out at certain moments, perhaps for decades (or even vanishes for good), and thickens at others. It is not an abstract time that is inherent in the work or that can be accounted for simply by listing years of publication.[5]

Translators, being both readers and writers, are perhaps the single most consequential makers of the time of a literary work (after it has been written by the author). The event of translation not only means that a literary work exceeds inherent limitations of comprehensibility; it must also be understood as a negotiation between the work and the moment in which the translator is situated. The event of translation *intervenes* in the duration of the work, sometimes decisively. It provides an intensification of this duration, but will also change it, redirect its flow by rewriting the work in another language and, not infrequently, by recoding its generic function. In his delightful essay "Mother Courage's Cucumbers," Andre Lefevere (1982) demonstrates to great comic effect how early anglophone translations of Bertolt Brecht transformed this alien German author into something of a Broadway playwright, partly through sheer mistranslations (turning cucumbers into the town of Gurken, for example), but above all by introducing rhymes and rhythms far removed from the German original. Lefevere argues, however, that this cleared the ground for Brecht to be received in an anglophone theatrical context that had been wholly ignorant of his work; it thereby enabled "better," more faithful translations to be produced soon after. The early anglophone translations of Brecht intervened in the emergence of Brecht's work as world literature in such a way that more durable translations, and a more durable "Brecht," could be constructed and consecrated within anglophone cultures.

The duration of *Os sertões* and its translations, by virtue of being such a hybrid piece of writing, presents many examples of such redirections of both genre and circulation. I must digress here to explain more fully what we are talking about: Euclides da Cunha, a military engineer, accompanied the fourth campaign against an uprising in the remote hinterland of the Bahia region in north-east Brazil. A community – some would say a sect – had formed in the 1890s at a place called Canudos around a prophetic figure known as Antônio Conselheiro. For various reasons, most of them misunderstandings, this community came to be perceived first by the Bahia state authorities and then the federal government in Rio as a threat to the still rosy-cheeked republic (proclaimed in 1889). The Canudos community, for their part, quite accurately perceived the troops that were sent out to "pacify" them as a direct threat to their existence and fought valiantly to defend their autonomy. Unbelievably, it would take four attempts before the government finally succeeded in suppressing – that is to say, annihilating – Canudos. Women and children, in so far as they had survived the hardships of the war, were spared, but every last man in Canudos – out of a total population of roughly 25,000 – was killed (Levine 1992).

What Cunha saw during this fourth campaign shook him so profoundly that he set out to write not only the full history of the Canudos war, as far as he was able, but an all-embracing analysis of the Brazilian nation and the broader significance of the war. It was not just the brutality and violence that had shaken Cunha, but rather the outright contradiction between what he, as a highly educated inhabitant of Rio de Janeiro, thought he understood about Brazil, and what he encountered as he ventured into the *sertões*. The most critical of these contradictions concerned his positivistic and social evolutionist faith in the victory of progressive modernity over "backward" societies and "inferior" races.

Cunha tried his utmost to stick to his positivist and evolutionist beliefs. "We are condemned to civilization," he says in a famous passage, "[e]ither we progress or will become extinct" (2010, 62). But what he encountered during the campaign threw his faith in progress into disarray. The inhabitants of the backlands, the *sertanejos* who according to his racial theory were degenerate and backward, became the heroes of his narrative, while the federal army, harbingers of progress according to this same theory, turned out to be perpetrators of sheer atrocities: "In spite of three centuries of underdevelopment, the *sertanejos* did not rival our troops in acts of barbarism" (2010, 431).

What made this contradiction particularly painful for Cunha was his own loyalty to the fledgling republic. This is noticeable in the vacillating reference of the words "our" and "we" in the sentences just cited. He speaks of "the *sertanejos*" on the one hand and "our troops" on the other. But the "we" in "[w]e are condemned to civilization" refers to the whole nation of Brazil, *sertanejos* included. In brief, the Canudos experience forced Cunha to confront the fact of radical difference within the imagined community of Brazil. The vast national impact of his work in Brazil could therefore be ascribed, with a term borrowed from Jacques Rancière, to its capacity to enable a new *partage du sensible*, alternately translated as the "distribution" or "division of the sensible" (2007, 12).

How, then, do we move from this irreducibly Brazilian understanding of *Os sertões* to reading it as world literature? Or to use Jauss's terms, how has it managed to strike "new resonances" through time that enable it to achieve that particular transformation? I return here to the Second World War and Stefan Zweig, the Austrian author quoted by Putnam. Zweig, who came from a secular Jewish background, was one of the most celebrated and widely read European authors in the 1920s and 1930s (and has recently enjoyed a revival – witness Wes Anderson's 2014 film *The Grand Budapest Hotel*). His work was in itself a translational phenomenon, reaching readers not only across Europe but in the United States and South America as well.

History, in the guise of the Third Reich, harshly intervened in his career, however. He left Austria for Britain in 1934, and then fled across the Atlantic in 1940. After a short time in the United States, he and his second wife Lotte Altmann ended up in Brazil. Despairing of Europe's prospects, Zweig fell in love with Brazil and wrote in a matter of months *Brasilien, ein Land der Zukunft*, published in 1941 (by a German publisher but in Stockholm, because of the war), and almost instantly translated into a number of languages, including French, Spanish, Swedish and English. Zweig's own future in Brazil was tragically brief: he committed suicide in 1942.

Brazil, Land of the Future is an enthusiastic, propagandistic, yet surprisingly well-informed portrait of Brazil, explicitly intended to remedy the ignorance of North American and European readers. Much of the book reads like a travelogue, with historical accounts and economic analyses thrown in. There is only one rather short chapter on Brazilian culture, and it is here that we find an even shorter section on literature. Indeed, Zweig discusses no more than two authors: Machado de Assis and Euclides da Cunha. In one lengthy paragraph Cunha is lauded panegyrically yet presciently in the following terms:

Comparable in world literature, perhaps, to *The Seven Pillars of Wisdom*, in which Lawrence describes the struggle in the desert, this great epic, little known in other countries, is destined to outlive countless books that are famous today by its dramatic magnificence, its spectacular wealth of spiritual wisdom, and the wonderful humanitarian touch which is characteristic of the whole work.

(Zweig 1941b, 159)

This is the *sum total* of Putnam's claim to the world literary status of *Os sertões* and his assessment that "[i]n no other instance, probably, has there been such unanimity on the part of critics of all shades of opinion" (v). But this was all that was needed. The combination of Zweig and the northern hemispheric malaise caused by the world war was sufficient to grant Cunha's magnum opus entry into the Europhone currents of world literary circulation, as I demonstrated earlier.

When this is done, the translations also effect a decisive generic shift that contains the work's strangeness. What Cunha presented as a rigorously scientific essay, and what certainly reads as an unruly, unsettled mixture of scientific, essayistic, journalistic and novelistic writing, is transformed into "literature," notably an epic, an operation already performed by Brazilian critics but consummated by the translators. In the Swedish translation Warburton unceremoniously, and without informing the reader, removes most of the "scientific" sections in parts one and two, and reduces the work to the narrative of the Canudos campaign. Already an established translator of British and American modernist poetry, Warburton was busy completing his Swedish translation of James Joyce's *Ulysses* when he chose to translate Putnam's translation of Cunha. He was, in other words, well-positioned in what Bourdieu (1993) calls the field of restricted production, and his translation of Joyce would secure his status as a important figure in Swedish letters. We could also turn to the blurb of the Swedish edition which clearly labels *Os sertões* as "a glowing epic about a barren and hostile landscape," which further demonstrates how the first wave of translations affects the duration of *Os sertões* by allowing it to be received as an epic rather than a Brazilian national treatise – but still underwritten by Zweig's internationally influential promotion of Brazil.[6]

Added to this, *Os sertões* is an indictment of the brutality of warfare. North American and European readers in the 1940s could relate to this without difficulty, while the remote setting served to displace the harrowing immediacy of these experiences. In a Swedish review of Warburton's translation, Tore Zetterholm writes that the war of Canudos, which results from the clash between "primitive fanaticism and power politics," also becomes symbolic of "the barbarism of war throughout the ages."⁷

It would appear, then, that these two early translations are largely indebted to Zweig's promotion of Cunha, but also, at a deeper level, to the turmoil of the Second World War. If it hadn't been for Nazi Germany and the war, Zweig wouldn't have fled across the Atlantic and discovered Brazil, in what turned out to be a vain search for a sanctuary. The war facilitated Zweig's own reception and mediation of Cunha. But it was also a factor in enabling the reception, limited as it may have been, of Putnam's and Warburton's translations. With time, the importance of this historical factor subsided. Following the logic of my earlier reasoning, one could say that after the 1940s and early 1950s, the duration of Cunha's work as world literature thinned out, only to become denser again in 1980, when the new Spanish translation by Estela dos Santos appeared, and again in the 1990s when Putnam's translation was reissued, Berthold Zilly produced the first German translation, and the new French translation appeared (1993). Elizabeth Lowe, whose all-new English translation appeared in 2010, is well aware of her own role in producing the continued duration of the work. In her brief note on the translation she admits that "[w]hile it is daunting to follow in Putnam's footsteps, the hope is that this rendition injects new life into *Os sertões*, bringing it to a new generation of English readers interested in how Brazil became a modern nation and curious about the role of journalism in times of war" (Lowe 2010, xxxvi). Lowe's emphases differ from Putnam's: no longer the rhetorical high ground of world literature, but rather war journalism and an interest in Brazil.

The texture of their respective translations reveals further differences. As a rule, Putnam tended to refine Cunha's style, while Lowe reproduces and even reinforces its abruptness. When Cunha writes "Valia a pena tentá-lo" (436), Putnam renders this as "It was worth trying, at any rate" (685), while Lowe, in lapidary fashion, simply writes: "It was worth a try" (448). We can see how this difference plays itself out by looking at two slightly longer examples.

First we have a paragraph from part two, describing the construction of Canudos. Cunha's original reads like this:

A *urbs* monstruosa, de barro, definia bem a *civitas* sinistra do erro. O povoado novo surgia, dentro de algumas semanas, já feito ruínas. Nascia velho. Visto de longe, desdobrado pelos cômoros, atulhando as canhadas cobrindo área enorme, truncado nas quebradas, revolto nos pendores – tinha o aspecto perfeito de uma cidade cujo solo houvesse sido sacudido e brutalmente dobrado por um terremoto.

(2005, 155–6)

Putnam translates the passage like this:

> This monstrous *urbs*, this aggregation of clay huts, was a good indication of the sinister *civitas* of the erring ones who built it. The new town arose within a few weeks, a city of ruins to begin with. It was born old. Viewed from afar, flung out over the hills and covering an enormous area, cut up into ravines and rugged-heaving slopes, it had the precise appearance of a city that has been rudely shaken and tumbled by an earthquake.
>
> (1995, 206)

Lowe, meanwhile, rewrites it as:

> This monstrous aggregation of mud huts clearly defined the sinister civitas of wrongdoing. The new town arose in a few weeks, a city of ruins. It was born old. Seen from a distance, spread out over the hills over an enormous area, split by ravines and rugged slopes, it had the appearance of a city that has been shaken and thrown about by an earthquake.
>
> (2010, 151)

Translation is always a matter of choosing between viable alternatives, as these excerpts show. Both Putnam and Lowe are, one could say, *selectively* faithful to Cunha's wording, but in different ways. Putnam retains Cunha's Latin "urbs" in the first sentence, and keeps something of its broken syntax by inserting a sub-clause that not only translates "de barro" ("of clay") but repeats and glosses the opening of the sentence. This is a premonition of how Putnam then continues to engage in what translation scholars call explicitation and amplification. Instead of simply "*civitas* sinistra do erro" we have "the sinister *civitas* of the erring ones who built it"; instead of just "já feito ruinas," we get "a city of ruins to begin with." Cunha's compressed syntax is made more fluid and readable by Putnam.

The last example is debatable, as the "já" ("already") could well motivate Putnam's "to begin with." Lowe, by contrast, just writes "a city of ruins," choosing the opposite of amplification: the temporal dimension of the "já" is implied rather than stated. Lowe seems in general to prefer syntactical reorganization and elision to amplification. The "urbs" is removed and the first sentence rewritten as one concise clause. Instead of Putnam's "precise appearance" – which rewrites Cunha's "o aspecto perfeito" – Lowe shortens it to "the appearance."

The second excerpt, deeply embedded in the war narrative, largely confirms these observations. I quote the three versions in sequence:

> Via-se a transmutação do trecho torturado: tetos em desabamentos, prensando, certo, os que lhes acolhiam por baixo, nos cômodos estreitos; tabiques esboroando, voando em estilhas e terrões; e aqui e ali, em começo dispersos e logo depois ligando-se rapidamente, sarjando de flamas a poeira dos escombros, novos incêndios, de súbito deflagrando. Por cima – toldada a manhã luminosa dos sertões – uma rede vibrante de parábolas ...
>
> (2005, 427–8)

> The effects of this terrific punishment were visible to the eye: roofs falling and, of a certainty, crushing those that were sheltered in the tiny rooms beneath; partitions crashing, with splinters and clods of earth flying through the air; while here and there, against the dusty background of the trash heaps, fresh conflagrations could be seen starting – separate ones at first, but soon becoming one huge blaze. Up above, the luminous backlands morning was overcast with a network of cannon balls.
>
> (1995, 688)

> The results of this horrific battery were visible to the naked eye. Roofs were falling and certainly crushing those underneath. Walls crashed down, sending splinters and clods of earth flying through the air. Here and there, against the trash heaps, fresh fires were flaring up. They were separate at first, but then they merged into one huge blaze. Over the bright backlands morning a canopy of cannonballs formed.
>
> (2010, 449–50)

Cunha's syntax and vocabulary combine here in striking, virtually cinematic, images of warfare. The passage is complex and challenging for translators. Putnam, again, remains faithful to the syntax but makes Cunha more prolix and polished than in the original. The last sentence, for example, explicates the "parábolas" by calling them "a network of cannon balls" and turns Cunha's incomplete clause into a full sentence. Lowe does something similar with that sentence, but contracts it by eliminating "Up above" ("Por cima") and substituting the more concise "Over."

On the lexical level, it is clear that Lowe opts for a more standard and less Latinate register than Putnam: she writes "bright" instead of "luminous," "blaze" instead of "conflagration," "walls" rather than "partitions." This is a strategic choice. It is not motivated by Cunha's own text – his Portuguese is often obtuse and archaic even to his first Brazilian readers – but makes him more accessible to the contemporary, globally dispersed readership targeted by the current Penguin edition. By simplifying his prose, Lowe's translation could possibly be described as more domesticating than Putnam's high style, but it is not a domestication on behalf of a restricted *national* readership. It is rather a *cosmopolitan* domestication that conforms to the transnationally viable mode of the Latin of our current global moment: English.

Added to this, Lowe's version is also shaped by a contemporary, and not nationally restricted, literary and political sensibility that differs radically from Putnam's 1940s. Lowe's Cunha in 2010 should be read post "new journalism" and post postmodernism. It speaks to the "war on terror," the Canudos campaign being an early example of how a government frames a rebellion as "terrorist," and resonates quite obviously with the post-millennial ascendancy of Brazil (although this took a dramatic turn for the worse after 2010). Or put differently: because of Brazil's new global prominence around 2010, it became viable also among English-speaking readerships to appeal to a specific interest in Brazil as nation, but unapologetically so and also with a comparative angle. Situating Cunha's narrative in the broader framework of war, rebellion and nationhood, Ilan Stavans writes in the introduction to Lowe's translation that

> [a]ll modern nations are born from sacrificial blood. The atrocities Cunha witnessed as reporter were beyond belief. Like the use of napalm in Vietnam by the U. S. Army, the Brazilian military spread kerosene on villages, then threw dynamite bombs on them, creating hellish scenes in which the Canudos population was burnt alive.
>
> (2010, xii)

Stavans is also entirely frank about Cunha's racism. There is no need today to "rescue" this aspect of his work. In the century since its first publication, the combined work of translators, critics, and of history itself has enabled *Os sertões* to accumulate a sufficiently substantial and widely distributed duration for it to be read discriminately. This observation runs counter to the previous claim that Lowe domesticates Cunha. But there is no deeper contradiction: while Lowe domesticates Cunha's *style*, at least on the lexical level, his polyphonous text is (re-)presented unabridged, even when it is awkward in relation to contemporary political values. A possible conclusion, akin to Lefevere's take on Brecht, is that as the time of translation does its work, strangeness becomes more acceptable. It becomes less important to secure, up front, the acceptance of the work according to target standards and genre expectations. If Warburton, in his Swedish translation, slashed large chunks of *Os sertões* so as to present a coherent epic to his readers, and if Putnam refined Cunha's style, then Lowe produces a rough-and-ready version of Cunha with his contradictions, inconsistencies and racist pronouncements intact. This could be taken as a sign – alongside the canonization of Clarice Lispector – that Brazil's relative isolation within the world republic of letters is diminishing, but it should also serve to emphasize the complex temporality of such a process and the multiple degrees of translational transformation involved. For other genres – poetry in particular – this translational process has an even harder time getting off the ground. In the case of *Os sertões*, it is clear that without Putnam, without the long duration of *Os sertões* in various languages and adaptations, and without Brazil's post-millennial moment, the Penguin publication of Lowe's translation would have been unlikely. Arguing a counter-factual case can be self-defeating, but the positive evidence of the accumulated duration of *Os sertões* presented here confirms a central argument in this book: "world literature" can never be a neutral given, but is always historically produced. As such, it may indeed challenge and change the very notion of the literary itself, as the generic peculiarity of *Os sertões* demonstrates. The cosmopolitan desire of readerships is nonetheless generated at the crossroads where ideology, economics and aesthetic traditions meet. Where this cosmopolitan desire then leads is unpredictable.

Notes

1 Venuti's terms have also been criticized by, among others, Maria Tymoczko, Mona Baker and Michael Cronin. See Myskja (2013) for an overview.
2 This means that Walnice Nogueira Galvão, when recounting the story of the late German translation of *Os sertões*, is slightly off the mark when claiming that it otherwise had been translated into "every European language" (Galvão 2009, 23).
3 Márai and Marchal are mentioned in Ventura 2002, 12.
4 As we have been arguing in this book, publication data on a global scale are seldom just there for the taking, which the unreliable aspects of UNESCO's *Index Translationum* show. Each listing of translation events of a given work requires a great deal of cross-checking between databases – and even then, one cannot be sure that one has managed to compile an exhaustive list. What such databases *do* allow, nonetheless, is a gauging of broad tendencies.
5 It should be noted, moreover, that there is a third aspect of time and translation that I don't have space to address here: the flourishing and waning of

translation efforts through history, such as the late medieval Toledo school, German romanticism, post-Second World War UNESCO-supported translation, or the current wave of translation into Mandarin. It is through such periods of translation that world literature, as substantial sets of texts, comes into being. As translation sociologists will tell us, however, most translation exchanges occur between a mere handful of the world's scripted languages.

6 "ett glödande epos om en karg och fientlig natur" (Cunha 1945, back cover).

7 My translation of the following passage: "Kriget, som blir följden av dessa båda principer, den primitiva fanatismens och den politiska maktlystnadens problemlösning, blir samtidigt en makaber symbol för det krigiska barbariet genom alla tider" (Zetterholm 1946, 169).

References

Alvstad, Cecilia. 2014. "The Translation Pact." *Language and Literature* 23, no. 3: 270–284.

Andrade, Mario de. 1948. *O empalhador de passarinho*. São Paulo: Livraria Martins Editôra.

Apter, Emily. 2013. *Against World Literature: On the Politics of Untranslatability*. London: Verso.

Auerbach, Erich. 1952. "Philologie der Weltliteratur." In *Weltliteratur: Festgabe für Fritz Strich zum 70. Geburtstag*, edited by Walter Muschg and E. Staiger, 39–50. Bern: Francke.

Bassnett, Susan and Harish Trivedi, eds. 1999. *Post-Colonial Translation: Theory and Practice*. London: Routledge.

Berman, Antoine. 1984. *L'Épreuve de l'étranger: culture et traduction dans l'Allemagne romantique: Herder, Goethe, Schlegel, Novalis, Humboldt, Schleiermacher, Hölderlin*. Paris: Gallimard.

Bhabha, Homi. 1994. *The Location of Culture*. London: Routledge.

Bourdieu, Pierre. 1993. *The Field of Cultural Production: Essays on Art and Literature*. New York: Columbia University Press.

Casanova, Pascale. 2004 [1999]. *The World Republic of Letters. La république mondiale des lettres*. Paris: Seuil.

Coetzee, J. M. 2002. *Stranger Shores: Essays 1986–1999*. London: Vintage.

Cunha, Euclides da. 1938. *Los sertones*, trans. Benjamin de Garay. Buenos Aires: Mercatali.

Cunha, Euclides da. 1945. *Markerna brinna*, trans. Thomas Warburton. Stockholm: Wahlström & Widstrand.

Cunha, Euclides da. 1947. *Les terres de Canudos*, trans. Sereth Neu. Paris: Juillard, and Rio de Janeiro: Caravela.

Cunha, Euclides da. 1948. *Oprøret paa højsletten*, trans. Richard Wagner Hansen. Copenhagen: Westermann.

Cunha, Euclides da. 1953. *Brasile ignoto (l'assedio di Canudos)*, trans. [unpublished data] Milano: Sperling & Kupfer.

Cunha, Euclides da. 1954. *De binnenlanden: opstand in Canudos*, trans. [unpublished data] Amsterdam: Wereldbibliotheek.

Cunha, Euclides da. 1994. *Krieg im Sertão*, trans. Berthold Zilly. Frankfurt am Main: Suhrkamp.
Cunha, Euclides da. 1995 [1944]. *Rebellion in the Backlands*, trans. Samuel Putnam. London: Picador.
Cunha, Euclides da. 2005 [1902]. *Os sertões*. Rio de Janeiro: Lacerda.
Cunha, Euclides da. 2010. *Backlands: The Canudos Campaign*, trans. Elizabeth Lowe. New York: Penguin.
Damrosch, David. 2003. *What Is World Literature?* Princeton, NJ: Princeton University Press.
Galvão, Walnice Nogueira. 2009. *Euclidiana: Ensaios sobre Euclides da Cunha*. São Paulo: Companhia das Letras.
Hayles, N. Katherine. 2004. "Print Is Flat, Code Is Deep." *Poetics Today* 25, no. 1: 67–90.
Heilbron, Johan. 1999. "Book Translation as a Cultural World-System." *European Journal of Social Theory* 2, no. 4: 429–444.
Helgesson, Stefan. 2010. "Clarice Lispector, J. M. Coetzee and the Seriality of Translation." *Translation Studies* 3, no. 3: 318–333.
Helgesson, Stefan. 2018. "Translation and the Circuits of World Literature." In *The Cambridge Companion to World Literature*, edited by Ben Etherington and Jarad Zimbler, 85–99. Cambridge: Cambridge University Press.
Hermans, Theo. 2007. *The Conference of the Tongues*. Manchester: St Jerome.
Holmes, James S. 1988. "The Name and Nature of Translation Studies." In *Translated! Papers on Literary Translation and Translation Studies*, James S. Holmes, 66–80. Amsterdam: Rodopi.
Jauss, Hans Robert. 1982. *Toward an Aesthetic of Reception*, trans. Timothy Bahti. Brighton: Harvester.
Lawall, Sarah, ed. 1994. *Reading World Literature: Theory, History, Practice*. Austin: University of Texas Press.
Lefevere, Andre. 1982. "Mother Courage's Cucumbers: Text, System and Refraction in a Theory of Literature." *Modern Language Studies* 12, no. 4: 3–20.
Levine, Robert M. 1992. *Vale of Tears: Revisiting the Canudos Massacre in Northeastern Brazil 1893–1897*. Berkeley: University of California Press.
Lindqvist, Yvonne. 2018. "Translation Bibliomigrancy: The Case of Contemporary Caribbean Literature in Scandinavia." In *World Literatures: Exploring the Cosmopolitan-Vernacular Exchange*, edited by Stefan Helgesson et al., 295–309. Stockholm: Stockholm University Press.
Llosa, Mario Vargas. 1981. *La guerra del fin del mundo*. Barcelona: Plaza & Janes.
Lowe, Elizabeth. 2010. "A Note on the Text." In Euclides da Cunha, *Backlands: The Canudos Campaign*, trans. Elizabeth Lowe, xxxv–xxxvi. New York: Penguin.
Meylaerts, Reine. 2011. "Translation Policy." In *Handbook of Translation Studies*, vol. 2, edited by Yves Gambier and Luc van Doorslaer, 163–168. Amsterdam: Benjamins.
Moore, David Chioni, et al. 2013. "An African Classic in Fourteen Translations." *PMLA* 128, no. 1: 101–192.

Moretti, Franco. 2000. "Conjectures on World Literature." *New Left Review* 1: 54–68.
Moretti, Franco. 2003. "More Conjectures." *New Left Review* 20: 73–81.
Munday, Jeremy. 2008. *Style and Ideology in Translation: Latin American Writing in English*. New York: Routledge.
Myskja, Kjetil. 2013. "Foreignisation and Resistance: Lawrence Venuti and His Critics." *Nordic Journal of English Studies* 12, no. 2: 1–23.
Niranjana, Tejaswini. 1992. *Siting Translation: History, Post-Structuralism and the Colonial Context*. Berkeley: University of California Press.
Putnam, Samuel. 1995 [1944]. "'Brazil's Greatest Book': A Translator's Introduction." In Euclides da Cunha, *Rebellion in the Backlands*, trans. Samuel Putnam, v–xxvii. London: Picador.
Pym, Anthony. 2009. "Humanizing Translation History." *Hermes* 42: 23–48.
Rancière, Jacques. 2007. *Politique de la littérature*. Paris: Galilée.
Sakai, Naoki. 2009. "How Do We Count a Language? Translation and Discontinuity." *Translation Studies* 2, no. 1: 71–88.
Sapiro, Gisèle, ed. 2008. *Translatio: Le marché de la traduction en France à l'heure de la mondialisation*. Paris: CNRS éditions.
Siskind, Mariano. 2014. *Cosmopolitan Desires: Global Modernity and World Literature in Latin America*. Evanston: Northwestern University Press.
Stavans, Ilan. 2010. "Introduction." In *Backlands: The Canudos Campaign*, Euclides da Cunha, translated by Elizabeth Lowe, vii–xxiii. New York: Penguin.
Thomsen, Mads Rosendahl. 2008. *Mapping World Literature: International Canonization and Transnational Literatures*. London: Continuum.
Toury, Gideon. 1995. *Descriptive Translation Studies and Beyond*. Amsterdam: Benjamins.
Ventura, Roberto. 2002. *Os sertões*. São Paulo: PubliFolha.
Venuti, Lawrence. 1995. *The Translator's Invisibility: A History of Translation*. London: Routledge.
Walkowitz, Rebecca. 2015. *Born Translated: The Contemporary Novel in an Age of World Literature*. New York: Columbia University Press.
Zetterholm, Tore. 1946. "Brasilianskt epos." *BLM* 2: 169.
Zweig, Stefan. 1941a. *Brasilien, ein Land der Zukunft*. Stockholm: Bermann-Fischer.
Zweig, Stefan. 1941b. *Brazil, Land of the Future*, trans. Andrew St. James. New York: Viking Press.

7 Unfinished business
A dialogue

Stefan Helgesson and Mads Rosendahl Thomsen

1 Language in the twenty-first century

Mads Rosendahl Thomsen (MRT): Language and translation are a good place to begin. A further consolidation of English as the dominant scholarly language has taken place in the past decades, and it has become the relay language for many works in translation that are not translated directly. As Erich Auerbach wrote as early as 1952 (in German), the dominance of English would both fulfil and destroy the vision of a world literature. We would have a shared language but we would lose nuance. A shared language makes it possible for comparative work to reach broadly, but under these conditions, is it also fair to ask if linguistic diversity still can be nurtured?

Stefan Helgesson (SH): Linguistic diversity, as I see it, is not disappearing at all. With increased mobility, many societies have become more, not less, multilingual. But the conditions under which diversity prevails have changed dramatically. Buttressed by borderless digital media and the continuing global hegemony of the US culture industry, individual speakers navigate this multilingualism increasingly through English alone, to the detriment of learning other "foreign" languages. On such an understanding, the pragmatic dominance of English rests on the edifice of Babel, and it needs to be conceived of as a language that interfaces with myriad other languages. This means also that we need other approaches to language than the standard normative identification of languages with labels such as "English" or "French," among others.

MRT: I agree, and abandoning the idea of pure languages and pure identities both in theory and practice is really very important. The turn towards world literature studies in the pragmatic sense of reading across traditional borders, and more emphasis on the importance of translation, makes that very clear. I like the idea of having interfaces with other languages, but still one might worry about the fate of minor languages as

Unfinished business: a dialogue   153

the future of language departments in academia is increasingly uncertain. In the mid-1990s, French, German, Italian, and Spanish typically had a solid foundation in departments around the world with researchers working in linguistics, culture, history and literature. Today departments have been reduced significantly or closed down completely, obviously resulting in a loss of competencies. And those were just some of the larger languages – the smaller ones are often wiped out completely of university education. How does this affect global literary studies? Have comparative literature and globalization changed the idea of committing to one culture or one nation and thus actually been a part of the decline in language departments? What new goals can institutions set for themselves?

SH: There are pragmatic as well as more principled matters that come into play here. There does seem to be a general downturn in language studies. One hears this complaint frequently from colleagues in Europe and North America. In a case such as South Africa, only a smattering of students study African languages, although the country has 11 official languages (or 12, including sign language). This obviously brings about a crisis of sorts for the philological mode of literary studies, grounded as it is in a notion of the historical specificity of each language. Then again, the absolute numbers of students in higher education across the world are steadily on the rise, and this is also reflected in the increasing specialization of research in the humanities. Niches for Classical languages, African languages, Byzantine studies, Finno-Ugric literatures, etc. will in other words not only remain but possibly also thrive. What world literature can and should contribute here (as we've been trying to show in this book) is a keen meta-analytical framework for understanding the hierarchies, ecologies and inter-relations of literary languages of the world. This is different from opting simply to "teach everything in English." Pragmatism is unavoidable insofar as we must meet students where they happen to be, but this should not exclude a more principled, critical understanding of what is at stake in the linguistic transformations of our day.

MRT: Adding to this, the divide between research and didactics also continues to be a challenge. The scarce resources of university programmes and what can be read in a course stand in sharp contrast to the potentially endless demands of what should be considered in research. The conflict between the research-oriented distant reading of, say, Franco Moretti versus the selection of works for close reading in the classroom – in a transnational constellation such as David Damrosch has envisioned it – suggests two very different approaches, although they can be combined. Even then there are the institutional demands: most scholars cannot pick and choose but will have to work within a local curriculum that limits them, often to a single language. Just as there was a call for opening up the canon that gave birth to postcolonialism's institutional impact, I think that the "worlding" of other curricula is a serious task. If one believes that that is the direction to go in, of course.

2 Institutional transformations

MRT: Writing ten, 15 years ago, I believe I was too optimistic about globalization. Even though I was well aware that the economic effects would be both positive and negative depending on where you lived and how you had been educated, I believed that on a cultural level, globalization had and has much to offer. Now it feels like a more split time in history. On the one hand, diversity is getting a stronger foothold than one might have expected on issues of nationality, ethnicity, and gender. The effects of migration are also changing the self-identity of countries that have to rethink what they are, how they should educate their population, and how they can balance diversity with identity. That even goes for the corporate world, which has been quite vocal in supporting diversity. On the other hand, there is a new nationalism that also has strong support and which would like to put things in reverse, including the cultural artefacts that people are interested in. This is not least the case in countries that seemed to open up to the world after the end of the Cold War. And while there is nothing wrong with being interested in all things (and texts) from your own part of the world, I think it makes the interest in internationally circulated literature and art even more necessary and important.

SH: This is one question where we might have different points of departure. I was never quite so optimistic about globalization, having been sensitized by postcolonial theory to its longer history – that is, imperialism. Then again, already in my earliest work I insisted (in my Swedish context) on the need for global approaches to literature. The global – and I often return to Spivak's definition of globalization as "the imposition of the same system of exchange everywhere" – is in my view an historical predicament with very different consequences depending on who you happen to be in economic, social or "racial" terms. This predicament, and its resulting combined and uneven development, is for me a key motivation for world literature studies. We have been thrown into this situation – and literature, with its own logic of mapping, memory and movement, can help us to understand it differently than the social sciences do. But current developments (such as Hungary's expulsion of the Central European University, right-wing listings of "leftist" professors in the United States, or the catastrophic political turn to the extreme right in Brazil) could mean that academics need to struggle once again to uphold an internationalist, "world" agenda.

MRT: I certainly see ongoing globalization on many levels but it is taking a different form with the renewed sense of nationalism. The hopes for a strong cosmopolitan cultural involvement rather than economic globalization may have been let down, but the former is still an honourable ambition, given the alternatives. And in some parts of society the opening up of cultures has been immensely successful; just think of how the food culture has changed and become much more diverse in the past decades, certainly for the better in many countries, including my native Denmark. But literature is obviously a different medium.

SH: I agree that we can chalk up some successes for globalization. Hans Rosling (the author of *Factfulness*, 2018) has done a good job of demonstrating how life has improved for large populations across the planet over the last few decades. This needs to be remembered before issuing blanket condemnations of capitalism. But at what cost? The contradictions of globalization are extreme: alongside more opportunities there is tougher competition and increasing inequalities, growth and trade spell ecological devastation, generalized diversification also means homogenization. Literature produced in our age can and does, however, provide an expanding dialectical understanding of globalization precisely in its contradictoriness.

MRT: Good points. Of course, we should also consider that world literature studies has had a very varied impact across the world. There has, for example, never been a grand tradition for comparative literature in the United Kingdom, but now world literature in English has emerged as an important orientation for change in the discipline.

3 National ideals

MRT: Language teaching in primary and secondary schools has obviously been around for a long time, but I believe there has been a change in the way nations are very explicitly requiring that their citizens should know more than one or even more than two languages. It has become a much more pronounced ideal of *Bildung* not to be monolingual, and this is not just something that goes for the elites. The idea of a mother tongue will probably continue to exist, but people will increasingly be brought up with two or three languages. At some point this will have consequences for national literatures and world literature.

SH: Again, there are multiple and parallel developments that need to be considered: the global dominance of English; the increasing multilingualism of many societies; the growing number of translingual individuals. I'm not sure what you mean by the "new" ideal that citizens should be competent in two or more languages. This needs be looked at on a case-by-case basis. In African countries, multilingualism is mostly seen as a fact of life: especially in urban areas, people code-switch constantly between two, three or more languages. In present-day Europe, it seems to me that ambitions have been lowered by the assumption that it is enough to know English as a lingua franca.

MRT: Africa is special in that regard and in some ways an example to follow. With a "new" orientation I was thinking of nations that have until now seen themselves as very heterogenous with one official or very dominant language, beginning to be categorically clear that they want to raise multilingual citizens. It is also worth considering that even if one takes Beecroft's ecological system and brings the different spheres of circulation on an equal footing in the sense that quality can exist in many ways and for different audiences, the idea of world literature still ends up privileging internationally successful work. Which again can be for the better (because the works truly are extraordinary) or for the worse (they circulate widely because they manage to sell clichés). And there is something odd about saying, "This poem translated from Danish will probably not make sense to you, or seem particularly interesting, but trust me, to me it is fantastic."

4 The status of literature

MRT: It can be hard to make up one's mind whether this is the best of times or the worst of times for literature. There may be more readers than ever who are generally better educated, and there are more options for publishing than ever. However, literature does not have the status in culture it used to have, and we are just at the beginning of a digital revolution that may change reading habits radically, in ways detrimental especially to poetry (which has been given up on even by students of literature) and fiction. And one has to think about whether or how literary studies follows reading habits (as it eventually probably will, but with how much resistance)? Of course, value systems change, but even if literature has become less central, why cannot there still be great achievements in literature? And is the status of world literature as great literature changing towards, as Damrosch put it, a mode of reading?

SH: Interesting points – literary studies as divided against itself. Inevitably, I guess. My take on this question is to approach literature as both an historical concept and a polysemic one. On the one hand, "literature" is a recent Western invention, coinciding with the rapid expansion of European imperial influence. The Aristotelian division of genres into lyric, epic and drama; the Arabic notion of *adab*; Sanskrit's *kavya*;

Chinese *wen*; the oral genres of the Yoruba: all of these are older or even ancient, yet hardly equivalent to each other and not obviously the same as the notion of literature that was established before and after 1800 by, in particular, German, British and French thinkers. This understanding could be described as the old Euro-narrative. The long and short of it is the breakdown of classicist rule-bound aesthetics in the eighteenth century, and the subsequent valorization of originality, authorship, national authenticity and aesthetic autonomy (which also reconfigured the understanding of earlier periods in literary history). This is, in a nutshell, what has shaped the modern disciplines of literary studies. And it is indeed a recent development: the study of national literatures dates back to the nineteenth century. Cambridge's faculty of English (literature) was first established in 1919.

On the other hand, we are now at the other end of the shore, having experienced multiple revolutions in the conception of textuality, reading, literary value. Combined with the proliferation of new fields of study – such as African literature – these theoretical revolutions demonstrate the semantic mutability of "literature." To claim, now, that literature is merely a hangover from nineteenth-century bourgeois culture is to argue in bad faith. Better, then, to approach literature – as we said in the Introduction – as a cluster concept in the Wittgensteinian sense. It will never have a sharp definition, but rather a number of overlapping meanings – and that is perfectly okay. This, to me, is one of the hidden motivations behind the current upsurge of world literature. Our conditions of (literary) knowledge have transformed so radically over the last 50 years that this also invites new and hitherto unanticipated conversations around the productively fuzzy concept of literature.

Taking a different tack, one could argue that it is the conception of (relative) autonomy that is at stake here. Pascale Casanova certainly tried to argue that the world republic of letters aspired towards and even achieved autonomy (notably in the modernist era), and that its forms of domination and regulation must be distinguished from the political realm. I'm not entirely convinced by her argument, although I do accept that aesthetic dimensions of literature demand a repertoire of non-reductive modes of inquiry, also in the macro-context of globalization. (Again without claiming that the aesthetic definition of literature is the only valid definition.)

MRT: I agree that autonomy has played a huge role in defining literature, also bringing a very forceful and excluding narrative into the field of study. Autonomy also has a certain purity to it, claiming that art and literature should serve no other purposes than itself. Yet, what literature *represents* is also clearly a part of what makes it significant. Literature on traumatic events has shown that the intersection between ethics and aesthetics is extremely meaningful and that there are elements that cannot be separated by the insistence on a theory of autonomy. I have never been too keen on trying to define literature as such, but I do on the other hand have a hard time giving up on the idea of quality. Andreas Huyssen struggles with this as well in an article on global modernism, where he proposes to give up the distinction between highbrow and lowbrow in literature and art, but without abandoning the notion of quality. I'm all for that but it could also take us back to a sometimes futile discussion of what the criteria for quality are. This is where I place great faith in criticism as a practice: that there is an ongoing discussion of the nuances of works, of how they compare, of what makes them more or less strong. A discussion that ideally takes place across national borders.

SH: I also see criticism as productive in that sense, which makes it all the more important to nurture disciplinary spaces of conversation, where contrasting and clashing perspectives can jointly contribute to the formation of knowledge. World literature should not attempt to do "everything," but one thing it does at its best is to cultivate such multi-perspectivism. I must also reiterate that I am *not* advocating for rigid definitions of literature. On the contrary, within world literature studies I see a renewed appreciation of its sprawling, protean nature.

However, when speaking of the current status of literature from our Scandinavian viewpoint, it is also necessary to say something about the ongoing crisis in the Swedish Academy (in 2018). Fuelled as it has been by clashes between incompatible personalities, matters of principle and the force of the #metoo movement, it can also be read as a symptom of cultural changes that the Academy is ill-equipped to cope with. Founded in 1786 by the Swedish King Gustav III on the model of the Académie Française, the Swedish Academy was rather reluctantly persuaded in 1901 to administer the Nobel Prize for literature, as this prize had been defined in the loosely formulated will of Alfred Nobel. This chance occurrence placed the Swedish Academy in a central position in the world republic of letters. Here we can track some of the changes that the "republic" has undergone over the last 120 years. The prize begins as an exclusively European concern; makes its first, anomalous, digression beyond Europe with the prize to Rabindranath Tagore in 1913; canonizes an increasing number of North and South American writers from the 1930s onwards; opens up (somewhat) towards Asia in the 1960s and Africa in the 1980s; awards a rising number of women writers in recent decades. Disagreements, controversies, and an ultimately unshakeable Eurocentrism notwithstanding, the Academy has managed to uphold the authority of the prize. What happens now is anyone's guess. Following the choice of Bob Dylan in

2016, which left many wondering, the Academy was hit by a well-researched exposé of a sex scandal in November 2017. None of the members of the Academy were accused of misconduct, but extremely serious allegations were directed at a cultural player with close personal ties to the Academy. This individual has since been convicted in court on two charges of rape.

The implosion of the Academy that followed – including the postponement of the 2018 Nobel Prize for literature – is evidence that the rules of the cultural game have changed. If the social prestige and even mystique of literature previously served as a bulwark for the Academy (even when they fought among themselves), this idiosyncratic royal institution seems ill-equipped to cope with the age of the social media – to such a degree that its consecrating function in the republic of letters is threatened. It might yet weather this storm, but it might also be that its role – which has brought withdrawn, complex or "obscure" writers such Elfriede Jelinek, Herta Müller or Svetlana Aleksievich into the limelight thanks to a public agreement on the "literary" itself as a value – is waning, along with literature itself. As I write this in April 2019, however, the crisis in the Academy seems to have died down. A number of new female members have been elected, and the appointment of a new Nobel Prize committee (with five external members) is a promising development. The forecast now is that two prizes will be awarded in 2019.

MRT: Observing all this from another Scandinavian country, it has been a weird spectacle, farce and tragedy at the same time, yet ultimately with the sense that people actually care about the institution and its symbolic power exercised from the periphery.

SH: To which I would just add: from a rather privileged *semi*-periphery.

MRT: Sure, Stockholm is not doing badly, and we used to think of Sweden as the moral standard bearers of the Nordic countries (well, Strindberg and Bergman should have been enough of a signal).

SH: Ah yes, to think that Strindberg and Bergman have shaped the perception of Sweden. And now Nordic Noir ...

MRT: Still, the question of what it is worth fighting for and how should not be overlooked. One could accept that literature is on the margins of power, but also argue that the formation of international literary communities raises the awareness of injustice in several countries. World literature studies went hand in hand with globalization, but certainly with a more complex agenda than praising a global market. Nevertheless, world literature studies does not have an easily identifiable enemy in the form of class conflict or colonial oppressors. It seems to me that the positive vibe of being tolerant, inclusive, expansive and curious comes with a drawback of not having something worth fighting for. At least that is a critique worth considering. With growing nationalism, it appears as if there is a cause that is worth fighting for more than just a decade ago, namely cosmopolitanism. It comes in many shapes and forms but at least all of them can be discerned from nationalistic chauvinism. Insisting on broadening the curriculum, also in the official languages of a nation, and of laying bare the complex relations between national and transnational identities is important and political in the sense that there will be people who argue for the opposite.

5 The complexity of literature

MRT: Literature is essentially amazing because it relies solely on language and thus brings people as closely to the thoughts of others as possible, and it is democratic because so little is required to make art out of words (compared to other arts – film in particular). And there are all kinds of books, all kinds of stories, in an immense display of diversity. But are hopes for impact and hopes for diversity in conflict? There is an underlying love-hate relationship with best-sellers and canonical works. We appreciate that they are visible, lend prominence to literature, demonstrate that there are things that are shared, make conversation easier. Best-sellers are also often seen as dubious in terms of quality, authenticity, originality, and because they install a winner-takes-all logic when the strength of literature is diversity. This also goes for genres. The novel has reigned supreme in the past century and well beyond, and it is still the dominant genre in literature – so dominant that it even overshadows poetry and drama. But are there signs of a change in this status? Is non-fiction becoming more important? Can communication on social media also be a form of literature? Not to speculate too much, but two scenarios are possible: the decline of the novel or its continued dominance.

SH: You touch here upon Bourdieu's logic of restricted vs. large-scale production, which has a remarkable capacity to reproduce itself. The novel, being such a capacious non-genre, will survive – but not always in printed form. There's a case to be made for the contemporary TV series as the novel of our day. What does seem to be a trend today, however, is the academicization (is there such a word?) of literature. With the global expansion of higher education, not only literary reading but also writing is increasingly nurtured within the confines of the university. This creates knowledgeable but perhaps also streamlined transnational readerships and forms of writing.

MRT: TV series certainly are produced and consumed at a high rate these years, and as with novels, there is a lot of rubbish and some really good stuff. For all the similarities with the novel's long narrative and multiple stories, it is a different medium that is capable of doing things that novels cannot, but also lacks some of the novel's qualities: the ability to shift from the specific to the general, to make shifts in time and condense time in a way that is very different, and of course being focused on language. Images are fine, but there is also a case to be made against TV series and not happily talk of them as the novels of the twenty-first century. As for the increase in the institutional involvement with reading and writing, it should hopefully not turn into an ivory tower or a museum but a platform for making literature thrive broadly. This also goes back to the role of the critic: should s/he aim to be proactive or just an observer?

6 Postcolonialism

MRT: Postcolonialism and world literature are two big paradigms that relate to comparative literature and ways of framing literary studies beyond the nation. World literature studies, in its current revival, may even have been unthinkable without postcolonialism. But have they become more divided as the years have passed? Are they separate fields of inquiry? And what could bring them closer?

SH: Indeed, the revival of world literature – as we pointed out in Chapter 1 – can be attributed not least to Edward Said's engagements with Auerbach; it is also notable that Homi Bhabha in *The Location of Culture* discusses world literature appreciatively as "an emergent, prefigurative category that is concerned with a form of cultural dissensus and alterity" (1994, 12). So, the term can be located at the very heart of the institutional consolidation of postcolonialism. This is also my own take on world literature: its two macrohistorical motivations are globalization and decolonization; its task is (or should be) to develop alternatives to methodological nationalism and methodological Eurocentrism.

In practice, as we know, tensions between the two paradigms have sometimes been severe (Casanova 2005 and Huggan 2011 could be mentioned as cases in point – perhaps also your own earlier reading of Boehmer [Thomsen 2008]). I've written on this before, but the informal format of this dialogue allows me to address directly what has drawn me, as a postcolonial scholar, to world literature. The postcolonial field of enquiry is constitutively political. It is not defined by any single political *position*, but understood as the academic and theoretical afterlife of anticolonialism (this, to me, is what the "post" in postcolonialism really means), it always engages with the troubled legacies of colonialism. This is what gives it its force. But this is also what has sometimes led, to borrow a phrase from

Ben Etherington and Jarad Zimbler, to "the eclipse of literary technique" (2014, 281), eliding in this way multiple aspects of literary practice and history. Encouragingly, however, there are many recent examples of literary studies that overcome the divide between postcolonialism and world literature – I could mention Nathan Suhr-Sytsma's *Poetry, Print and the Making of Postcolonial Literature* (2017), Jeanne-Marie Jackson's *South African Literature's Russian Soul* (2015), Peter D. McDonald's *Artefacts of Writing* (2017), and Tobias Warner's *The Tongue-Tied Imagination* (2019) as four superb instances. The Warwick Research Collective's influential *Combined and Uneven Development* (2015) also achieves this, if from another, rigorously Marxist angle. But then there are a number of smaller skirmishes between the "camps" that often seem to be about position-taking in the North American academe.

In a recent response to one such articulate attack by Joseph Slaughter (2018) on the current agenda of comparative literature in the United States, Jeanne-Marie Jackson makes a useful distinction between wanting to do justice *through* literature, and doing justice *to* literature. Doing justice through literature implies using literature instrumentally to pursue one's political agenda. The risk here is that it might become "a form of inadvertent injustice in its own right, provincializing 'global' traditions by enforcing too literal or direct a relation between the world of action and the world of literary thought" (Jackson 2018, 256). Doing justice to literature involves instead stepping back to give literature its due – even if it does not comply with one's ideological desires. This is the approach I identify with (without claiming that I actually succeed). This is also why I increasingly wish to make my idiosyncratic positioning in a Scandinavian society visible in my anglophone work. World literature – which is always perspectival – is more accommodating, it seems to me, of such idiosyncrasies. Although it may sound counterintuitive, being up front about such positioning is one way to challenge the two methodologies of nationalism and Eurocentrism.

7 Gender

SH: Gender might possibly be the elephant in the room in world literature. If, as gender scholars claim, literature itself has participated both in the maintenance and interrogation of patriarchal scales of value (one need only think of the many women writers who used male pseudonyms in the nineteenth century), then this needs to be foregrounded in the world literature discussion. The male dominance in just about any version of a world literary canon is plain to see. (The nineteenth-century British novel would be a rare exception.) The selection of authors in my chapters in this book are also susceptible to this charge, I'm sorry to say. Besides selection, making the gender dimension in texts and institutions of evaluation visible is just as important. Patterns of dominance are not static and there are multiple historical causalities at work. In *La langue mondiale* (2015), Pascale Casanova makes the striking observation that the push for translation into French in sixteenth- and seventeenth-century France was driven in no small degree by women in the aristocracy – i.e. a social group that belonged to the literate minority, but had been denied formal education and was therefore unable to read Latin or Greek. In a later era, the emergent genre of the novel in Britain was nurtured by its female readership, while romanticist notions of the "mother tongue" and its literary value were obviously gendered. These aspects of literary history have more than a national and local interest – they invite instead comparative questions (how have readerships been gendered in different literary cultures?), as well as properly global or relational ones (how does gender factor into the translational ecologies of world literature?; what are the long-term trends in international canonization?).

MRT: Gender biases are still very significant in all societies, even though things are much better than just a generation ago in many societies (unfortunately, worse in others, like Iran). All research shows that many more women read fiction than men, but we have yet to see if that spills over into changing the canon. Perhaps not of literature written 150 or 200 years ago, but for post-First World War literature. Still, I am not too optimistic that a more equal canon will emerge in literary history before we get nearer to authors writing in the second half of the twentieth century and maybe not even then, although things are moving in the right direction. But not fast enough. A survey by Andrew Piper has shown that even though things have improved, the ratio 2:1 seems to have plateaued in terms of the attention given to males and females (https://txtlab.org/2018/06/gender-trouble-literary-studies-he-she-problem/).

On the other hand, resources for finding female writers are emerging with digitization, for example the project Women Writers in History (http://resources.huygens.knaw.nl/womenwriters). But it is sometimes hard to figure out what readers think of this issue. A class of Danish students I taught were quite reluctant to engage with the question, claiming that as long as the writing was good, it did not matter to them who had written it. (Eventually they found a lot of interesting female writers from all ages and around the world.) But from a political perspective, it is very important that there are female and male voices everywhere literature is written. And I really admire those who have written despite personal risks, such as the Lebanese poet and publisher

Joumana Haddad (born 1970), the European-based Chinese author and filmmaker Xiaolu Guo (born 1973), or the Iranian poet Forough Farrokhzad (1932–67).

8 Migrants

SH: Migration is where globalization and the aftermath of decolonization frequently intersect. Major names in postcolonial studies (Said, Bhabha, Spivak, Hall, Boehmer) have also thematized migration, but it exceeds the postcolonial framework. Hence, migration has been one of the richest areas for methodological and theoretical renewal in literary studies. The rubrics might shift – exile, diaspora, minorities – but in all these cases, post-Romantic assumptions concerning national provenance, the primacy of the mother tongue, and rootedness in tradition have been challenged. To my mind, one of the most promising fields under development concerns multi- and translingualism, or what Yasemin Yildiz (2012) has felicitously called "the post-monolingual condition." An important point here is to historicize post-Romantic assumptions about monolingualism and recognize that historically there has been no necessary connection between an author's first language and their language of writing. Yet, equally important is to identify what is *new* in the emergent literatures of our day, where different clusters of languages are mobilized in literary texts and the differentiation of comprehensibility (involving differentiated readerships) is used as an aesthetic strategy.

MRT: Agreed on the last point, and in general one should be very cautious about throwing around judgements about what counts and what does not. But I think the migrant experience is particularly interesting for a couple of reasons. First of all, much literature thrives on differences. Rich and poor, upstairs and downstairs, established and upcoming, and so on. The difference between capital and province has been reduced in many countries thanks to education and communication. The tale of a young man from the provinces trying to make it in Paris is not what it used to be. But the experience of the migrant carries with it that cultural divide that makes its mark in the stories. Artistically, the dual perspective of being inside and outside at the same time has been turned into a lot of very interesting literature. Secondly, even though it is only a minority of the world's population that can be said to be migrants or refugees, perhaps about 3 per cent, their cultural impact is huge, making communities more diverse and changing the idea of what is normal. To render that experience in literature and other artistic media is definitely an important task.

9 World literature and grand challenges: new directions?

MRT: Literary studies often has to defend itself as being a luxury in a world that has many bigger problems. But setting aside that art is one expression of the highest human achievement and a necessary element for developing rich cultures and meaningful lives, one can ask what literature and literary studies have to offer to global challenges. To the environment? Biodiversity? Human enhancement? Digitization? Migration? Conflict? Certainly, world literature addresses many of these darker sides of human history, also because they transcend cultural boundaries, but is that enough? What imprint can literature have? The optimistic view would be that education, empathy, complexity and engagement through stories, the sense of sharing perspectives, of a fundamental humanness, an historical perspective of continuity and change are actually extremely valuable and will enable politics, community building, cultural exchange and so on in ways that would not have taken place the same way without literature and the other arts. Certainly, ecology will be a very important issue for decades to come and with possibilities for a strong political engagement of literature, an issue that lends itself very well for an intercultural interest and dialogue.

SH: The challenges are of two kinds, it seems to me: disciplinary and existential. I think we have a fairly well-grounded sense by now of the disciplinary challenges of world literature. Besides requiring a combination of methodologies, some of which are still in their infancy (such as large-scale data mining), the biggest challenge is to approach literary studies as a collective undertaking. The heroic, individual figures of Auerbach or Said or Casanova can no longer serve as role models. World literature studies needs instead to be thought of as a meeting place, not unlike Léopold Senghor's "rendezvous of cultures," where scholars from the full spectrum of languages and literatures must participate in order for the field to become legitimate. The image is indeed idealistic, but its realization is a very practical matter – it is all about funding, networking, emailing, Skyping and endless sessions of editing. Our co-authoring of this book could be seen as one small indication of the collective nature of world literature; it could also be accused of being too limited in its outlook. Better examples are the plethora of companions, edited volumes and special issues that have appeared in recent years.

The existential challenges are of another order – hard to countenance without abandoning the language game of academic discourse, and obviously not the exclusive domain of any particular discipline. The recent turn towards the worlding capacities of literary texts (as in work by Ganguly 2016; Cheah 2016; Hayot 2012; Neumann and Rippl 2017) could nonetheless be read as expressive of a renewed interest in literature as an-*other* discourse, a parabasis (a term once used by Spivak), that offers us ways of grasping the staggering contradictions of human existence. Literature, broadly understood, is both *of* our moment (as a market phenomenon, an ideological tool, etc.), but also always *beside* it, enabling multifarious modes of knowledge, memory and experience otherwise occluded by the prevailing versions of common sense. If push comes to shove, this is where I ultimately place my loyalty and faith as a reader and literary scholar. This is part of my habitus, and it is a form of belief, as Bourdieu would have insisted, and I don't see the identification of belief as necessarily de-legitimizing. We are living in an age of mounting, multiple and unprecedented crises – with climate change as the crisis of all crises – and to cope with that we need to engage to our fullest capacity the imaginative resources of human culture.

References

Bhabha, Homi. 1994. *The Location of Culture*. London: Routledge.
Casanova, Pascale. 2005. "Literature as a World." *New Left Review* 31: 71–90.
Casanova, Pascale. 2015. *La langue mondiale: traduction et domination*. Paris: Seuil.
Cheah, Pheng. 2016. *What Is a World? On Postcolonial Literature as World Literature*. Durham: Duke University Press.
Etherington, Ben and Jarad Zimbler. 2014. "Field, Material, Technique: On Renewing Postcolonial Literary Criticism." *Journal of Commonwealth Literature* 49, no. 3: 279–297.
Ganguly, Debjani. 2016. *This Thing Called the World: The Contemporary Novel as Global Form*. Durham: Duke University Press.
Hayot, Eric. 2012. *On Literary Worlds*. Oxford: Oxford University Press.
Huggan, Graham. 2011. "The Trouble with World Literature." In *A Companion to Comparative Literature*, edited by Ale Behdad and Dominic Thomas, 490–506. London: Blackwell.
Jackson, Jeanne-Marie. 2015. *South African Literature's Russian Soul*. London: Bloomsbury.
Jackson, Jeanne-Marie. 2018. "Comparison Re-Justified." *Cambridge Journal of Postcolonial Literary Inquiry* 5, no. 3: 255–261.
McDonald, Peter D. 2017. *Artefacts of Writing: Ideas of the State and Communities of Letters from Matthew Arnold to Xu Bing*. Oxford: Oxford University Press.
Mufti, Aamir. 2016. *Forget English! Orientalisms and World Literatures*. Cambridge: Harvard University Press.
Neumann, Birgit and Gabriele Rippl. 2017. "Introduction." *Anglia* 135, no. 1: 1–20.

Rosling, Hans, with Ola Rosling and Anna Rosling Rönnlund. 2018. *Factfulness: Ten Reasons We're Wrong About the World – and Why Things Are Better than You Think*. New York: Flatiron Books.

Slaughter, Joseph. 2018. "Locations of Comparison." *Cambridge Journal of Postcolonial Literary Inquiry* 5, no. 2: 209–226.

Sturm-Trigonakis, Elke. 2007. *Global Playing in der Literatur: Ein Versuch über die Neue Weltliteratur*. Würzburg: Königshausen & Neumann.

Suhr-Sytsma, Nathan. 2017. *Poetry, Print and the Making of Postcolonial Literature*. Cambridge: Cambridge University Press.

Thomsen, Mads Rosendahl. 2008. *Mapping World Literature: International Canonization and Transnational Literatures*. London: Continuum.

Warner, Tobias. 2019. *The Tongue-Tied Imagination: Decolonizing Literary Modernity in Senegal*. New York: Fordham University Press.

Warwick Research Collective (WReC). 2015. *Combined and Uneven Development: Towards a New Theory of World-Literature*. Liverpool: Liverpool University Press.

Yildiz, Yasemin. 2012. *Beyond the Mother Tongue: The Post-Monolingual Condition*. New York: Fordham University Press.

Index

Abakari, Salim bin 99
abolitionists 90, 91
abyss 84, 87
Achebe, Chinua 3, 4, 5, 32, 36–7, 69
adab 156
Aden 95
Adichie, Chimamanda Ngozi 5
Africa 3, 4, 9, 19, 27, 56, 87, 88, 94, 97
African literature 4, 5, 33, 105, 157
Agualusa, José Eduardo 66–7
Ahmed, Siraj 18, 96
Akkadian 50
Aleksievich, Svetlana 159
Alves, Castro 91–2
America (see also: Latin America and North America) 59, 88
American Comparative Literature Association 31
Americas 5, 88
Anand, Mulk Raj 36
ananda (delight, joy) 9
Andersen, Hans Christian 119, 123
Andrade, Mario de 133–4, 135
Angola 67
anthropology 2
Appiah, Kwame Anthony 24
Apter, Emily 16, 40, 48, 54, 132
Arab world 82
Arabian Nights 75
Arabic script 99
Arabic 45, 50, 52, 53, 95, 99, 100
Archer, Jodie 121
Aristotle 156
Asian literature 12
Assis, Machado de 134, 142

Atlantic Ocean (see also: Black Atlantic) 84, 86, 90, 93, 144
Auerbach, Erich 8, 9, 12, 32, 152, 161, 165
Austen, Jane 56
Austria 142
autonomy of literature 157

Bâ, Ahmadou Hampaté 12
Balzac, Honoré de 1
Bamman, David 123–4, 125
Bassnett, Susan 39, 134, 135
Bechuana dialect: see Setswana
Bechuana: see Tswana
Beckett, Samuel 14
Beecroft, Alexander 15, 20, 50, 51, 53–6, 84, 105, 156
Beira 102
Bellos, David 116
Bengal 7, 10, 18,
Bengal renaissance 10
Bengali (Bengalee) 9, 45
Benjamin, Walter 127
Bergman, Ingmar 159
Bergson, Henri 45
Berman, Antoine 135
Bermann, Sandra 39–40
Bernheimer, Charles 31
Bhabha, Homi 32–3, 161, 164
Bhagavadgita 50, 104
Bhattacharya, Bhaidik 18, 19
Bible 7, 71, 101, 139
Bildung 155
Bjørnson, Bjørnstjerne 57
Black Atlantic 85–92, 93, 104, 105

Bloom, Harold 3, 62–3
Blyth, R.H. 70
Boehmer, Elleke 35–7, 77, 161, 164
Bolaño, Roberto 73
Bombay 95, 102
book markets 47
Borges, Jorges Luis 72, 74–5, 109,
Bourdieu, Pierre 14, 143, 160, 166
Brandes, Georg 45, 66
Brazil 91, 133, 136, 141, 142, 144, 147, 148, 155
Brazilian literature 133, 136, 137
Brecht, Bertolt 140–1, 148
Brink, André 87
Britain 10, 46, 56, 90, 142, 163
British empire 4, 101
Brown, Dan 71
Buescu, Helena 15
Buffon, Comte de 7

Cairo 95, 102
Calcutta 7, 63
Calvino, Italo 62
Camões, Luís de 86, 87, 105
Campbell, Roy 87
Camus, Albert 118
canonization 4, 59
canons 7, 14, 24, 59, 62
Canudos 141, 143, 144
Caribbean 85, 88
Carretta, Vincent 89
Carroll, Lewis 71
Caruth, Cathy 64
Casanova, Pascale 13–14, 15, 18, 133, 157, 161, 163, 165
Catholicism 55, 82
Cervantes, Miguel de 57
Césaire, Aimé 86, 90, 105
Chande, Selemani bin Mwenye 99
Cheah, Pheng 16, 17, 48, 166
China 25–26, 53
Chinese: see Mandarin
Church Slavic 52
CIA 13
circulation 4, 47–54
civilization of the universal 11
Clarkson, Thomas 90
classical languages 46
Coelho, João Paulo Borges 94
Coelho, Paulo 71–2, 133

Coetzee, J.M. 140
Cohen, Margaret 84
Cold War, the 8, 12, 13, 154
Cole, Nicolas 113
Collin, Christen 57
colonialism 2, 4, 10, 19, 93, 101
Columbus, Christopher 7
Communist Manifesto 8, 48
comparative literature 13, 14, 16, 19, 29–32, 53
Condé, Maryse 88, 90
connected histories 83
Conrad, Joseph 84
Conselheiro, Antônio 141
Constantinople 90
Coovadia, Imraan 94
cosmopolitan desire 148
cosmopolitan literature 53, 105
cosmopolitan reading 138
cosmopolitan values 45
cosmopolitanism 137
Couto, Mia 82, 93, 94, 97, 98, 99, 104
Craveirinha, José 88
creolization 87
Cromwell, Oliver 55
Cunha, Euclides da 134, 136, 137, 138, 141–2, 143, 144–8

D'haen, Theo 6
Damrosch, David 14–15, 30, 36, 39, 47, 49, 68–69, 139, 153, 156
Dangarembga, Tsitsi 36
Danish 114, 137, 138, 156, 163
Dante Alighieri 18, 53, 57
Darwin, Charles 7
decolonization 50, 105
deconstruction 62
DeepL 116–17
Delhi 131
DeLoughrey, Elizabeth 84, 92, 104
Desai, Gaurav 83, 94, 96
Díaz, Junot 75–6
Dickinson, Emily 118
didactics 153
digital humanities 2, 52, 109–29, 131
digital media 2, 3, 17, 20, 50, 52–3, 100, 152, 154
distant reading 7, 14, 49, 110, 125–7, 153
domestication 132, 147

double consciousness 89, 90, 93
drama 1, 31, 40, 57, 156, 160
Du Bois, W. E. B. 89
Duchamp, Marcel 131
Durban 93, 102, 104
Dutch 137, 138
Dylan, Bob 158

Ece, Ayse Fitnat 41
Eckermann, Johann Peter 6, 7
Eco, Umberto 72
ecology 165
Edmond, Jacob 67–8
Egypt 45, 82, 96
Emerson, Ralph Waldo 103
emic approach 54
enchantment 71–5
Engels, Friedrich 8, 48
England 56, 92
English 3, 4, 5, 45, 51, 55, 99, 102, 133, 136, 139, 142, 144, 147, 152, 155
English literature 54, 55, 57
epic 74, 86, 104, 143, 148, 156
epiphany 128
Equiano, Olaudah 88, 89–90, 105
Estonian 133
Etherington, Ben 162
etic approach 54–5
Étiemble, René 12
Ette, Ottmar 31–2, 41
Eurocentrism 158, 161, 162
Eurochronology 93
Europe 5, 6, 7, 10, 18, 25, 27, 33, 45, 52, 56, 57, 59, 75, 82, 88, 96, 142, 153, 156, 158
Even-Zohar, Itamar 51
evolutionary theory (evolutionism) 7, 141

Fanon, Frantz 32, 34–5
Farrokhzad, Forough 164
Felski, Rita 29
Finnish 45
foreignization 132
France 11, 92
Frank, Anne 71
French 45, 51, 133, 134, 137, 139, 142, 144, 152, 153
Freyre, Gilberto 134
Friedman, Susan Stanford 29

Frobenius, Leo 11, 12
Frost, Robert 38

Gadamer, Hans Georg 77–8
Gama, Vasco da 86
Gandhi, Mathatma 93, 101–4
Ganguly, Debjani 16, 17, 98, 166
Garay, Benjamin de 138
gender 162–4
genre 14, 62
Gentzler, Edwin 40
German East Africa 98
German 99, 137, 152, 153
Germany 56
Ghosh, Amitav 85, 93, 94, 96, 98, 99, 100, 104
Gikandi, Simon 36
Gilroy, Paul 83, 88, 89, 91
Glissant, Édouard 32, 85, 87, 89, 92
Global Anglophone literature 54
Global South 16
globalization 2, 10, 13, 19, 20, 46, 49, 50, 51, 97, 154–5
Goethe, Johann Wolfgang von 4, 6, 7, 8, 9, 11, 12, 24–5, 28, 32, 57, 77
Gogol, Nikolai V. 69, 131
Gollancz, Israel 45, 56
Goodreads 117
Google Books Ngram Viewer 118,
Google Translate 113–6
Google Trends 119
grand challenges 165–6
Greece 53, 92
Greek 45, 50, 51, 55
Grevenius, Herbert 132
Grieco, Agrippino 136
Griffiths, D. W. 58
Guillén, Nicolas 88
Gujarati 102
Gumbrecht, Hans Ulrich 75
Gupta, Pamila 83
Gurnah, Abdulrazak 93, 100, 104, 105
Gustav III, king of Sweden 158

Haddad, Joumana 164
Hafez 7
Haggard, H. Rider 82
haiku 69–71
Hall, Stuart 164
Hardy, Thomas 45

Harry Potter-series 25, 123
Hayles, N. Katherine 111
Hayot, Eric 16, 166
Hebrew 45, 137
Hebrew script 95
Heilbron, Johan 51, 134
Heinemann (publisher) 2
Heise, Ursula K. 31
Hemingway, Ernest 131
Hemon, Aleksandar 38–9
Herder, Johann Gottfried von 8
Herford, C. H. 46
Hermans, Theo 134
Higginson, William J. 70
Hindi 102
Hitchcock, Peter 16
Hodapp, James 99
Høeg, Peter 72
Hofmeyr, Isabel 83, 92, 93, 97, 101, 102
Holiday, Billie 88, 105
Holmes, James S. 134
Homer 1, 50, 57, 84, 85
Huggan, Graham 5, 66, 161
Hughes, Langston 88
Hugo, Victor 57
Hungary 154
Huyssen, Andreas 31

Ibsen, Henrik 132
Iceland 45
Igbo 3, 5
Imru al-Qays 57
Index Translationum 117
India 7, 45, 56, 63, 82, 94, 96, 102, 103
Indian Ocean 82, 83, 84, 85, 92–104
Institute for World Literature 15
intertextuality 3
Ireland 45
Isabelle, Pierre 116
Islam 99, 100
Italian 137, 138, 153
Italy 92

Jackson, Jeanne-Marie 162
Jameson, Fredric 71–2
Japanese 45, 132
Jauss, Hans Robert 140, 142
Jelinek, Elfriede 159
Jianbo Gao 122–3, 125

Jockers, Matthew 121, 125
Jones, William 7, 18, 19
Joyce, James 113–14, 127, 132, 143

Kafka, Franz 14, 63, 66, 114–17
Kant, Immanuel 7, 49
kavya 156
Kertész, Imre 36
Khair, Tabish 37–8
Kipling, Rudyard 45
Kong, Shuyu 25
Kuhn, Roland 116
Kundera, Milan 26–7
Kyunyŏ 53

Laachir, Karima 83
Lagos 2, 3, 4
language 152–154
Larsen, Svend Erik 39
Latin 45, 50, 51, 52, 53, 55, 147
Latin alphabet 132
Latin America 19, 27
Latin script 99
Lazarus, Neil 35–6
Le Clézio, J.M.G. 94
Lee, Sabrina 124, 125
Leerssen, Joep 28
Lefevere, André 135, 140
Lessing, Doris 18
libraries 47
Lindqvist, Yvonne 134
Lispector, Clarice 72, 133, 148
literary ecologies 18, 20, 46, 47, 51–4, 105
literary markets 5
literature, status of 156–8, 160–1
Llosa, Mario Vargas 137, 138
Lodge, David 110
London 2, 3, 4, 13
Lowe, Elizabeth 138, 144–8
Lukács, Georg 76
lyric 1, 3, 156

machine translation 113–6, 131
Mandarin (Chinese) 45, 50, 51, 132
Mangalore 95
Mani, B. Venkat 15
Mao Zedong 71
Maputo (Lourenço Marques) 88, 105
Marchal, Lucien 138

Mária, Sandor 138
Márquez, Gabriel García 12, 73
Marx, Karl 8, 9, 48
Marzagora, Sara 83
Mayakovsky, Vladimir 18
Mbembe, Achille 87
McDonald, Peter D. 162
McLean, Alastair 73
media studies 2
Mediterranean 85
Melville, Herman 84
Middle Eastern literature 12
Middle Passage 87, 88
migrants 164
Milton, John 55
minor languages 152–3
Mitchell, Breon 115
Mitchell, Margaret 71
Mo Yan 74
Moretti, Franco 14, 15, 18, 30, 36, 47, 73, 110, 126, 133, 134, 153
Moulton, R. G. 56–7, 58
Mozambique 97
Mufti, Aamir 18, 41, 65, 96
Mukherjee, Neel 63–5
Müller, Herta 159
multiculturalism 31
multilingualism 46, 102
Munday, Jeremy 138
Murakami, Haruki 68, 72, 119
Mustafa, Fawzia 99

Naipaul, V.S. 32, 94
national literature 24–29, 53, 105
nationalism 6, 20, 25, 27–8, 56, 154–6, 160, 161
Nesbø, Jo 1
Neu, Sereth 138
Neumann, Birgit 166
new journalism 147
New York 13
Nielbo, Kristoffer L. 122–3, 125
Nigeria 2, 4
Nobel, Alfred 158
North America 5, 75, 153
Norwegian 132, 137
NovelTM 110

Okri, Ben 74
Ong, Walter 111

orality 53
Orientalism 7, 10, 18
Orsini, Francesca 83
Östergren, Klas 132
Ottoman empire 90
Oyono, Ferdinand 139

Pamuk, Orhan 41, 72
Paris 11, 13, 131
Pascal, Blaise 11
Patel, Shailja 94
PEN International 13
Persian 45, 50
philology 18, 19
Piper, Andrew 110
Plaatje, Solomon T. 58–9, 88
Plato 11, 104
poetics of Relation 85, 89, 92
poetry 31, 38, 40, 69, 70, 72, 75, 76, 92, 93, 100, 120, 143, 148, 156, 160
Polish 137
political economy 48
Pollock, Sheldon 50, 53
Pontoppidan, Henrik 71
Portugal 137
Portuguese 86, 134, 147
positivism 141
possible worlds 17
postcolonialism (postcolonial studies) 15, 19, 20, 32–9, 161–2
postmodernism 147
Prendergast, Christopher 15
Protestantism 55
Proust, Marcel 127
Putnam, Samuel 136, 138, 142, 143, 144–8

Quran 101

race 12, 50, 58, 97
racial categories 89
racism 88, 89, 147
Rahimi, Atiq 66
Rancière, Jacques 142
Rediker, Marcus 85
remediation 31, 40, 103
Richter, Sandra 15
Rippl, Gabriele 166
Rosling, Hans 155
Rowling, J.K. 71

Rumi, Jal al-din 18
Rushdie, Salman 65, 74, 118
Ruskin, John 103, 104
Russia 56, 99
Russian 131

Said, Edward W. 18, 32, 96, 161, 164, 165
Saint-Exupéry, Antoine de 71
Samuelson, Meg 83
Sanskrit 7, 18, 45, 50, 52, 53
Santos, Estela dos 144
São Paulo 133
Sapiro, Gisèle 51, 134
satyagraha 102
Saussy, Haun 15, 29, 41–42
Scarry, Elaine 64
Schlegel, August Wilhelm 10
Schleiermacher, Friedrich 132
Schlözer, August Ludwig von 6
Schopenhauer, Arthur 10
Senghor, Léopold Sédar 11–12, 165
serial collective 139
Setswana (Bechuana dialect) 45
Shakespeare, William 128, 45–6, 56–9, 85, 105
Sharp, Granville 90
significant geographies 18, 83–4
Silveira, Dom Gonçalo da 81, 82, 86, 104
Slaughter, Joseph 162
slave trade 91, 105
slavery 87, 88, 93
Sousa, Noémia de 88–9, 90, 105
South Africa 45, 59, 87, 101, 103, 153
South Asia 9, 19
Soviet Union 13
Spain 92
Spanish 142, 144, 153
Spivak, Gayatri 16, 32, 49, 154, 164
Stanford Literary Lab 110
Stavans, Ilan 147
strangeness 62–3, 66–8, 71, 73, 76–8, 143, 148
Strindberg, August 159
Suhr-Sytsma, Nathan 162
Swahili literature (poetry) 93, 100
Swahili 99, 100, 105
Swedish Academy 158–9

Swedish 57, 59, 131, 132, 139, 142, 143, 148

Tagore, Rabindranath 9–11, 12, 45, 158
Tamil 102, 131
Tenen, Dennis Yi 124–5
tertium comparationis 131, 132, 139
textual zone 139
Things Fall Apart 3–6
Thiong'o, Ngugi wa 33
Tihanov, Galin 50
Tin, Maung 57
Tippu Tip 99
Tiwari, Bhavya 10
Tolkien, J.R.R. 71, 119
Tolstoy, Leo 103, 104
Touré, Ahmed Sekou 12
Toury, Gideon 135
translatability 16, 51
translation 5, 9, 12–3, 20, 29, 47, 131–49, 151
translation studies 2, 16, 18, 39–42, 134–5
Tswana (Bechuana) 58
Turing test 116
TV series 160–161

Underwood, Ted 120–1, 123, 125–6, 127
UNESCO 11, 12, 117
United States 7, 52, 57, 136, 137, 154
universalism 66–7, 93
untranslatability 132

Varsava, Jerry 29–30
Vassanji, Moyez 94
Venuti, Lawrence 39–40, 132, 134, 135
vernacular (language, traditions) 18, 46
vernacular canon 54
vernacular ecology 53
vernacular literature 54, 105
vernacular values 47
vernacularism 134
vernacularization 53
Vierke, Clarissa 100
Virgil 11
Voyant Tools 127

Walcott, Derek 32, 85, 87
Wales 45
Walkowitz, Rebecca 134
war journalism 144
Warburg, Karl 57
Warburton, Thomas 138, 139, 144, 148
Warner, Tobias 162
Warwick Research Collective 18, 162
Weltliteratur 1, 6, 8
wen 157
Wergeland, Henrik 57
West Africa 9, 89
Wikipedia 118
Wilkens, Matthew 121–2, 123, 125
Wittgenstein, Ludwig 1
Woolf, Virginia 1

Wordsworth, William 55
world (concept) 16–17
world literature in English 34
world-system 18
Wyllie, David 115
Wynter, Sylvia 88

Xiaolu Guo 164

Yeats, W.B. 2
Yildiz, Yasemin 164
Yuan Yuan Tan 131

Zanzibar 102
Zetterholm, Tore 143
Zilly, Berthold 144
Zimbler, Jarad 162
Zweig, Stefan 136, 142, 143, 144